FAMILY AWEIGH

They lived the dream

MICHAEL HOLT

ISBN: 1502976250
ISBN 13: 9781502976253
Library of Congress Control Number: 2014919246
CreateSpace Independent Publishing Platform
North Charleston, South Carolina

TABLE OF CONTENTS

DEDICATION

I dedicate this book with all my heart to my wife
Rosemarie. One day, and rather to her surprise,
she found herself metamorphosed from housewife
and mother into first mate, cook and much, much
more than bottle-washer, on a sea-going boat with
attendant crew. The serenity, courage, and exceptional array of skills with which she coped with
these new demands rise out from this story.

Prologue

The story told in 'Family Aweigh' is about a family with a Dream. With three teen-age children, we dreamed of leaving home to live on a boat in the Mediterranean. We managed to live our Dream. And although the story took place some years ago I believe its power to entertain will never fade. It is a timeless story.

The lure, the challenge, the dangers, and pleasures of the sea are timeless. And while our 'Jernica' was a motor yacht and big by some standards, the hands-on owners of yachts of all shapes, sizes and kinds will recognize the common, timeless, threads: anxiety facing difficult seas, problems of ship handling, hard slog dealing with maintenance, an exhilarating sense of freedom in heading out into open seas, and the incomparable feeling of peace and contentment on entering an Arcadian anchorage after a rough passage.

The cruising grounds, tranquil bays, and safe anchorages we found around the Med are timeless too, whether for sailboats or motor cruisers. 'Development' may well have changed their faces – but those basic characteristics of nature which have made them a magnet for sailors of every kind of craft over the centuries will never change.

This is a story for many landlubbers too. The Dream that drove us is timeless.

We met so many people in harbours around the Med who said, 'You're so lucky! I wish we could do this too'. I always replied, 'Well, do it.' They would reply, 'But we've got our work, and children at school.' I replied, 'We too had our work, and children at school. But we did it.'

And there too, in the problems to solve, and their solutions, surprisingly little has changed over time. How to leave home, and how you will finance the adventure. (Make sure you can finance the time you plan to be away.) How to find 'your' boat, turn a townie family into skilled mariners (a boat is very demanding, the sea can be very dangerous), much is unchanged.

Some solutions indeed are more easily found today. For education, we did well, but remote computing via the internet today offers educational solutions even on the move which were never available to us.

 Modern technology can also extend your enjoyment of our story. In the Epilogue you will find the name of a website where you will be able to see photos of 'Jernica' and its crew, hard at work, at play, and in some of the dramatic incidents described in the book.

Some of our readers may one day find themselves sailing though Jernica's cruising grounds. If so, I hope you will remember us. It would be wonderful to know we had partners in creating a truly timeless document, the continuing adventures of a 'Family Aweigh'.

Michael Holt

GOING,
GOING - OOPS - GONE!

"Next on the right", said Rosemarie, looking at the map. "It should be just coming up."

I frowned at the hedgerow on our right, devoid of openings as far as the eye could see.

One of the kids in the back said, "You ought to know Mum by now. She means left. Here!"

I stood on the brakes. Tyres squealing, we made the turning. The sign said, "Boulevard de L'hotel des Myrtes" our destination.

"I told you so," Rosemarie said with the feminine logic which makes the liberation of the species quite superfluous.

She opened the window to lean out and half our home tried to cascade out past her ears. Nicholas, being senior teenager, expertly organised stuffing everything including his mother back into the car.

It - the debris, not Rosemarie - had been trying to escape or rearrange itself for about a thousand miles; since we'd rolled off the ferry at Calais; as we'd diced with macho death-dealers on the dodgem circuit described as a ring road round Paris; and much further south as I took my eyes off the road to point at beloved bottle labels transformed wondrously into road signs as we passed through the vineyards of Bourgogne and Beaujolais.

Within striking distance of the Mediterranean coast, where bleak razor-ridged hills screen the tough and historic port of Marseilles we turned east.

As we travelled the rolling green-and-ochre patched contours of the Provencal hills our excitement mounted. The autoroute was leading us steadily towards the resorts of the Cote d'Azur and our final stop, St. Raphael.

What matter if our belongings overflowed the roof-rack, bulged out of the boot, crept under our behinds, cascaded around our feet, and tried to flop out of the windows? We forgot we'd been cramped and tired.

We craned for a first glimpse of the villa we'd hired as our temporary home and first stop on an unknown road leading to a new life afloat.

Carolyn was first to spot the villa nameplate.

"There it is!"

She flung out her arms creating an avalanche inside the car. Carolyn, like most fifteen year-old girls was capable of peaks of excitement quite enough to cave in any roof.

I stopped the car and Carolyn fell out to open the green wrought-iron gates. "I can't believe we're really here, at last," said Rosemarie.

But at this moment she knew it had all been worthwhile; first the years of uncertainty; finally the month-long wear and tear, every day packing the lifelong possessions of a family of five; every day cutting another lifeline tethering us to a known income, known home, known friends, known schooling.

We'd hired the villa because it was the cheapest we could find. We'd wondered why so cheap. Now the evidence was clear. It was superficially attractive with a high arched entrance and wooden veranda under a sloping red tiled roof. But the wood and tiles were faded and the windows unpainted. The garden was large and overgrown with straggling weeds. We all looked at it in some trepidation. Carolyn pushed on the gate.

"It didn't fall off," Jeremy observed as it swung easily on its hinges.

Jeremy was the down-to-earth one. Just coming up to fourteen, he was our self-taught mechanic and electronics expert. He was self-taught by necessity as I had difficulty even fixing a fuse.

Rosemarie was practical too, of course. But having Jeremy was good organisation on my part as it gave Rosemarie more time for cooking, at which she excelled.

Today I probably need to explain that we were married in an age when a chauvinist was only a normal kind of Frenchman. No tag except "lucky so-and-so" could be attached to the guy bright enough to persuade a beautiful girl with a degree who was also a great cook, to marry him.

I drove in switched off the engine and looked around, breathing in new home. The road we were in was thick with oleander bushes and pines. They perfumed the air over which lay a tranquil silence.

Through the dense green foliage we could catch only a glimpse of the red roofs and green-shuttered windows of surrounding villas.

Our villa was towards the bottom of a hill. No more than two hundred meters away were blue Mediterranean waters. As we found later, within ten minutes we could walk to the centre of busy St. Raphael, a sizeable town.

But this special January morning, we saw only a quiet green country road with secret perfumed gardens.

It was two years since we'd all agreed we'd sell our home, pull the kids out of school and me out of business life. Then we would go to live on a boat on the Mediterranean Sea.

There were a number of reasons, but one central theme. We wanted a total change in environment. We lived in a comfortable house in London, with everything taken for granted.

A boat can't be taken for granted. We'd been voracious readers of every yachting book that came within reach. Any friend or acquaintance that'd even sniffed salt air was lured home and drained of knowledge.

We learned a boat must be cleaned daily, and de-rusted and painted frequently; its bilges and bottom kept cleaned; its working parts tended with affection. On voyage moreover it requires its nose to be pointed in the right direction, avoiding sharp projections. And the elements can no longer be ignored, for a boat is one of their creatures.

In a boat you must come alive to the world moving around you. If we tackled everything ourselves we'd have a daily challenge, which we welcomed. Our home wouldn't be any longer a comfortable anaesthetizing box; our days maybe no longer a series of repetitive reflexes.

We'd acquired the taste for a simpler life, closer to nature on Continental holidays in a caravan. We would wake in the middle of silent, fragrant fields. A pair of shorts, we were dressed. Housework was minimal. Returning home, I would be more conscious of the bad-tempered stranger rising inside me after a bad day at the office. I wanted to get rid of him.

Rosemarie loved the air and freedom of these holidays. She wasn't looking for an absence of work: she was something of a workaholic making me feel guilty, peering over my newspaper as she busied herself with umpteen jobs I never knew existed around the house. But she also longed for a release from working within closed walls.

The kids meanwhile were struggling on crowded, rush-hour tubes each day for school. I don't think it's natural that at the height of a human being's physical and mental powers - schooldays – he or she should be asked to sit still all day, say nothing, and listen. Teachers are human: that is, very ordinary mostly, worried by their bills, their sex lives, the sometimes boring and repetitive nature of their work, the fidgety audience.

It requires rare skills and talents to command any group's attention for more than a few minutes, let alone an hour.

These qualities are found in only a few born, gifted teachers.

Schools at that time had also become test-beds for social theories. Teachers no less than children, had no idea where they were going, or why. Or if they did, it changed the following week. To be bright and enquiring, it was made known, was to want to be superior - the word was "elitist".

The idea of going away to live on a boat, to be responsible totally for their own environment, to travel, was embraced by the children with enthusiasm. It was worth the wrench even of leaving their friends. Jeremy at the age of 13 had just gained competitive entrance to the highly regarded University College School. I asked him which of the two lives he wished to choose.

Jeremy looked at me as though I were barmy, and said so. "I will be the one looking after the engines, won't I?" he enquired, rather threateningly. "Yes," I said. "Then, what do you think!" he said. (Jeremy dropping out allowed Hugh Dennis, who later became a famous UK comedian to take his place - which we found out when he dropped Jeremy's name in a newspaper article about his life some years later).

Nicholas, our oldest, was doing well at Marylebone Grammar school (as it was), had a love of Russian authors – and their work was easily transportable.

After we'd made up our minds we assumed we'd be away to clear waters in a few months. But the loose ends to be tied up stretched on and on. Leaving home, business, school and fixing finance we discovered were not menial tasks.

Mariner fever took over the household and kept our spirits fresh even as get-away plans dragged. Cooking, homework and working papers, nightly interrupted the principal family activity of tying sheet-bends, clove hitches, and recognizing buoy shapes and colours.

Every weekend we took off to breath in salt air and warm engines in marinas along the Hamble and south coast. We were looking for "our" boat. Rosemarie soon knew the smallest detail of every craft for sale. It was just as well.—Boat agents are no different from house agents - except they are called "brokers". Many have no idea about the boats they are selling, but will happily send you to the farthest corner of the kingdom to buy it. "Just what you're looking for," they'll assure you. Rosemarie's encyclopedic knowledge saved us many a wasted journey.

With the whole family due to be afloat I thought maybe somebody ought to know what they were doing. I began studying for a yachtmaster's certificate.

One evening I let out a yell. Rosemarie came running in. I remember she had her mouth open, and a whisk held in one hand from which egg white was dripping on the floor.

"What? What is it?" she cried in alarm.

"I did it!"

"What? What have you done?" She looked round for the damage.

I pointed triumphantly at the chart on the kitchen table. "I made it into Boulogne!" Rosemarie grimaced, shook her head sadly and withdrew to whip the eggs a bit harder.

The thrill of navigating via a lightship, a few buoys and some coastal landmarks safely into Boulogne was exhilarating, even when start and finish was on the kitchen table.

Then I was doing it for real. The kitchen table became Chichester harbour where the ringing beat of halyards against masts signaled every burst in the breeze. We were greeted on board by Jim, our yacht-master-tutor and owner of the motor yacht.

"You look a bit young for a yachtmaster's course," he smiled at Jeremy. But the thirteen-year old was there mainly for the engines and had soon disappeared into his Aladdin's cave to admire wonders of twisted met-al, throbbing cylinders and gasping pipes which this mechanically retarded father regarded as dangerous beasts best left alone in the dark -or in the care of some fearless soul prepared to tame them.

I would genuinely never have continued with our sea saga if I did not have full confidence that our thir-teen year-old son was a knowledgeable hero.

It was a chill November night as we crossed the bar and crept out to a dark sea.

As the lights of home disappeared and all was black on the bow we entered a new world. We were borne into the sealed capsule of a wheelhouse at sea.

It was hypnotic. The soft glow of dimmed lights, a translucent scatter on the radar screen, a meandering compass needle, a rhythmic background of engines, other dim shapes - one over the wheel, another shuffling hands and rulers over charts; finding a new balance to the uneven motion underfoot. There was a hiss, and a faint translucence forward as water was thrust off the bow.

On this and other wintry winter nights Jeremy and I followed buoys and lights up and down the broad and sheltered reaches of the Solent and sailed in and out of Cowes, Chichester and Portsmouth harbours.

One frosty night we were berthed just across the water from what seemed like the whole of the royal navy in Portsmouth harbour. I could not imagine how any one of the massive vessels had found its way in, let alone a fleet.

As we had entered our instructor said, "Follow the leading lights". All I could see was Portsmouth. Every street light, hotel, house and apartment had its lights blazing to greet us.

"Where?" I asked trying not to sound desperate. The patience and courtesy of any yachtmaster instructor is unmatchable. The bearded and anoraked figure by my side carefully pointed an arm along my line of sight.

"There, see..just get them in line, one above the other."

I battened hopefully onto a distant red light. It changed suddenly to amber and then green and the stationary bright white lights adjacent became a tide of moving car beams.

We berthed somehow. The courteous voice said, "Well done. You won't find any difficulty picking out the lights once you've had more practice." I really didn't believe him.

It was freezing. We discovered heating was not mandatory on all boats. I had brought along long johns as a daytime precaution. I now donned them under my pyjamas. I put on a sweater over my pyjama tops; then added an anorak.

Jeremy was performing similar antics, in and out of his berth. He mustered a grin. Even freezing to death is fun on a boat. We slept soundly under the big guns.

We thought we'd better be sure we enjoyed life afloat as a family. We took off on a yacht we chartered in the Channel Isles. The weather was poor and the seas roughish but nobody wanted to go back home.

We learned again the desirability of doing everything for ourselves. The charter crew included a cook dug up at the last moment. Norman had a very prominent nose, so inevitably he became Norman the Nose. He was sick crossing the channel.

Rosemarie it was who, imperturbable as ever, occupied the heaving galley and made the sandwiches.

We'd crossed the channel on our kitchen table charts; and indeed on real ferries. But arriving in France was never the same as on our own boat. We'd never before noticed the salt of the air, the yapping of the gulls, other small boats busy about a port's business.

We'd never noticed the water in fact. It slapped and gurgled and carried pieces of wood and led us to low quays with weather-beaten faded French notices and faded weather-beaten Frenchmen complete with berets.

Our gallant cook recovered in harbour. He served up a meal of dried-up potatoes, tinned peas and tinned meat. Our second and third repast was to the same standard of inspiration.

We'd insisted we wanted to work on the boat; but I asked Norman, "Do you think you can cope with the cooking?"

He scratched his beak while he considered how best to break the news. "Well, you might get bored with it."

"What" Rosemarie enquired by way of discovery, "is your specialty?"

He contemplated a moment. "Anything out of a tin." Divining that some further explanation might be in order, he revealed, "I'm usually a delivery skipper".

We agreed we might get bored, and the prominence departed. Rosemarie took over the cooking.

The kids' rope-handling and knots came on apace; and not long afterwards I had my yachtmaster's certificate. It's a very small step on a long road to understanding the sea. But the neighbors could have been excused for believing I'd been made Admiral of the Fleet by the family reception committee waiting on the doorstep when I arrived home from the final test.

And to tell the truth, I probably wouldn't have felt more pleased if I had have been!

The dream was coming more into focus.

Meanwhile friends who knew about our plans told us how lucky we were. They'd love to do it too, but they had a house, kids, their work etcetera, so they couldn't do it.

Everybody we met in the following years told us how lucky we were, but they had a house, kids, work, etc so couldn't do it themselves.

We started to attack the loose ends of our departure plans. The only way to get things done, we thought, is to do them.

What to do, most importantly, about the kids' on-going education? We looked into tried and proven correspondence course and selected two, covering the "O" and "A" level subjects the children would have taken at school.

We bought the course books, and didn't send the kids back to school in September. Instead we tried out the courses. By December we declared the new educational system a success. The children couldn't wait for their marks to come back in the post. This was all their own work. If they failed, it was them, not teacher. They were bright-eyed instead of bored with their learning.

We knew some academic groundwork would be lost from opting out of the conventional system. But the self-discipline in learning they'd already begun to display told us much about what they would gain.

A voyage to new horizons and peoples would have further educational value - and couldn't be found within the concrete boundaries of schools now forcibly dedicated to the art of mediocrity.

We'll only get to do something, we told ourselves again, by doing it.

We were so unitedly determined to "do" that we very nearly moved from London with nowhere at all to go. We had decided to solve two other problems in one; those of selling the house - (the market was dead - it always is of course when you want to sell) and income by letting the house.

The tenants had signed the lease and were due to move in within three weeks. Rosemarie was working on the floor surrounded by packing cases and our belongings. Suddenly she stopped and looked up. She'd been sorting and stowing for a week, working from dawn till the early hours.

"Tell me why I'm packing all these things", she burst out. "I must be bloody mad! Where the hell are we going?"

"We'll find somewhere," I said. It appeared that this oft-repeated philosophy had now reached its natural limits as a shoal of villa brochures were flung at my feet.

"Find something!" she sat with arms folded.

"Where?"

"France."

We had not looked seriously at France. Too expensive, crowded and sophisticated.

"After all," Rosemarie went on, "it's only a base for a few months while we find Jernica." We didn't have a boat but we had a name - first letters of Jeremy, Nicholas and Carolyn. It was Carolyn's inspiration, as she was always liable to remind us.

We thumbed through France, looking only at prices. "Here's one we can afford," I said.

13

"Where is it, French West Africa?" Rosemarie asked not in the warmest of tones.

I double-checked. "Well, the advert says," I paused and checked again, because at the price it seemed to good to be true, "it says, it's only a few minutes from the sea, at Saint-Raphael, on the Côte d'Azur."

There was a rush for the atlas. "At that price it'll be in French Sahara," was the general drift. The atlas proved it wasn't in the Sahara. On the contrary the town seemed to be within easy striking distance of just about every major marina and port on the Mediterranean coast.

We hardy slept that evening for fear our heaven-sent find would be let. But the agent said it was free. There wasn't a catch - "Although the furniture's a little antiquated."

"Can you see the sea?" we asked jokingly. "Oh yes, from the verandah." What! Was the unanimous shout. Our deposit was in the post. Within minutes.

Our last morning in our London home dawned. We'd only let the house, but we didn't expect to be coming back to it. The weather was January London, grey with hints of rain. For once, it wasn't necessary to prod and cajole the kids out of bed.

The previous evening we thought we'd stuffed the last of our belongings into hold-alls, but that morning an earthquake seemed to have strewn gear all over the ground floor. Rosemarie crept downstairs and gazed at the debris. We were due to catch an early cross-channel car ferry.

My, to that moment in our married life, totally unflappable wife said, "Oh, my God" and sank into a chair.

She had spent a frantic month of days and nights ceaseless battling to be ready for this moment. Now we were heading into the unknown but not quite ready, it seemed.

We all set to transform the earthquake into nothing worse than an overloaded car.

Then I noticed Carolyn trying to hold back tears. "It's tough leaving your friends," I said. She shook her head. "Is it Floppy?" I finally guessed. She gave a slight nod. Floppy was a three-foot high teddy bear. It was nearly as big as she was when we'd bought it seven years earlier. The children had had to make agonising decisions about what to leave behind. Floppy was too big and bulky, Carolyn had agreed.

"We'll get Floppy in somehow," I said now.

"It's alright", said Carolyn wiping her eyes, "It's just I didn't like to think of him sitting there all alone when we've gone; but it's alright really." We stuffed him into the melee. Floppy and Carolyn looked a lot more cheerful.

Friends came to see us off, and were soon waving us goodbye. We were sad to see them disappear from view, but we had been curiously unmoved at the prospect of not living in our comfortable home again.

Now here we were. We were in France. We were on the Cote d'Azur. We were on the threshold of our villa, and a new episode in our lives. As we continued to uncrease our legs, somebody said, "It looks fine."

It wasn't a modern box. A centre arch supported on a couple of pink stone columns created an entrance hall flanked by two low wings. It was simple, classic, built in 1914. A deep-south type verandah ran along the frontage.

We entered. The rooms were large. The furniture was antiquated as promised, and sagged. We liked it.

Under a bright blue winter sky and with unfamiliar sweet smells around we began to unload the groaning car.

As we were all dumping bags inside, somebody remarked, "It's very cold in here!"

We stood still, suddenly appreciating the stark contrast with the pleasant temperature outside. Rosemarie disappeared into the bedrooms and emerged with a grim expression. "The beds are wet!"

"What's that? I asked the bloody agents to put the heating on a couple of days early," I said in a rage.

"Well they haven't," Jeremy said, springing out of a cellar which nobody else had realised existed, "the boiler's stone cold."

"And don't swear," Nicholas and Carolyn advised me, together.

(I had in fact discovered, quite by accident, that the way to stop my children swearing was to swear oneself. They were therefore running a campaign to stop me swearing and Rosemarie from smoking. We were both very difficult to bring up.)

The euphoria of the first few minutes slipped away. Rosemarie began a more careful examination of the place. I heard metallic noises which sounded like Jeremy dismembering the boiler.

We dumped the last of our belongings in the hall. The floors were bare wood, or tiles. Large damp balls of fluff clung to them like barnacles. "There's a sort of smell of ..?" Carolyn was sniffing the air, searching for words.

"Mouldy wood?" Nicholas contributed.

Carolyn opened a wardrobe door and let out an affirmative "Pooh!"

A mattress walked out of a room. The legs looked like Rosemarie's.

"Right, let's get cracking," a voice commanded from somewhere in the mattress.

For the next couple of hours our human chain worked like angry ants. Through the bushes we found a large area of unkempt lawn, unscreened by trees. Into this blessed sunlit pool we marched backwards and forwards carting the contents of the villa.

Mattresses, blankets, sheets, pillow cases and chairs were exposed and in the hours that followed we turned them over, and over again, like frying eggs.

Between times I phoned the local French agents, who -so we had been informed by the English agents who had actually taken the money - would attend to our needs. There was a long discussion during which the entente became less cordial.

"Ce n'etait pas a nous, l'occasion," they explained,

And so, they continued, as they themselves had not let the villa, although they might have said they would turn on the heating, why should they?

I said, yes, yes, quite, but I understood they were the local agents for the villa.

"We are. But we didn't let it."

"Alors," I compromised, "Voulez-vous nous envoyer quelqu'un pour marcher en route le chauffage."

My school French needed tuning. I wondered if I might have asked them to send an army driver, or hot water bottle instead of somebody to attend to the heating. I gathered they might send somebody but not before six o'clock. It was now eleven in the morning.

"We are frozen and our beds are wet," I hoped I said in French.

"Oui. Six o'clock."

"Merci beaucoup," I snarled.

We were beginning our French education. The French are reputed to be a highly logical race. This may be so in the Academies of Paris.

In the south, where Provence touches azur seas, Mediterranean logic begins.

A business provides customers with a necessary service. Customers will therefore be grateful. A proper customer will accept that the time, and the conditions under which a service or product is provided is best decided by experts -those who run the business. Certainly not by the customer, the favoured one.

Such times and conditions may change from one telephone call to the next. Why not, when nobody is in a hurry, and there's always tomorrow?

As I slammed down the receiver Jeremy sprang from some nether region. He was wearing the complacent look which precedes news of a practical man's success.

Having waited for my "Well?" he said, "The boiler's working." He had found a number of buttons switches and valves and had attacked them in the correct order.

At his words we all stood stock still, listening. From beneath our feet came the lovely muffled reverberations of a boiler commencing to "marcher en route." Practical Jeremy once more basked in family glory.

From the kitchen came an almighty clatter. Rosemarie hadn't stopped to listen. She was throwing out junk from the store of alleged kitchen utensils.

Our chain of human ants recommenced, morale uplifted. From time to time a hand would take time off for a furtive feel of a radiator. They were warming, but too little, too slowly. The penetrating chill remained.

By way of thankfulness Carolyn uttered the family formula to cope with all tragedies: "I'll make some tea."

It was now late afternoon. The sun was fast fading. We sank into the old chairs. There came a loud cracking sound, Nicholas's tall figure slowly subsided through the sagging framework of his chair, depositing him on the stone floor.

"I've been deaded!" cried our longtime Goon fan.

We made a closer examination of the furniture and it was clear that its faded glory would be maintained only so long as it was not actually sat upon.

There came, now, scraping noises from the kitchen and an explosive squeak or two. It was either large mice or Carolyn in trouble. We all made for the kitchen. We found Carolyn busy turning knobs, lighting matches and muttering threats and incantations.

The kettle stood cold on the stove. As Jeremy approached, Carolyn squawked, "I can do it!" He withdrew. But time passed and still we had no gas. Everybody seemed surprised but then I was the only one who had spoken to the agency.

I called "Jeremy!" and Carolyn reluctantly gave way.

Our secret anti-agency weapon began searching around and under the stove, in and out of cupboards. Before long there came a clicking noise from some other nether region whence he had disappeared.

There came a muffled, "Try it!" We had gas. Tea at last was served. We took it outside. The balmy evening air enveloped us even more sweetly coming from the dank, chill interior. The bedding was still wet.

I telephoned the London agents. They had, after all, copped the commission. They agreed it was terrible, these French agents. They too were desolate. But since there was nothing they could do wouldn't it be a good idea if I 'phoned the owner?

Oh, there was one other piece of advice. "If I were you I should treat yourself to a good stiff brandy," the hearty voice from London said.

I spoke to the owner. He was helpful and considerately invited us to spend the night at a local hotel at his expense. The can-carrier is invariably the one who picks it up, not he who kicks it out. The London agent later advised the owner he had been too generous.

The following night we were able to stay at the villa.

Those friends consumed with envy at our Mediterranean frolics would have been more cheerful could they have seen us. The boiler was working (madly consuming expensive fuel oil) but the heating wasn't.

We were fully dressed in our scanty supply of winter clothes. And we wore blankets over the clothes. After all, only mad dogs and Frenchmen employ winter coats in the Riviera of the brochures. We certainly hadn't brought any along.

There was one toilet in the bathroom. We needed another. This problem was also solved. In the darkest corner of the cellar Rosemarie found an old toilet. It was dirty, spidery, and bunged up with paper and what preceded the paper. Nobody would go near it.

Rosemarie was observed proceeding in the direction with pail, mop, broom, cloths, rubber gloves, and a fixed expression. The calls of "want any help?" were less honest than usual.

An hour later I opened the new facility with a proving pee and a stiff whisky for Rosemarie.

As we shivered that evening, our minds at least were warmed with expectancy as we huddled over the map on the floor. We'd bought some nautical charts showing all the harbours and marinas in the region, none more than an hour's drive away.

Jeremy was planning a technological assault on the boiler, having turned down my suggestion of hob-nailed boots. Nicholas was into a novel, somewhere in Russia with the Karamazovs. That left the enthusiastic Carolyn on her hands and knees, finger prodding eastwise along the coast. Each time she found a name on our list her finger jabbed triumphantly and her voice rose another tone.

"La Rague!" A moment later, "La Napoule!" And so we proceeded up the scale to Cannes, Pierre Canto, La Callice, Antibes, Nice, Baie des Anges, St. Jean Cap Ferrat, Beaulieu, Monaco, Menton. Harbours with myriad makes and designs of craft not available in the U.K.

For years they had been names in an unlikely dream. Now they were a few hours sleep and a short drive away.

The children beat us out of bed in the morning. "Not another coffee," the normally book-bound Nicholas snarled at us over breakfast, "we'll never go." It was eight o'clock. We bundled into the car.

The skies were the clear deep blue of winter, not the milky haze of summer, as we wound along the Corniche de L'Esterel.

Large red sandstone bluffs, like a miniature Grand Canyon loomed above us on our left; to our right, or starboard as the kids insisted - wooded escarpments fell steeply towards the sea. And yes, only one description was possible - azur. We passed only one other car on this beautiful scenic road which in summer is nose to tail metal.

We began to descend to the plain leading to Cannes. Suddenly we rounded a corner and were looking down on a forest of masts above ranks of gleaming white hulls. It was La Rague.

We slowed and stopped, to take in our fill of hulls, superstructures, and sails white and beckoning in the sun,

"Look! Is that the one we're going to see?" Carolyn exclaimed hopefully pointing to the largest sleekest yacht on view, miniaturized from our high viewpoint.

"Well over a hundred feet long. Probably got a helicopter. Just what we want," I said.

"Oh," said Carolyn, to family chuckles at Mademoiselle's haute tastes.

A few minutes later we entered the marina, nestling under the eastern arm of the Corniche cliffs. Richard, the English agent due to show us around the boats we'd short listed, was waiting.

We followed him past jetties full of boats, old and new. There were the solid-looking sea-battling North European jobs - De Vries, Van Lent, De Beers from Holland – old British Silvers and Nicholsons, their wheelhouses set solidly above no-nonsense hulls; and then the Italians - Baglietto, Benetti, Amiral, smart designer-boats, styled like jet planes and designed not to fight the seas but to skim over them at speeds to impress.

As we rounded the jetty we recognized many of the boat names. After years on agents' lists (much to their despair), Rosemarie in particular with her memory for detail was in her element. Ah yes, that was the boat with one cabin too few; that was the one without an aft deck; this one had engines with a rapacious fuel consumption, and so on.

What we wanted was a good sea boat; and a livable one. Small enough for a family of five to handle, but large enough for teenagers and parents to get away from each other sometimes.

Richard signaled us to stop. "Here we are. She's got everything you want. But she's been let go a bit." He indicated a scruffy boat moored mockingly between two smart Italian outer-space jobs.

We'd pinned a lot of hopes on her. A good sea boat from an English yard; well equipped; the accommodation we needed - four cabins. And she was within our price range.

The reason for that was clear as we stepped aboard.

"Did Richard say she'd been let go - or dropped off the Eiffel Tower?" Nicholas enquired.

It is always depressing to be aboard a badly cared-for boat. Varnish and decks alike were peeling. Brightwork was rusting.

I entered the wheelhouse. It was cramped and the chrome and wood panels addled with sea and neglect. The design suggested switches knobs and pieces of equipment had been tossed in the air and stuck where they fell.

Carolyn was frowning around the saloon. "I suppose it's alright for a holiday, but it's a bit much for living in, and doing schoolwork," she said, obviously fearful that I might fall for the first bridge that fluttered a spoked wheel at me.

But this raddled old lady had long lost her charms. Jeremy walked out of the engine room with hunched shoulders which needed no commentary.

We returned to the car a little chagrined. We were prepared for a boat, in our price range, which required love and care to restore to the pristine state of yesteryear. But this gave us no chance.

"Well that was our white hope, that was," Rosemarie said.

Richard frowned, sharing our disappointment. "She was in good nick when I saw her only a few months ago," he said, and we all mused silently on the significance of that remark. The sea environment is unforgiving.

Richard pointed. "There's a De Vries motor-sailor. Only eight knots. But it's in lovely condition."

We followed his finger. We saw a classic motor-sailer with canoe stern and gleaming paint and brightwork. We sped the car around the jetty and we were all cheerful hope again.

Our disappointment this time was that the cabins were for occasional use by midgets, not for permanent use by our adult-sized, still growing teenagers. But we remained in better humour. There might yet be attractive boats available within our range.

As we departed Richard said, "Don't worry. I'll do a tour of the ports. I'll find what you want, I'm sure I will."

We liked him and he inspired a confidence not shared by other agents we'd met..

So at dinner that evening in the villa we opened our bottle of vin de table, and with some cheer raised our glasses to Jernica.

Carolyn's small glass of wine did nothing to remove her impatience. Gloomily she said, "We'll never live on a boat. I just can't believe we will." And then with questionable (albeit familiar) logic she added, "I wish we were on the boat now. I just can't wait!"

"You can't wait!" Jeremy exclaimed indignantly, clearly thinking that the wait for his engines was on a higher plane.

The central heating was a mess and it took us a cold month to discover it was pumping expensive hot water under the foundations. But we had all the warmth we needed in the excitement and expectations around the table that evening.

THE VAR - CHASING
PAPER AND CHEDDAR

I n the weeks that followed, Rosemarie would serve up meals of the quality and quantity which the children and I regarded as our Natural Right. In between times she was leading the scrubbing of paintwork, walls and cupboards and polishing floors.

We found the local shops, and the local markets. A collapsible bike, ready for the boat, carried Carolyn in the mornings to the boulangerie. She could have visited any one of about four within the same short ride.

The French never did believe nonsense stories that bread makes you fat. And if it were to be true, they would not believe it. They make it delicious and eat it in all sorts of varieties. Life is for living. Bread is the staff of life.

Carolyn returned triumphantly from her first visit in negotiating a purchase in the mysteries of the French language.

"They were really nice," she said of the shopkeepers. "Wanted to know what English people are doing here this time of the year."

She then plonked down before her slavering parents and curious brothers a very long, very thin needle of bread. Various noises of disbelief arose.

Brits are brought up on a diet of consumer-complaint. When abroad, look for the rip-off. "They knew you were English alright. I'd better go next time," said big brother Nicholas, drawing fierce abuse from a defensive but defiant Carolyn.

Next morning, Carolyn and Nicholas went together. We discovered that the brand of long, torpedo-shaped bread, proud trade-mark of France was, locally at least, not a baguette, but a "restaurant." Ask for a baguette, and you get a needle.

A baguette is no less tasty. But as parents we discovered yet another fact of modern life. As Rosemarie and I rhapsodized each morning, the kids looked on in some disgust, and moaned nostalgically about English sliced bread; that's right, the white plastic stuff.

What can you do? Or as we were beginning to say, Que faire?

Helping us say it in French was our regular morning diet of the "Nice Matin." This is the daily bible on the Riviera with separate editions for the departments of the Var, and the neighbouring, more fashionable, Alpes Maritimes.

It is a cross between the most provincial local 'paper, and a national. Most eagerly awaited locally are the scores of photos of local groups, children, dignitaries;

and ceremonies with the mayor, of which there is never a shortage.

We noticed that it wasn't a campaigning paper. We began to learn about the Med.

In later months, and years, we became aware that somewhere, as our family had travelled down the A8 Autoroute an invisible and magic line was crossed.

We remained in France. But we - and all northern travelers like us -including the northern French, who are no less affected - enter another region.

It is one timelessly affected by the heat, and the indolence, of the Mediterranean climate. The mores that breed in this hothouse environment are not those of the cold lands of Viking, Saxon or Norman.

The first superficial signs are the Provençal twang. We learned to amend our schoolboy French. We asked not for the Nice "Matin" but the Nice "Mataing". For the very useful word "enfin"- at last - we learned to say with a nasal twang, "enfang".

As to another difference, reporting, sure, the activities of local political bigwigs, mayors, senators, businessmen are there to be reported. But if they are not perfect, this is not for nobodies to criticise. Anyway, what can there be to criticise?

After all, this is the Cote d'Azur. Or to some, the Riviera. Either way it's the coastline running from Marseilles to St. Raphael, comprising the Var coast; and then from Cannes, skirting Monaco and on to the Italian border at Menton, the Alpes Maritimes. This is home to the fashionable of Europe as well as the world's dictators fat on Swiss bank accounts. (An easy way to annoy any citizen of the Alpes Maritimes is to tell them they live in Provençe - which they do. 'Ah, non monsieur, that's the area to the west inhabited by peasants.')

The seas are genuinely transparent azur. The hinterland is a world of valleys, mountains for hang-gliding, sweet-scented maquis and ski slopes and superb restaurants tucked away in old hillside villages. The weather is long on the warmth, and indeed intolerable heat craved for by sun-starved northerners.

The choice of fresh local foodstuffs in the markets is mouth-watering in spring and summer-even though in winter it's back to the supermarkets for vegetables.

On the Cote d'Azur, the harvest of all this munificence is free-spending tourists. They arrive in summer. It is then steamy hot and so of course one must only amble about one's work.

True the visitors are not there in the winter; but why hassle to scratch around for a little more at a time when the climate is perfect for leisure, and summer anyway pays for all?

It is such an agreeable arrangement of nature. What fools would want to disturb it? It is accepted as facts of life and a total lack of surprise that politicians are likely to be corrupt, and rich men will have mistresses.

There is only one original sin and that is upsetting the business of earning a good living in this blessed clime. Upset the commercial shakers and movers, and you upset god's business.

We could find no echo in the local editions of "Nice Matin" of scandal stories carried in British newspapers about Nice's then famous mayor, Gaston Medecin (who later did a runner to South America). The attacks on Medecin by Britain's most famous local expatriate, Graham Greene, then living in Antibes, rang round the world, but had all the impact of a damp squib on the Cote d' Azur.

We discovered the word "plastiqué" from the Nice Matin. Not infrequently there were short reports that this restaurant, that club or bar or disco had been "plastiquéd." We first assumed that their frontages were being reshaped by plastic. But then the accompanying pictures of wreckage began to sink in. Reshaping was right - but the plastic was of the explosive kind, the administration of which ensured the owners realized they really did need protection. No thunder from the editorials. Not even a squeak.

The effects do not touch the golden geese - the tourists, except indirectly. The major Casino in Nice was closed down for some years as a result of indiscreet gang infighting which became too public.

We gave up twitting our French friends about these events on their doorstep.

Shrug, palms up, lips pushed out, eyebrows raised, head on one side. "C'est la Côte d'Azur, n'est-ce pas?"

When we raised our heads in the mornings from the "Nice Mating", and had finished the 'restaurant' bread, the butter croissants (only truly crowned by French apricot jam) and the steaming bowls of coffee, we could enjoy the garden.

Some weeding had revealed irises in the flower-beds and doves in the trees. These birds had a throaty call which the family decided sounded like the croupier's , "Faites vos jeux!"

After all, they were French doves and if they didn't actually play roulette they'd know about it. Thereafter any member of the family going about their work could be heard humming unconsciously, "Faites vos jeux!" to the call of the doves.

Funds were short. But on rare occasions, in between schoolwork and boat-seeking we could enjoy the charms of St. Raphael.

We enjoyed best sitting at one of the cafes facing the old port in late evening, the sun in our eyes, an aperitif - or coke -in our hands. The red-lit skies of the fast-dropping sun, together with the painted hues of the local fishing boats made a vast shimmering coloured canvas in the waters of the port.

Shopkeepers were pleasant. If they weren't, a prime cause was our inability to phrase perfect grammar, or pronunciation; or, horrors, get the gender wrong.

For some French - the bourgeois in particular - France is the centre of the universe, and the whole civilised world speaks perfect French. If that doesn't include you, tant-pis.

We always visited one chemist in the town with some trepidation. The first time I walked in and asked for "un bouteille" of something or the other, the mature, immaculately-dressed and coiffed lady shop-assistant looked out of the window and said she hadn't any, when I could see it on the shelf.

Some time later, after several abject pleadings, she took the bottle down, handed it over still looking stonily out of the window and said, "Ah, vous voulez UNE bouteille.." of whatever it was.

In such cases, humiliation is mandatory before service.

One Sunday morning Rosemarie and I crept out of bed early, to avoid the children and bloody tourists. We were making for the food market.

We set off along the palm-fringed sea front. Within ten minutes we reached the pretty crescent bay and could look down where in summer waiters would be busy preparing tables at the restaurants backing the sandy beach.

Across the road, cafe tables with brightly-coloured umbrellas had already lured the early apperitif drinkers. Glamour was added by the gambling Casino standing on the corner where 007 himself would not have looked out of place.

We set off along a side street for the heart of the town and the covered market. It was populated mostly with local women. The men sat in the adjacent bars sipping their morning Ricard, watching and assessing the passing parade, nodding, smiling, their words playing second fiddle to their arm gestures.

We later found that even in mid-season, at that time in the morning there would not be a tourist in sight. We hoped that by now we were well camouflaged as locals.

The stalls were laid out with a variety of fresh foodstuffs. We avoided the popular horse-meat stall. We could have found our way to the cheese stall blindfold.

At the fish stall we chose an enormous section of dorade, which with a Provencal sauce is the most typical fish dish to be found in the local restaurants; Rosemary then lost herself in the wide variety of lettuces, mesclun, blett - a sort of winter cabbage - and herbs of all kinds - parsley, thyme, basil, herbes de Provence.

At one stall an old lady dressed in an old woolen belted winter coat, wool hat and wool mittens had laid out a small selection which was obviously fresh from her garden, rather than a farm. In the spring we would see her with a variety of herbs, little piles of dandelion leaves, haricots, peas and beans, which she would be busy shelling ready for her buyers.

Rosemarie by now was ready when in Provence to do as the Provençals do. She took the metal pannier offered by one of the stall holders; then she gently pushed and prodded and lifted the various produce for inspection before placing it in the container to be weighed.

Her fellow buyers would have been outraged at the strange English-market notion that you may examine and touch what you're going to eat only after you've paid for it.

One English food we couldn't replace. One day Rosemarie was in the local supermarket, before an enormous display of French cheese.

"Cheddar, s'il vous plaît," said Rosemarie.

"Les anglaises, alors," said a glowering lady queuing behind. "With all these delicious French cheeses, you still choose a mere English cheese. Quelle horreur!"

No French lady would think of guarding her tongue at such a scandalous moment.

Rosemarie explained. "Desolée, madame. But for making the Welsh rarebit, there is no French cheese that can match the Cheddar."

The French lady was taken aback and the queue ended up in an animated discussion agreeing they'd never heard of "Lapin Gaulloise", Welsh rabbit.

The kids made use of the sea on their doorstep. We hired diving gear and they went out on the local diving boat to learn the craft.

This wasn't possible at the time if they'd been back in England. The British Sub-aqua club's minimum age for learning was fifteen - only Nicholas would have qualified.

In the shop we met a stocky man with a leathery face. He was, as we learned, a quartermaster in charge of discipline on France's major aircraft carrier.

Jean was chunkily built, crew cut, with twinkling eyes, He was a genuine tough guy, the quiet kind that need no front or bulging biceps to prove their point.

He now took charge of our teen diving incompetents.. He was always calm, and, as to be expected, highly competent. As it turned out it was just as well. The French school's methods would have earned a few raised eyebrows in England.

There, the children had discovered the beginner must spend months in a swimming pool learning how to use his gear before being allowed in the sea.

With Rosemarie and me as passengers the dive-boat chugged out one morning to the little Lion island, just off the marina of St. Raphael.

Jean showed our three learners on board how the breathing equipment worked. Then the kids donned wet-suits and masks and clambered down the ladder into the sea.

We thought they'd go down a few feet and get used to using the equipment. So did they.

They were taken down to the seabed, fifty feet below the surface.

The instructor took off his face mask and gestured to them to do the same, showing them how to clear it and put it back on. Jean was watching.

Jeremy: "I took mine off, tilted it, blew it to clear it as we'd been shown, and put it back on again. But there was a load of water and sand floating in it. I could see Jean finger wagging. I tried again, same result - finger still wagging. It all went misty."

He hadn't got the band of the mask off from the back of his head. Jean fixed it.

Next time they thought they'd go down fifty feet but went down further. Carolyn came up with Jean in close attendance and arrived on deck with a bloody nose! Jeremy staggered about a bit.

Rosemarie and I plastered grins on our faces to cover our fright. Jean laughed at seeing our concern. "Oui! They look like they've been in a war! But it's only diving!"

Rosemarie and I remained concerned. The kids loved it. Rather to our surprise, they stayed alive, and not to our surprise, become competent divers before they could have begun at home.

What Rosemarie and I most enjoyed about the diving was the drinks that followed with Jean and his friends at our cafe opposite the old port.

We asked him about the diving training methods.

He laughed and said, "You call it throwing the deep-end, heh? Your kids good."

We were content to drink to that.

The villa was beginning to shape up to Rosemarie's ideas of a family home. A major problem remained. We'd been able to bring few clothes and books in the car; and our hired kitchen was miserably equipped. These were early days of the Common Market.

In London we'd packed ten tea chests to follow us out. We assumed their arrival would be speedy. But we now received from Customs an enormous bundle of literature, in French.

"But we're in the Common Market now!" Rosemarie pointed out, "Free movement of goods and all that."

"There appears to be free movement," I said, thumbing through the literature, "for ten ton trucks, industrial boilers and the like. And for the French moving to England. But for goods headed in the other direction, especially our kid's books and our clothes we have to get permissions and rubber stamps from everyone in the French telephone directory."

Rosemarie collapsed into a chair; and I made the world's classic mistake, typical for a northern European come south. I decided to do everything by the book. Worse, I said, "We'll get a lawyer to sort it out."

The lawyer's walls in Cannes were covered with impressive certificates and it did cross my mind that perhaps he couldn't afford wallpaper. I showed him the documents.

"We'd like you to make sure we do everything right, and quickly," I explained. "We need those tea chests."

His English was clearly deficient, as he babbled back at us in French. Rosemarie picked up the gist.

"He wants a £500 retainer," she muttered. We didn't have the courage to walk out, and she dug into her handbag which tends to double up as a family goods carrier and wallet.

As Rosemarie handed over, the lawyer addressed us in fluent English. "I've dealt with this problem before," he said reassuringly. "You must first go to your local Town Hall to get a resident's certificate, and then take it to the tax office for their stamp. You do that and leave the rest to me."

We were both enormously relieved to learn how simple it would be. As he was showing us out I asked, "Are there likely to be any problems?"

"No - although of course the tax office won't give you a certificate. They never do."

The door and my mouth were half open. "But you said we needed their certificate," I pointed out.

He smiled and shrugged. "I'll deal with it. Leave it to me."

"How long will it all take?" Rosemarie asked before the door closed. "Ten days. Maybe two weeks."

Rosemarie grimaced but he was disappearing behind a broad smile and his broader door. Rosemarie said, "He's very charming."

Some time later he sent us forms to sign.

We returned them; and he sent them back to us for some signatures he'd forgotten to ask for.

"Never mind," I said, "he's charming."

We went to the Town Hall and were told to return in a week. It took three weeks of constant visits but they did produce a certificate.

Meanwhile Rosemarie was beginning to develop my habits of bad language and I was beginning to develop hers of smoking. But we were now free to go to the tax office.

"But there's no point," said Rosemarie. "The lawyer said they won't give us a certificate."

"We'll have to try," I said. The kids had no books; we'd been wearing the same clothes day after day. We had to wash up pots from one dish before Rosemarie could prepare another, as the least of her kitchen problems.

Behind it all was the infuriating knowledge that if our car or caravan or van had only been big enough, exactly the same goods could have accompanied us without a form in sight.

We knocked on the door of the tax-office. A girl appeared and we explained our mission. She pointed to another door. We moved towards it. "But the inspector only deals with applications on Wednesdays," she called after us. It was Monday.

"Isn't he in then?" I asked.

"Certainement! But only on Wednesdays, your business."

"Merci," I said, and Rosemarie said something else under her breath in her new found role as family assistant- swearer. We knocked on the door indicated. A harassed-looking man opened it and glared at me. I explained we wanted a certificate from him.

He snarled "Mercredi!" and went to slam the door.

Before he could do so, Rosemarie appeared smiling behind me. He stared, the door was thrown open, and then he almost fell backwards in his haste to smilingly beckon her in. I was allowed to stay too, grudgingly.

As Rosemarie spoke he listened beaming, nodded vigorously, began writing and finally flourished a gigantic rubber stamp with which he smacked on our certificate.

"Voila!" he said, his face wreathed with smiles at Rosemarie. He seemed reluctant for us to depart but finally we backed out.

"What a charming man," Rosemarie said. It is a mistake in Mediterranean countries to use lawyers; much better to use pretty women. They can clear problems of any kind in an instant.

Happy at last, we posted the certificates and waited for the succour of the packing cases. Instead, forms continued to arrive in shoals from the solicitor; we'd return them, and then he'd send them back to us for more signatures.

After six weeks, in desperation and with threats of divorce I was back in London chasing our cases.

I made another terrible mistake, still following "the book." I fixed an appointment with a French bureaucrat, an official at the French consulate in London.

A bulky fellow, he was known unofficially, I learned, as Hardy. I looked around but couldn't see Laurel.

He waved me into a chair. Before him was the formidable pile of documents we had amassed. They weighed about as much as the tea chests. For ten minutes I sat in obedient silence as he fingered through them, fondling and nodding at the pages. I waited for him to work his rubber stamp, and then hand them back so I could be off.

He looked up, impressively bulky. "It is very serious."

He spoke with great deliberation and looked at me for an explanation. I, of course, had none; I had only a great ringing in my ears of alarm bells.

He handed me the forms slowly, in the careful manner of one entrusting valuables to an idiot. "See there!" His pudgy finger poked at the page.

I could see nothing of significance, except paper.

Finally he sighed and said slowly and distinctly, "You see. Your lawyer has sent a photocopy of the certificate."

"Good," I said.

Shaking his head he said, "We must have the original."

I launched into an explanation of our needs, kitchen equipment, books for the kids' schooling, clothes- we were freezing, and sorry about the lawyer but the certificate was obviously genuine wasn't it?

He handed me very carefully five more forms all identical. He indicated a dozen lines which required completion - my age and the children's, purpose of visit, nature of goods, value, etc.

"But these details are already on the forms you have," I pointed out.

He shook his head, and my heart sank.

"Alors?" I said, hoping that mercy might be extended to a French-speaking member of the EEC.

"You must fill in the other forms."

"With the same information?"

"Even so."

"Of course! Why not? Ha ha," I laughed.

Some time later with cramp in my fingers and hate in my heart I finished.

He slowly inspected and fondled each page with the kind of attention which would have seemed possible only for a Sultan inspecting a new batch for the harem. When satisfied, he would stamp them, sometimes two whacks to a page.

At last he replaced the stamps, sat back, and gave a glacial smile, saying nothing.

"Toute va bien?" I said, with a sinking feeling it wasn't.

"This is a note I've written for French customs," he said pointing.

"Ah? Why?"

"It points out that the certificate is a photocopy."

"Alors?" I enquired, not wishing to overwork my vocabulary.

"So, they may not accept the documents when your goods arrive," he explained, and for the first time in our encounter looked positively happy.

When I arrived back at my London quarters a message was waiting from a transport company I had contacted. An hour later I met the proprietor in a pub in Notting Hill.

He took the sheaf of papers, admired the stamps and heard my story.

"You say you told the lawyer you'd soon be living on a boat - and would cruise the whole Mediterranean?" he enquired.

"Yes."

"Well these forms are no good to you. They allow you to import personal possessions into France free of duty - but you can't export them for two years."

I spilled my beer.

He looked at the list of goods. "Nothing of real interest to customs here. No great values. We'll list some of it, pay twenty five per cent duty and have done with it. I'll have the goods with you in three days."

We paid, they were.

Northern politicians may one day understand that there is an uncommon understanding by Mediterranean Europe of the munificent words, "Common Market."

What is given, will be taken in common. What is due, will commonly and cheerfully be administered to death.

JERNICA FOUND

With our state of siege lifted and the villa growing more habitable we could spend more time looking for Jernica. The marinas were packed with attractive vessels. It seemed impossible we wouldn't find her.

But we were handicapped by our price tag. I telephoned a leading French agency. A girl took details, breathing politeness. Then she asked, "How much do you want to pay?" I told her.

There was a lengthy pause. She appeared not to have heard very well for she asked me to repeat the figure. There was another long delay. Then she said, as icily as only a French business girl can when dealing with importuners, "We can offer you a 1935 Camper & Nicholson."

I made the noises of gratitude appropriate to a pauper wasting the time of a girl waiting to do her nails and then asked, "Anything more modern?"

"Oui. A Silver 1950." She rapped out the details and then put the phone down remembering another urgent call. Forget Brigitte Bardot. French office girls can be tough.

Campers and Silvers were classic boats. But too old can mean too many problems unless one is very lucky. We were hoping to buy a boat not so much old, as oldish.

The Campers was in Paris, but the Silver was in Antibes. We always journeyed to this old Port with hope: like pilgrims on their way to Jerusalem.

The visitor to the town bursts through the thick traffic, down the hill, and the port opens up before him. An old fort dominates the northerly rampart of the massive sea wall. Forming the other leg of the harbour is the old wall of Antibes, on which stands a church and terraces of houses built from massive stone blocks.

At a view are hundreds of boats. They include the loveliest and largest to be found. And some of the ugliest. We found our Silver. She had long slipped out of the 'loveliest' category. From the quay, caulking could be seen taking leave of decks, and woodwork was blackened with water.

We didn't know what she was like under the waterline, but we reckoned she would sink anyway if it rained hard enough. There wasn't much chatter on the return journey.

Out of the silence Rosemarie said with wifely prescience, "You're thinking that that's what we have to expect in our price range."

"More or less," I said. That was exactly what I'd been thinking but I didn't want her to develop the habit.

We went to see a converted MFV (motor fishing vessel) at Beaulieu. MFV bespoke sea worthiness and the details suggested the accommodation was good. We travelled with that special kind of hope which descends as a mantle on seekers-after-boats; it is unquenchable in face of successive disappointments in face even of the plain facts of life and money.

Beaulieu is perhaps the most attractively sited of the French marinas. The bay in which it lies just east of Cap Ferrat is composed of steep, rich green rolling escarpments enfolding the boats nestled below.

We drove into this grand setting and looked around hopefully at the boats - all spotless. It is a very expensive, trés-snob marina. Rosemarie gave a little shake of the head.

"I know what you're thinking," I said with husbandly prescience. "The setting's too rich to discover Jernica." She nodded.

Our boat had stopped being an MFV. A small flat had been built on the aft deck. A very sweet French lady showed us clusters of divans, chests of drawers. And a grand piano. Three different owners had all added their own design of pipes, valves and other bits and pieces in the engine room which Jeremy regarded with a worried frown.

We dutifully bowed and murmured, "Fantastique", and withdrew before she could demonstrate the magnificent tone of the piano. None of us played anyway. We lingered to gaze at other boats which were either not for sale, or too expensive for you, M'sieur, and drove away.

The days turned into weeks and then a month was gone. The kids slogged unbidden at their correspondence courses - which would have surprised at least one very good friend and headmaster who had assured us that a stick was a necessary companion to carrots. But there was now no teacher to blame if their studies went astray. The responsibility was theirs alone. They got on with it with a will.

We had time to enjoy the company of good friends we'd made of several French families. Luckily they were as anxious to improve their English, as we our French.

But our thoughts were always longingly on Jernica, wondering as each day passed if we weren't really asking too much.

One morning the telephone rang. It was Richard. He had, as promised, scoured the coast. "I've found the boat for you. In Cannes."

"Oh yes." My voice was as flat and toneless as I felt. We'd heard the phrase before.

Richard caught my tone. "She really is," he insisted. He gave me some encouraging details about the accommodation.

I called Rosemarie. She picked up the earpiece which the French telephone service thoughtfully provides for boat-hunting families.

"It's a 65ft De Vries Lentsch. Her accommodation could have been designed for you. It's just what you want."

"How old?"

"She was built in 1961. But she's in beautiful condition."

"Good sea boat?"

"A De Vries Lentsch! She's got to be! And steel."

"Price?"

"More than you want to pay. But it's open to an offer!"

The tone of my voice and Rosemarie's animated face had caught the children's attention. As I replaced the receiver I was peppered with excited questions.

"Could be it!" Rosemarie told them beaming. "Richard is someone who actually knows what we're looking for!"

I was prepared for more disappointment. I tried the nonchalant Provencal approach. I raised up my eyebrows, turned down my mouth, lifted my arms, and shrugged. But I hadn't been trained long enough.

"Richard certainly seems to think it's for us," I heard me say.

Sleep that night was difficult. We set off next morning along the golden road to our ports in a mood of excitement.

We hadn't visited Cannes before for boat hunting. La Croissette, the broad parade of Cannes is famous for its topless starlets and millionaires, in that order. Wide beaches are backed by broad promenades with sleek expensive boutiques. It all threatens to drown in a torrent of snarling traffic, but never quite goes down.

We entered Cannes from the west along the Quay St. Pierre, a broad attractive boulevard. On our left a mixture of sailors and yacht-crews various - some known less elegantly along the marinas as boat-bums- sat at tables in front of the rows of cafes and restaurants.

In some of the restaurants only the very rich would be eating later at their candle-lit tables. Far above soared the ancient streets of the old port: looking out to sea and affording an early glimpse of a loved one returning home. Spectacular when floodlit at night, it was even more enchanting to us at that moment.

Yachts were stern-to on our right. This was the old port.

The millionaires' yachts - very large, eye-catching Sleeping Beauties waiting for their summer Prince and a brief kiss of life - were more likely to be found midst the boutiques off the several huge marinas sited around Cannes such as Pierre Canto and La Napoule.

But here, apart from an odd infiltrator or two, the boats looked more workmanlike. They looked as though they saw more of the sea. They didn't look out of place alongside the fishing boats moored at the far end. On the quayside the fishermen were working nimbly at their nets as their forefathers had done for generations before - although they'd now have TV at home and their catch now cost more than prime beef.

As we drove the last few yards there was some ribaldry about at last finding our perfect boat, until Rosemarie said, "There's Richard! He looks so enthusiastic."

"That's because he hasn't known us fusspots too long," Carolyn observed, thinking of all the agents who'd fallen by the wayside in our two years' search. We'd become regarded as professional 'lookers'.

We got out of the car and greeted Richard. We looked along the mooring trying to spot the boat he had in mind. He smiled and said "Come on."

We passed several boats where we were all thinking "surely not that one," before he stopped at the end of a gangplank and smilingly pointed.

Our first sight was of an inviting teak deck aft, and a wheelhouse resplendent from the outside with shining varnish.

The skipper, a dark rather sad-looking Frenchman was waiting to welcome us on board. We removed our shoes and walked slowly aboard.

Anybody searching for a house has had the same sensation. One looks and looks; you count on your fingers each of the features you must have. Then one day you enter a door. You stop counting. You don't care what the individual features are. You know simply you want this one.

After two years and about thirty false hopes, this was what happened to us. All of us. We were home. We wanted this beauty.

The wheelhouse was large and airy with all-round vision. The interior filled the eye with beautifully varnished wood, deeply satisfying after so many plastic vistas. The decks and fittings were well cared for, the metal shining.

I stood behind the gleaming brass and wood wheel, handling it, looking over the bows to the rippling waters.

Rosemarie had disappeared below. I waited anxiously for her to reappear. She was bound to find something wrong. Why did I marry someone so practical?

She reappeared in an excited flurry and punched me on the shoulder. "It's just what we want! It could have been built for us." She dragged me off the wheel. "Come and see the cabins and the galley."

Everywhere down below fine handicraft was visible in the handsome deeply-grained woodwork of bulwarks and cupboards. The dimensions had been calculated to the millimeter to provide ideal accommodation for us.

Rosemarie pulled me along. "Come on!" The galley was an extension of the lower saloon, on the same level.

There aren't many women ship's architects which probably explains why the galley is too often in the bowels of a ship, leaving it to the cook's imagination to work out if the sun or moon is shining aloft; and requires food to be humped up steep steps.

"Look how well you can see out," Rosemarie said, dancing about. There was a stove, sink, even a fridge. And Rosemarie was opening lockers and cupboards galore. "What fabulous storage!" said the practical one.

Forward of the galley was a large fo'c'sle with its own shower and toilet ideal for one of the kids. We moved aft.

On many yachts this area is consumed by a vast owner's cabin - or "stateroom". It's an effective way of tickling a prospective owner's ego so that he reaches for the cheque- book. Anybody else is then accommodated in bunks squeezed into adjacent cupboards.

This owner's cabin was a comfortable size, but it left room for two smaller but well-proportioned cabins.

"Look how well I fit," Carolyn beamed at me meaningfully, sitting at the built-in table in one of the smaller cabins.

Rosemarie was like a magician, finding and opening wardrobes, drawers, lockers, in all sorts of places. "Storage, storage!" she kept exclaiming excitedly.

Jeremy appeared at the double. Carolyn swept an arm around, "Look! Isn't it great."

"Yes, yes," said Jeremy making a great show of looking around. "Come and look at the engine room."

We climbed down a vertical iron ladder from the wheelhouse. We entered a large space running the beam of the boat and about fifteen feet long. The gleaming cylinders of two large diesel engines - GM 6-71s -dominated the area. Each was 147 horsepower. There was also a very large diesel generator.

Overall, my untutored gaze registered a fearsome mass of pipes, knobs, hoses, valves and switches. But even I could see the proportions were right; stand-up room, and just space enough to work around the intricate network of metal.

My heart sunk as I looked at my thirteen year-old. I suddenly saw us on a raging sea with all the pipes and joints springing leaks," Will we be able to handle all this?" I asked, meaning, "will you?"

But Jeremy was far away, Midas in his counting house. He rummaged around the engines. "These must be the fuel filters - oil filters here - heat exchangers.... "he went on, touching the parts like a priest laying-on hands.

"First though," he said. "It'll need some de-rusting, and a jolly good clean up. Then we can paint it."

His confidence eased my nerves and I retired hastily aloft leaving Jeremy in a state of high excitement.

Richard had been looking under floorboards. He held some up so I could look at the bilges. The hidden areas of the boat were clearly as well tended as those in sight. A tour of the decks confirmed the same care had been taken of the fittings.

I stood again behind the large wheel. It was a romantic wheel, brass-spoked, and varnished, not one of those tiny black things created by some ergonomically-crazed modern designer.

The family was now gathered in the wheelhouse, looking, touching, gazing out to sea.

It suddenly hit me that a yacht with these features would never be available at our price.

"Oh God," I said aloud. "We won't be able to afford her."

"Richard said you can make an offer," said Rosemarie anxiously.

"I can't see the owner accepting what I can offer," I said waving an arm around at all the marine loveliness.

"Oh Dad! Don't be like that," Carolyn admonished, in her exasperated -with-the-old-folks tone.

But this, it appeared, was not the only problem.

The middle-aged French skipper's dark eyes were melancholy. I felt for him. At fifteen years of age the boat couldn't have looked very much better when she left the builder's yard. But we had told him we would be our own crew.

"How is she as a sea-boat," I now asked him.

To my astonishment he shook his head vigorously.

"No?" I queried falteringly.

"After all, M'sieur, she is not a trawler."

I said as cheerfully as I could, "But if you're out in a bit of a breeze, no real problems?"

He held out both hands and moved them violently from side to side.

"The stern goes like that!"

We had to have a good sea-boat. With that there could be no compromise. We'd have aboard a family and our home.

Carolyn had picked up the conversation and must have seen the expression on my face. She said "After all dad, we're not doing single-handed around the world stuff."

"You know how often we've agreed we must have a good sea-boat," I said, and Carolyn hurried off to attend to more important matters.

Further questioning couldn't shake Gaston's gloomy appraisal of the boat's seaborne qualities. "The rudder's been changed" he suddenly added. "It could fall off."

We had been speaking French. I checked over in my mind vocabulary learned at school and more recently from "Nice Matin". I decided I hadn't understood him very well.

"Fall off?" I faltered unbelievingly?

He nodded his sad eyes even sadder.

Rosemarie appeared wanting to know what Gaston was on about. She'd been poking about happily, discovering even more storage space.

I started to explain to Rosemarie that, after all, alors, she wasn't a trawler. My tone must have been reassuring or more likely she wasn't listening for she skipped away for further explorations. Gaston was meanwhile rummaging around amid some charts and documents.

He tapped my arm. When he had my full attention he traced a finger over some drawings he'd pulled out. He stopped at the rudder.

"In heavy seas..." he didn't finish his sentence. Instead he waggled one hand in rudder style, then smote it sharply with the other. I saw the rudder disintegrating.

Jeremy had now emerged from below. I grasped Gaston's hand and mumbled "Au revoir." Richard had departed earlier for another appointment.

We left the boat and waited to cross the busy Quai St. Pierre.

Jeremy asked, "Will it take long to buy her?" his face aglow.

Rosemarie was beside herself with delight. "We really could live on her!"

Nicholas said, "It's great, when will we get her?"

As he had spent time looking over her when he could have been dipping his nose into Disraeli's "Vivian Grey" we knew he really meant it.

"Skipper says she's not a good sea-boat," I said, as we made our way to the car. The excited chattering stopped. They looked at me as though I'd taken leave of my senses. I knew how the Ambassador felt who brought bad news to the Pharaohs and was strangled for his pains. I told them what Gaston had said about her.

Jeremy was first to answer. "What? A de Vries Lentsch?"

Built by a famous yard; beautiful workmanship; lovely lines. How could she also be a lousy sea-boat?

Jeremy was right. We desperately wanted to believe there had to be something wrong with the skipper's story, and we decided there was. Much of the gloom lifted.

A little niggle persisted.

Some friends, Douglas and his wife Pamela, accompanied Rosemarie and I a few days later to look the boat over. He'd been years at sea and they'd lived aboard a ketch in Antibes for two years. As with so many yachtsmen and women, helping others on boats was a kindness which had become second nature. We would treat his opinion with respect.

We introduced him to Gaston. Douglas looked the boat over. He listened to the skipper's description of the deficient qualities with polite interest.

Gaston produced his plans and traced again the suspect rudder. In his down-to-earth Yorkshire accent Douglas said, "I can't see how that could be a problem."

Gaston paused in mid-breath, but he was lost only for seconds.

"Well yes," he said "after all, we've only lost one." He turned away with a deep sigh.

I could think only of the old comedian's challenge "Follow that!"

Douglas did. He just patted the skipper on the back and said consolingly, "Never mind."

Pamela emerged from below with Rosemarie. "There's such wonderful space," she said. "It will be perfect for you!"

As we came ashore Douglas looked back from the quay surveying our heart's desire with knowledgeable eyes. He said, "There's something about her I like." He grinned at me. "Absolutely no problems at sea!"

A glow fell over us such as must envelop a condemned man when embraced by the hangman with news that he is reprieved. Richard meanwhile had conveyed Gaston's fears to the owner. He threw a fit. He'd been out in all sorts of rough seas with her including Mistrals, "and weather I wouldn't contemplate with other boats."

Rosemarie and I travelled again to meet Gaston. We conveyed his owner's state of mild shock.

"Mais oui," Gaston shrugged. "As I was saying, it's only a yacht - so it shouldn't be taken out in a gale." Then he looked at us with a grin. "But if you should get caught out, d'accord, there isn't a safer boat around!"

I looked at him, but saw no cause to quarrel. We were more than happy to accept that the story was now straight, and fitted every visible piece of evidence.

Gaston's actions were understandable. He had given the boat love and devotion. That was clear from its condition. He was going to lose her. Of that we were now certain.

It is commonplace that all boats are compromises. We started off seeking all the virtues, Beauty, reliability, economy, space, sea-worthiness; and not expensive, please.

But to look for perfection in a boat is as idle as to seek it in a human being. She must be judged in the round.

We had few illusions after our years of searching, about perfection. But we had found the boat we wanted.

"There's no doubt this time," said Rosemarie as we departed from our final talk with Jacques, "we've found Jernica."

On this occasion the children had been left to their schoolwork and there were long demands for details when we arrived back. We told them the seaworthy bogey was finally laid.

I stilled the excited chatter. "Remember we've still got to persuade the owner to accept our figure. He's got to drop a lot, before we have a chance. And we've still to arrange a marine mortgage."

Carolyn was downcast, "I'll never believe we'll ever live on a boat. We're just, kind of, nowhere."

I said, "We're somewhere, we've found our boat. Before, we didn't really believe she existed."

"That's true," Rosemarie said. "But if somebody else steps in she won't exist again."

We thought it would be days. But it took weeks of hectic days on the telephone and restless nights to clear the complications of non-resident sterling mortgages.

During that time we all imagined cash-ready buyers swarming over our "Jernica", and bidding frenziedly; and the more we tried to push the thought away the more certain we were she'd be gone.

We found that most outings ended driving slowly past her, and if we saw a strange figure on board we would continue on our way slumped in gloom.

Then one day, to great excitement, the mortgage loan was made available. At last we had the means to make some kind of bid. I picked up the phone to contact Richard's firm.

He said, yes, she was still on the market. The family was hanging on my every word and we all breathed out in relief.

I made an offer. It was to the limit of our capacity, yet it sounded ludicrously low when I heard myself making it. I expected Richard to laugh and say 'pull the other one'. But he just said "OK" and rang off.

He rang back not very much later. The family gathered silently around the telephone, like townsfolk gathered to hear the news from the front.

"Sorry. The owner won't accept your price. But he will come down a bit."

"I'm really unable to go any higher," I mumbled truthfully. Richard made appropriate noises of sympathy.

I replaced the receiver to the silence which normally only precedes news of the end of the world. There was no way we could increase our bid.

I said "She's a lousy sea-boat. The rudder falls off."

Nobody had the heart even to say 'shut up'. Some hours later I suddenly found myself on the phone again explaining why our bid was a good one, and there was this other boat we had to make up our minds about ("Dad!" from open-mouthed and virtuous kids) and please try again. Richard said he would try.

I put the phone down to a deep depression passing over the family. The owner wouldn't come down. When the phone rang later we scrambled like Spitfire pilots in the films. There was a fight for the earpiece.

Sure enough it was Richard. "I've some good news for you. I've been on to the owner in Geneva. He's accepted your offer. Of course it's subject to sea trials and a survey." He added cheerfully, "We'll soon find out if anything falls off!"

I put the phone down, and was draped around with arms, hugs, squawks, beams. Champion of the World. We hauled out the Chateau bottle we'd brought from London ready for this moment and opened it. (We never did find where to find a good Chateau bottle in France. Presumably it's all exported.)

The kids, allowed one coke a week, finished off two weeks' rations. We toasted everybody we could think of, but especially Jernica.

Rosemarie and I pulled out our surprise package. Two years earlier at the Southampton boat show we'd bought T-shirts with "Jernica" embossed; we'd hidden them ever since.

Now we produced them still in their original wrappings. From somewhere a Breton fisherman's hat was slapped onto my head.

So, suitably dressed and with at least one moist eye from a young female unbeliever we toasted Jernica, our boat, at last coming into view over the horizon.

However, finding Jernica had been love at first sight, and we should have known better than to expect such an affair to run smoothly.

Our offer accepted, a few days later we fell upon Jernica for the day. As we strolled up the gangway on the Quai St. Pierre it was difficult to believe that she was likely to be ours.

Rosemarie measured and burrowed around. Jeremy got lost below, wooing engines. I wooed Gaston. The resultant diagrams I drew of the boat's systems as understood by me from Gaston' technical description in French would have made Heath Robinson green with envy, and caused Jeremy to scratch his head. But I thought they were great. It was a start to not leaving things to electricians and plumbers and handymen anymore, but to doing things ourselves.

Lunchtime, and we ate the first meal aboard prepared by Rosemarie. We rode back to the villa on a passing cloud.

To mounting excitement the momentous day arrived of our sea trial aboard Jernica. And there we were, unbelievably, heading out to sea, Cannes astern, just like that.

We all felt very emotional, but we also had a job to do. Gaston was at the helm. I asked him to turn the wheel sharply, all ways, putting the sea forward, astern and abeam.

Finally, I said to Gaston "Voila! Le rudder ne tombe pas!" He grinned. We did enough in a couple of hours to confirm that she was all the sea boat we wanted.

And then we were through to the final stages of the purchase, with our boat hauled out onto the slip. To nobody's surprise the survey was successful. At our request, the surveyor telexed his approval to the marine mortgage company in London to speed the matter. We were up and away over the last hurdle of our long journey. It was Friday.

On Monday morning I departed for Cannes. I was going to collect some money from the bank. But my prime purpose was to phone the marine mortgage company to confirm they'd received the telex and had issued our loan. I needed the cash which had arrived at the bank Friday to pay the yard where Jernica had been slipped for the survey. No pay, no boat was their very prudent rule.

I entered the bank and found a cashier. The girl started form-filling and counting money. "What's the rate for sterling today?" I asked, to make conversation. She gave me a catastrophic figure.

The look on my face prodded her into an explanation. "Nobody want it. Eet just 'appened ce matin today!"

I blew out in relief. "What luck! My money arrived on Friday."

She looked at me strangely. "But we change your money at today's rate. Monday."

It was the first prank of the Day of the Gremlins. I tried not to think what this collapse of the pound would be costing us for the boat. I strode off grinding my teeth.

"How did it go?" Claire at the yacht brokers asked. I explained, and she grimaced. I asked her to phone the mortgage bank in London, the prime business of the day.

The mortgage had been agreed subject only to survey. And the finance company knew now the survey was good. I picked up the phone. I was soon through to the man in charge and announced myself.

"Ah yes," he said.

"I've phoned to enquire about the marine mortgage," I said.

"Oh yes," again.

"When do we get the money?"

"Well, to tell the truth I'm not familiar with your file."

"You've had the details for about two months," I protested. "Now you've had the surveyor's report. What more is there?"

"Yes, but someone else has been dealing with it. I haven't had time to familiarise myself with it yet."

"When will you be able to study the file and give me an answer?"

"I'll phone you this afternoon, "he said. I gave him the villa number. I should have known, I told myself, no self-respecting bank ever gives a proposal to the executive who has to give the O.K. It goes first to somebody down the line. He is supposed to sort things out, ready for decision.

But when the moment comes, the man making the decision wants to sort out for himself, starting from scratch. The lengthy interval imparts an air of great study, and the method serves admirably to increase employment, and fees.

A cheerful chorus of "How did it go," awaited me on my return to the villa.

I told them. The grins were replaced by disbelieving groans.

"Not problems still," moaned Jeremy and Nicholas in unison.

"Well, I'm not believing <u>anything </u>till it happens," stormed Carolyn for the umpteenth time, but we were beginning to believe she knew something, as she wandered out into the garden.

"Merde alors," was Nicholas' comment demonstrating at least that he was passing his time with his new-found French friends instructively.

"I'll never get at those engines, I can tell," Jeremy grumbled fearfully.

Carolyn suddenly reappeared, obviously upset. "Come quickly! There's an injured bird in the garden." She led us outside.

Each twilight a flock of sparrows would fill the branches of the evergreens, cork-oaks and pines above our heads with their fishwives' chatter. This little bird's port wing dragged helplessly on the ground.

"Can we make it better?" Carolyn pleaded.

Injured birds can only be dealt with by being put out of their misery. By whom? Only Rosemarie had the backbone.

She had turned pale and. wouldn't look at us as she returned. We sat around on the veranda, at a loss. There was a sudden scream. We rushed inside. Rosemarie was in the kitchen, laughing hysterically.

"After the dead bird, now I've got to put the bloody chicken in the oven!" We could see it lying cold and still and naked in the tin.

We crept into bed, early. Later, the phone sounded. We didn't answer.

More days of waiting, telephoning and agonising followed, watching our price climb as sterling continued its decline and the Chancellor kept explaining all the benefits of nobody wanting pounds.

We were paying in U.S. dollars. So every time the pound weakened, we had more to find. We had time to contemplate the puzzle that while we paid more, the owner got the same.

Here surely was a financial black hole, sucking in money which had to be paid, but benefitted nobody.

The time dragged heavily. As each day passed we were convinced the owner would run out of patience and offer our lovely boat to a higher bidder.

But one day the end of our long beleaguered state was signaled by the sound of the telephone bell.

The mortgage was fixed. At last, we would have our live-aboard yacht.

We could soon be labeled jet-setters. Yet we were paying, after careful search, no more than the cost of a modest semi-detached in London. The only difference was that this house would move between sea and sky at our command. And would require a lot more work from its inhabitants on maintenance. They would often be able to depend on nothing for support but their own inbuilt resources.

We arranged for Gaston to deliver the boat, our boat, from Cannes to the marina at Saint-Raphael. We needed her there to load our belongings - reinforced since the early days by visits from friends.

Saturday was the day fixed for the boat's arrival. In the early hours of Saturday morning Rosemarie heard me padding around the bedroom.

"What are you doing?" she called.

"I'm stuffing paper in the doors and windows to stop them rattling. There's a bloody-great wind started to blow."

Saturday morning we arose very early and craned our necks at the appropriate angle to view the sea.

Herds of white horses were frothing and galloping in legions across the sea. The dreaded Mistral - the north-westerly gale of the region, had struck.

It was the first really big blow since we'd arrived. Gaston cancelled the day's event. He sounded uncharacteristically cheerful.

"Tomorrow, then," I said on the telephone.

"Non, non." Tomorrow was Sunday. So it would have to be Monday, Mistral permitting. We hunched and grunted our way through that day, a very bad-tempered family.

Sunday morning we awoke, craned our necks and grated our teeth. The sea was flat calm. But thankfully, so it was too on Monday morning. Spruce and cheerful children greeted our bleary eyes at six in the morning. By seven our little group stood waiting on the cliff top a couple of miles along the road to Cannes, straining our eyes out to sea.

The moment came when we saw the unmistakable profile of Jernica appear around the point, about a mile out to sea. As she surged into full view we admired her beauty, waved and shouted and didn't particularly care if any passers-by thought we were loopy.

Then we piled into the car and raced back to St. Raphael marina, to welcome her in.

Or at least the kids piled in and I hobbled. The gremlins were having a last fling, being reluctant to depart a scene where they'd been having so much fun. I had a severe pain in my balls. I could move only with difficulty.

This occasioned some hilarity and much impatience as we walked along the sea wall in St. Raphael marina. Jernica rode towards us about half a mile out, cutting stylishly through the sea. We waved and cheered some more.

She then sped straight past the harbour entrance, until we could see only her stern. The stern became very small.

Rosemarie cried out, "Oh the twit! He's taking her to the old port!" That's where the boat was heading. But a dire fate for Gaston was aborted as Jernica began to turn towards us.

Within minutes she was at the entrance. Gaston waved merrily back and sounded the foghorn. As he was tying up he explained that he had been maneuvering to let us take pictures. We told him we thought his sense of humour was most interesting.

Then all was ready for us to go aboard. Rosemarie dropped a few tears from behind a happy smile; a fierce hug from Carolyn served to hide more wet eyes.

With the growing dignity of almost fourteen years Jeremy smiled his way aboard. Nicholas' comment, "This is our boat then. I never had any doubts we'd make it," expressed his own pleasure.

After two years of plans which had sometime seemed futile, and frustrations which had sometimes seemed insurmountable, we'd arrived.

We settled around the table in the wheelhouse with Gaston and opened the bottles we'd brought.

As we drank to beautiful Jernica my lightly spinning head at least neutralised painful lower regions.

I clambered through the boat with Gaston, trying to learn how things worked. I nodded my head vigorously in the engine room as Gaston expounded, but saw as always only a worrying tangle of valves, pipes and tubes.

I had no doubt however that Jeremy would see a fine working instrument.

That evening we dined aboard. Rosemarie and I became very merry, and there was a lot of noise. The next day I couldn't move, for nether reasons, but Jeremy seemed no less cheerful for being able to rummage around the engine room without amateur interruption.

A doctor came, prescribing drugs for which Carolyn returned from the pharmacy with one franc change out of £50, and it was only the thought of the additional cost which prevented me also having a heart attack.

"Is your father a big man?" the chemist had enquired when handing over the bundles of drugs and looked perturbed when Carolyn told him I wasn't.

This assortment was shot into me daily, there being a fervent Gallic belief that as the Lord designed the behind as a pincushion there is no need to prescribe oral medicine. The cure is achieved for fear that it might continue.

After a few days I was able to don trousers to a ribald cheer from the crew. There were already subtle changes in decor and the engine room looked shinier and Jeremy dirtier.

I hoisted our Royal Yachting Association burgee, and purchasing screw-on letters - nobler hand-painting to come later - the name "Jernica" was spread proudly across our stern for the first time.

A debugged skipper was now ready to lead an eager crew to sea.

VIRGIN SAILOR MAKES
MAIDEN VOYAGE

The day we had chosen for our maiden voyage to Baie des Anges dawned with blue skies and a breeze. It was April, and we were bound for our berth at the marina of Baie des Anges on the outskirts of Nice, where we had decided we would refit Jernica.

In our various tours in and out of marinas and on and off potential boat-homes we had made numbers of acquaintances and several friends especially in Baie-des-Anges.

One was Chris. He was skipper for a lovely old motor yacht, a 'Silver' berthed at Baie des Anges. The yacht, a wooden classic of the 30's hadn't been quite the one for us. Especially when he told us that to reverse gear he had to leave the wheel, run down to the engine room, engage reverse there, and speed back to the wheel praying that nothing had appeared across his stern in the meantime; and a repeat of the operation to go forward again.

He told us these facts with the wry grin he always seemed to wear, and accompanied by the chuckle that accompanied the tales accumulated from his long experience as a yacht skipper and diverse jobs, not always legal.

Burly, but with spectacles and balding, he looked more like a teacher than action man. But he was one who would turn his hand to anything, especially if it was likely to be dangerous or unconventional. For his company as well as his work, we had readily accepted Chris' offer that we should berth near him at Baie des Anges. We had decided on the work we needed to do on Jernica before we could begin our cruising, and we were happy for him to take charge of it.

Now we were ready to go.

I was fit, Jeremy was like a jumping bean, and Carolyn wouldn't leave my elbow, ready to be given her first sea job.

"You cast off astern with Mum," I commanded, masterfully I hoped. Nicholas was to be action man releasing the ground chain at the bow. (We were berthed, like all boats in Med. marinas, stern to the quay. The bow was held firm by a line which we had winched aboard, the other end being tethered to the sea bed. This was the "corps-mort", or ground line.) Rosemarie was hassling around below checking that all was well stowed. The Red Ensign of a British yacht was streaming proudly aft as it had done each morning since we boarded.

I went to pay the bill at the Capitainerie. "You're leaving? Where's your ship's passport?" the official asked. I explained it hadn't been handed over by the agents for the previous owner. I didn't add they'd told us it wasn't really necessary.

"It's illegal to travel in French waters without the ship's passport, you'll have to go to customs and get one," the official said. One of the ways we had made friends was by asking at the local Chamber of Commerce to be introduced to a local family with kids to swap English for French conversation. One of the families was the Naerts. The cheerful Monsieur Naert was at the marina to see us off. He volunteered to come with me to Customs. We hurried round to their offices in the old port.

I made what I thought was a brilliant exposition of our situation to the customs officer, concluding "May we please have our new passport?"

"Eh bien. But where is the old passport?"

"We're waiting for it," I explained and spread all the papers we had on his desk - Bill of sale, registration, birth certificates for everybody, marriage licenses, and others, enough to make any good bureaucrat think it was Xmas.

He looked at me stonily and not at all at the papers. "Where," he said, "is the old Passport? Without that you cannot get a new one."

"Mais," I spread my arms like a good Francophile, "I have all the papers to prove we are the new owners n'est-ce-pas? And I said in a tone of reasonableness nobody could resist, "we are all ready, and waiting to leave."

He stared at me even more stonily. "Pas possible, M'sieur."

That strong feeling crept over me which had started to become standard reaction when meeting the facts of bureaucratic life in the Mediterranean. I wanted to knee the official in the crotch.

Like everybody else, instead I fixed my face with a warm and friendly smile; at least I hoped it was, as on earlier such occasions my family had advised me it was an unmistakable dirty look.

Suddenly Monsieur Naert at my elbow hailed an official in an adjacent office.

"Ah! Ca va?" he called. They were friends who hadn't met for years. They were soon engaged in warm discussion. Then came a few sheltered nods in my direction, followed by whispering and mutterings.

Within minutes we had a new passport. A vague face-saving promise was extracted from me to return the old one later. I thanked M. Naert with all the respect due in the Mediterranean to one who has bureaucrats for friends, and can therefore perform miracles.

We returned to Jernica. Jeremy was scarcely visible behind a huge smile as we waved the paper, his bottom half already poised to plunge into the engine room.

"What are we waiting for?" Carolyn was waiting, ready to dash to her lines.

We were waiting for me to catch my nerve. I'd be handling our boat for real for the first time, a green skipper helped by an all-green crew.

It hadn't been planned this way. We had asked Gaston, the previous skipper, if he would like to accompany us.

He had said "Mais certainement," but now, long overdue, was nowhere to be seen.

We looked for him along the quay a last time.

"Doesn't seem to be any option. I'll have to take her," I said.

Rosemarie said, "I suppose it'll be alright." She then perked up. "Anyway, Jeremy will be looking after the engines." At this, everybody looked more cheerful.

I said, "Start the engines Jeremy."

"At last," he said, with enormous feeling. Jeremy wasn't having any modern nonsense about pressing a button in the wheelhouse. He wanted to check his precious system in person as it sprang into life for him. Rubbing his hands like a miser about to receive a gold bar, his face a picture of joy, he descended the steel ladder to his engine room.

After a short pause, there came an exhilarating throaty roar and throb of life from our two 147 HP General Motors' engines. Our 13-year-old engineer, Jernica, and her devoted crew were in business.

Jeremy poked around and finding no oil or water gushing or other disasters pronounced Jernica fit for sea.

Back aloft I found Rosemarie and Carolyn standing by the stern lines.

We were berthed, like all boats in Med. marinas, stern to the quay. The bow was held firm at St Raphael by a line which we had winched aboard, the other end being tethered to the sea bed. This was the "corpsmort", or ground line.

Nicholas I had designated as action man on the ground and anchor chain at the bow. After all, he was the oldest of the kids. But this was a case of handing the tallest teen on the boat the shortest straw. If the anchor was in use, every time we raised it, some luckless soul needed to be crouching in that cramped, dark, airless space of the fo'c'sle reserved to store the anchor chain. The chosen-one's job was to receive the chain as it rattled down the hawser and flake it round and round as neatly as possible so that when we next anchored, the chain would play out without snagging or sticking. It wasn't a job to win many votes, at the best of times. The worst of times depended on the constituents of the sea-bed; but that unique element of our learning curve was yet to come.

Nicholas transferred himself forward ready to release the ground line. Carolyn had secured the dinghy in its davits over the stern. She and Rosemarie hoisted the gangway. A breeze ruffled the air. I watched the girls beginning to release the stern lines, I bawled, "Cast off", to Nicholas to release the ground line, and then went forward to the wheelhouse.

I engaged the engines, keeping the revs down in case the girls had any problems with their new job. I strode a few paces aft to make sure the lines were clear then started a dignified saunter back to the wheel. Half way there I saw that, with the engines barely turning we were drifting fast to collide with the adjacent boat.

Sang-froid changed to sang-chaude as I dashed to the wheel. The adjacent boat was a smart Italian outerspace job. It had arrived a day earlier.

The owner had enjoyed a champagne lunch on his aft deck with a pretty girl, and then both had disappeared. A curtain was drawn across the ports of the aft stateroom disappointing our children that nobody gave a thought for their further education.

It now crossed my mind that the owner would be very disgruntled, not to say pugnacious if his amorous cruises had to end before the season was out.

I dived for the throttle levers. Champagne Lunches looked no more than an inch off our starboard bow. I pushed the starboard throttle forward, port aft. Minimum revs. That ought to be right. Jernica seemed totally unaware of such expert handling. She continued to drift. Champagne Lunches looked like becoming afters.

I opened the throttles. There was an answering roar from our engines. We shot forward missing C.L. by a whisk of paint. Then we were hurtling for the harbour exit as lively as any destroyer commanded to battle, "with all possible dispatch." At least we were out of our berth.

And then Rosemarie came leaping and stumbling into the wheelhouse shouting her head off. My heart sank, I thought "My God. I've hit something after all." I slammed the motors into neutral.

"What is it? What is it?" With beating heart I looked round in alarm.

Rosemarie shouted at me "All clear aft!" and beamed in delight.

In family discussions on ship handling we had agreed the need for close coordination and communication between wheel and warps. Rosemarie had obeyed. I turned my snarl of, "You frightened the life out of me!" into a grimaced "Thank you," and returned to the wheel.

"Jesus!" was reported to have been my next exclamation. Engines still only partly opened and with insufficient forward motion, the breeze was drifting us down onto the skein of mooring lines along the right/starboard side of the fairway.

I turned the wheel and opened the throttle a little more. All that happened was our rudder and propellers edged further towards the threatening lines. I corrected. Nothing.

I slammed the throttles forward. Response - we were hurtling out of the harbour again, in our role of auxiliary destroyer.

Nicholas' said in my ear, "There's a big sign. The speed limit in the marina is three knots."

"That's for French boats," I snapped. A number of Gallic figures aboard local boats and on the quay were dancing up and down and bawling at us no doubt cheering us on our way. Then, somehow or other, we were down to a sedate speed, and making, we discovered, for the middle of the exit.

I had been saving the wearing of my yachting hat ornamented with Royal Yachting Association badge for this occasion. In the huff and puff of Customs and take-off it had been forgotten. Now Rosemarie with a proper sense of occasion jammed it over my ears. (Membership of the RYA cost only £2 p.a. at the time and outstanding value for the badge, and burgee (just a little extra) alone. Landlubbers we found were likely to assume we might be something a bit special showing such illustriously-named colours.)

So it was that Jernica departed the last few meters at least of the pleasant marina of St. Raphael with some decorum and the crew with a little style.

We were out to sea. We felt very good. There appeared the cup of tea which celebrates such moments in our family.

Jeremy disappeared again into the engine room. Before doing so he donned an old ski hat of mine, ear muffs down. It kept out the engine noise. It also explains why anybody might have seen a boy with a fur snow-hat on a boat on blazing hot days in the Mediterranean.

Outside the harbour walls, the stiff breeze made its presence known. The seas were whipping up. We were delighted with the way Jernica rode them, her semi-displacement hull riding like a patrol boat rather than a trawler.

Jeremy appeared from below. "There's smoke coming into the engine room from the exhausts." His face disappeared only to reappear anxiously moments later. "More smoke."

Nicholas happily took over the wheel and I went below with Jeremy. The first frowns of responsibility were heavy on his young brow. Smoke hung over the engine-room. The exhausts had been repaired as part of the work following the survey.

He poked around. Then he said, "I think it may be OK. I think it's only the dust drying out from the work they did."

I found so much smoke for such small reasons difficult to believe, but Jeremy, as usual, proved to be right. The smoke started to clear.

I went thankfully back to the wheel and decided it was time to try her with the throttles full open. I concentrated on equalising the revs on both motors, eyes fixed on the counters.

"We're heading for the shore," Nicholas murmured some moments later. I pulled my head up from the rev counter. We'd made a half circle and were heading for rocks. I turned the wheel. Our course hardly changed. The rocks loomed closer.

I throttled down, leaped down from the seat, bent my knees and applied leverage. Jernica's large rudders were demonstrating a will of their own.

Rosemarie appeared, looking at the rocks with a startled expression. "You practicing?" she enquired anxiously.

"Of course," I said, but as I was gritting my teeth, making throaty noises, and heaving with all my might as I said it, I might not have been totally believable.

Reluctantly, no doubt because she was having fun, Jernica came round. We missed the rocks.

"Wouldn't it be better to practice further out?" Rosemarie asked.

I agreed that sounded like a very good idea.

At least I was able to show the kids what not to do as they took turns at the wheel.

A little further on round Cap Rossa the sea got lumpy. Jernica rode through it with style. We pointed out landmarks on the Corniche de L'Esterel which we had passed so often by road. They looked so different, so much more important from the sea and gave us a deep feeling of having crossed into new horizons. And from a couple of them, the little tower of La Chretienne, off Antheor, and the Pic de L'ours light a few miles west of St. Raphael, I got great satisfaction from using the hand compass to practice taking our first-ever precise fix of Jernica's position at sea.

We pressed forward. Past La Rague, then La Napoule, Cannes and successively the other harbours we had haunted; somehow never quite believing we would see them as now, marking our sea passage.

When we headed round Cap d'Antibes we were on the last lap. We turned due north, into Baie des Anges. The final leg of our course had put the easterly blow, a good five now, on our beam. Jernica began to roll, but not too unkindly. I was happy with the good behavior of my lovely boat.

We could understand why we were in a bay of Angels as we made for the marina entrance of Baie des Anges. Though half hidden in the heat haze the Alpes-Maritimes soared in the background like a stage setting; the blurry outline of Nice beckoned further up the coast. The impressive pyramid apartment blocks with their hanging gardens which flank the marina merged into the frame of the mountains beyond.

Then we were through the entrance, into the port. It was an added delight to arrive at our first journey's end to be greeted by our friends M. and Madame Naert who had volunteered to bring our car. We saw them waving furiously.

The family bustled excitedly and competently about their business as crew, though I noticed one or two fingers still working out their clove hitches as they tied the fenders.

Chris appeared alongside in a dingy. "Berth alongside my yacht," he called. We all looked hard to see where he was pointing. We could see his yacht but no noticeable gap.

"Where?" I shouted at him.

"There - beside me," he shouted back.

"But there's no space!"

He laughed. "You'll be surprised. Have a go," and went away chuckling. The opening he'd indicated appeared to be about three feet wide. Our beam was sixteen feet.

Nicholas said, "No. I think he'll be surprised"

"You'll never get her in," Carolyn said in a horrified voice, speaking for the crew.

"I can't see how I can get her in there!" I replied, speaking for me.

The marina was rather open to east winds. The flags of all nations strung on the sea wall were nastily horizontal, and stiff. Spray flew over the wall. There was a ringing and slapping of halyards on masts. Boats were dancing at their moorings.

This was not encouraging for berthing a boat I'd never handled before. But I had time to glimpse the romance of it all. I also noticed the rather large numbers of other crews, gathered cheerfully to watch what the infallible grapevine would have told them was my virgin marina berthing.

I concentrated my attention on swinging Jernica's stern into the indicated slot. I adjusted throttles and turned the wheel and had the nasty feeling that Jernica wasn't taking too much notice of me. She wavered and wagged her stern towards our destination, and I was grateful for the sausage-like fenders we'd lowered over the side to prevent scrapes alongside other boats. Then mercifully our lovely steed began to edge into her slot. Aha, it was possible. Nicholas got ready to heave the ground line aboard. I relaxed and felt I'd done alright, first-time berthing astern with Jernica.

At that moment there were loud shouts from adjacent foredecks. Rosemarie popped out of the wheel-house to listen and popped in again.

"Chris forgot to tell us we've got to drop the anchor as well as pick up the ground chain," she announced. "You'll have to start again." It was one of the few marinas where both ground-chain and anchor were required for mooring.

We retraced our path towards the anchor drop point. We were broadside to the wind. I used engines and rudder to stop the drift. Or at least that was the idea. But Jernica was stubborn, with a mind of her own. She didn't feel like going where I wanted. She was getting some un-fair help because the closeness of other boats and their mooring lines meant we had little way on.

She reminded me of when I'd been learning to ride a horse. Every time the instructor said, 'Turn right' or 'left' I nearly fell off. I had been easily the worst in the class which included kids who could hardly walk.

The instructor said, "Next time I say 'right', turn left." I did so and stayed on with ease. The instructor explained that, as well as me, the horse had been lis-tening to him, and when he gave his order had deliber-ately gone on the wrong foot to throw me off.

The horse knew he had a learner on top. I gave up riding. When you have a beast twenty times your size and twice as intelligent, it's time to quit.

Jernica knew she had a mug aboard. She listened to the wind, not me. She liked being broadside to the wind. It was comfortable for her. She'd turn some other time, when it suited her. Broadside meant drifting. I tried to encourage my stubborn sea-borne steed towards the an-chor dropping point.

Suddenly a little harbour workboat shot out from a berth close by to the spot we were maneuvering into, and scuttled round us to the opposite side of the har-bour. As it did so I glimpsed a face peering anxiously at us out of the wheelhouse.

My story later was that the captain must have been of a very nervous disposition; the family had a simpler suggestion - he was intelligent.

Certainly there were vague signs of stress now around the crew. Smiles looked a little cheesy. At this critical moment, a familiar face suddenly appeared alongside in a dinghy. "Can I help?" It was Chris.

As I shouted as cheerfully as I could, "I can manage, thanks," eager hands were helping him aboard.

With a word or two from Chris in my ear Jernica, my marine steed, realised her bluff was called. We chivvied her into position and our now trusted bow hand, Nicholas, dropped anchor. We eased astern once more, the girls threw their lines adroitly, friendly hands grabbed them, and we were fast in our berth. We all gave each other a hug and many smiles.

The Naerts climbed aboard to join Chris in our saloon, the kettle was on for tea and glasses were filled, according to taste and age. Some of the glasses were bubbling and so were the crew.

We all settled down for the evening on the aft deck, wine or Coke in hand shared with new friends. Or nearly all of us. Through the wheelhouse windows I suddenly spotted Jeremy vanishing below floor level.

I leaped up and poked my head through the door. "Where on earth you going?"

"I'm going to take up the engine room bilges to see what oil's got down there."

I said, "For goodness sake! Do it tomorrow."

"What am I supposed to do all evening," he glowered. "Twiddle my thumbs?" He disappeared.

It was home. But it was different. It was Jernica.

TERRORS OF
TERENCE-TRIPOD,
MOLLY-MULE

The day after our arrival was very hot. The sea was glassy. It was the kind of day we'd all imagined we'd be lazing in some deserted bay. In fact we were up to our eyes, literally, in dust and sweat.

We'd come to this marina to refit and redo. A well-filled marina and near to Nice it was backed by all the workshops and skills we'd need to employ. We were determined Jernica would never look like some of the sad derelicts we had visited.

We calculated the work would take us two weeks. Then we'd be off, sailing around the Med.

We got cracking with enthusiasm. New specialties developed.

Varnishing in particular is a skill requiring careful preparation and great patience. We had lots of glorious wood around the wheelhouse and superstructure.

The varnish must be applied in many layers, after rubbing down laboriously each time with wet-and-dry sandpaper. Rosemarie became our expert. The work is never-ending. The salt environment is ruthless in its demands. If they are not met, the penalty is severe.

Carolyn became the champion filler of undulations, and painter of hull and coach-roofs. She came expensive. One daub of paint for the boat, and two for her overalls. We could have got a good price for them as a modern canvas.

After much effort and nagging by Jeremy we obtained an English version of the General Motors manual for our diesel engines. It was open at all times - by the side of Jeremy of course; during the day, in the engine room: at night it went to bed with him.

Nicholas and I were Jacks of all trades, deck and hull scrubbers, sanders, painters and rust scrapers. Ours was a steel hull. Search and destruction missions against patches of rust hoping to lurk and spread in dark, obscure corners were a continuous task.

Improving Jernica was a full-time task. But time was set aside every day for the kids to tackle their correspondence courses. Rosemarie and I were monitoring. They were making good progress.

We spent several days cleaning Jernica's behind, as befits a new baby. Below decks aft on Jernica was a large lazarette – a very large toolbox. Rosemarie found rust there where nobody had realised there was boat.

"Come and look," she invited me in siren tones. I descended the ladder looked around, but couldn't see rust. Rosemarie demonstrated the proper way to look for rust. I followed and copied.

I propelled myself horizontally backwards, then folded my stomach so that my upper parts were vertical. A few inches from my eyes I then beheld rust. A small band ranged the width of the boat. Grunting and creaking I returned to the light and air above.

"We need pot-holers," I suggested, Rosemarie disappeared upside down again, this time with acid and scraper.

Sometime later we perceived the arrival on deck of an apparition like something out of the Water Babies. It appeared to have a face and hair and arms but they were covered by sweaty layers of black grime. The whites of eyes looked out at us and then a pair of scaly hands reached towards me. As I backed away they placed a scraping knife into my hand.

"Here, have a go," said a voice recognisably Rosemarie's but in tones no water baby would ever have employed.

I descended and contorted. It was our first introduction to the inflexible law that all work on boats must be done upside down, or bent double, or even treble. I could scrape only at eyeball level. As I scraped rust filled my nose and eyes which smarted painfully as they became soaked with sweat.

While clambering about I discovered a number of greasing points I hadn't realised existed. Nor had anybody else, by the look of them. It pays to pot-hole on your own boat. Nicholas later took over. He asked for a Davey lamp.

Next day Rosemarie started laying out on deck all the accumulated years of clutter from the lazarette.

Tools, tubes of gunge, pipes, ropes, chain screws, shackles, wires, hoses, metal and plastic bits, wood, bolts, old tins of paint, varnish and stripper and scores of mystery parts, usually covered in grease or rust.

Our proud teak decks looked like a derelict junk-yard.

Rosemarie and Jeremy sat in the middle of the detritus like grubby street urchins, picking, sorting, wiping. We worked out what some of the more esoteric items might be. Some were a puzzle.

Rosemarie went to fling overboard one rusty piece of anonymous metal.

"Whoa!" shouted Matt, the skipper of neighbouring "Blue Finn", who happened to be on board at that moment.

"Why keep a rusty tin opener?" I enquired.

"That bent and rusty tin-opener is a fuel-injector remover. You'll need it!"

We became respectful and even worshipful thereafter, of even the dirtiest and most misshapen bit and bob.

The lazarette dominated proceedings for several days. Then Jeremy disappeared into its maw for a day. Having painted it silver and black, it was, he declared, good enough to store tools again.

The lazarette's detritus had been meanwhile scattered on the aft deck. Rosemarie took up action stations and suddenly we had our pristine aft deck back again, with our workshop now stacked as neatly as a larder.

It was Rosemarie's birthday. No cooking was the order of the day.

We seldom ate out. Once we'd paid for Jernica's needs, funds could be scarce, as when money was called for, it invariably stuck in the pipeline on its way to us. Banks seemed to have no difficulty in cabling funds more slowly than a coach-and-four could have hauled it in days of yore. Everybody we ever met told the same story.

But this was birthday-treat day. I pointed out the Savoy grill was too far away. We set off for the "Casino" supermarket self-service restaurant in party mood. Work for a few moments forgotten we enjoyed three tasteful courses for a few pounds per head.

Rosemarie looked at the remains of her birthday table, "That was jolly good," she pronounced. The kids began stowing lots of little plastic sachets into pockets.

"What're they?" I enquired curiously.

"Mustard of course!" they replied. Casino mustard was good French stuff, and sachets were always heaped in a basket at the end of the counter.

"For Gawdsakes," I remonstrated, "You'll have us arrested!" Nobody seemed to be listening. We ate at the Casino from time to time and never did buy any mustard in France.

Jeremy began an attack on the engine room. During the next month nobody bothered to ask where he was. Those of us working aloft started a tan. He stayed pale as milk. If he showed up above we asked him if he felt alright.

He was mastering the subtleties of his nether world. Indicator lights in the engine room warned we had electrolysis somewhere. Clashing metals activated by sea-water boring holes in the boat didn't appeal to anyone.

Friendly experts from other boats couldn't find a cause. Jeremy searched all day, surfacing with a growl, before descending again. Then he emerged with a satisfied grin.

"Well?" I asked, in my role of straight-man. He said, "There's a wooden chock in the battery box which has got all covered in electrolyte. It's been acting as a conductor. It's OK now."

I nodded my head in the wise fashion of the ignorant man.

And so the grind of bringing a boat up to, and maintaining it in pristine condition repeated itself day after day. Rosemarie sandpapered and varnished and looked after the household. Carolyn sanded and painted; Nicholas and I scraped and painted and did jack of all trades; Jeremy checked and changed and scraped and burnished every item, scupper and section of hull in his engine room.

For the kids, that wasn't all. Typically, once, in the early hours, after everybody had been at the usual day's hard labour, I poked my head into Nicholas' foc'sle where the light was burning, to find him deep in "Daily Life in Ancient Rome" - one of his exam subjects.

We had decided to remove our DC generator and install an AC Chris had found for us second-hand. We would then be able to use shore-based electrical devices

- most importantly, in that heat as far as Rosemarie was concerned, a freezer and washing machine.

The time came to set about this major task. When we'd agreed terms for installing the new machine with Chris we had assumed he would have a team of workmen helping him.

We were right. He had us.

But there were to be no Trade Union hours. Chris had his own boat to look after. His habit was to start on Jernica late in the evening, when we were just knocking-off from our daily grind. He would join us for dinner and would then often work through with us until the early hours of the morning.

Nicholas emerged as family hero on these occasions remaining as assistant to Chris long after the rest of us had collapsed wearily into bed.

The drawbacks to this system were substantial, but the theatrical benefits were substantial. These were the days of achievement — and terror! The terror devices, created and named by Chris were Terence Tripod and Molly Mule.

Our old Lister diesel generator, unsuitable for our needs, was a remarkable workhorse and would run day in day out for generations. It was also solid. And as we were to discover, hell to lift.

We raised the floorboards in the lower saloon, exposing the generator lurking in the engine room below. Now Chris could get to grips with the monster. It had first to be hoisted seven feet to the saloon floor then dragged aft to the quay.

He sat studying the problem. "I know what to do," he proclaimed finally. He returned in triumphant mood some hours later with what seemed to be, and no doubt once had been, somebody's telegraph pole. We watched with interest as he sawed it into three lengths, which he wired together.

He waved his hand at the contraption and beamed at us through his spectacles. "Terence Tripod is ready."

We helped him place his home-made sawn-offs around the hole in our saloon floor. It was like a rickety three-legged wigwam, without canvas. It sagged and wobbled to the touch.

"We can begin lifting," Chris announced, impervious to the somewhat horror-stricken looks from our side.

"H'm," commented Jeremy, as our technical representative.

We stood in respectful or rather fearful silence. Rosemarie appeared, frowned, looked at the device, and hastily disappeared back into the galley.

"Now to attach Molly Mule," Chris announced oblivious to the mounting terror his words were creating. Molly was a device with steel wires attached to a ratchet on a body no more than a foot long. She would lift one-ton weights, Chris averred. Molly was hung ungraciously from the apex of the tripod, as unlikely looking a strong man as one was ever likely to behold.

We couldn't place her directly over the generator, now named somewhat obviously as Jenny, so Chris created an ingenious network of knots which he assured us would allow us to pull her at an angle. We didn't recognise the knots. "Learned them in my days as a lorry driver. Very useful," he told us.

Molly was now set up to pull upwards, through a network of wires at an angle.

"Ready," Chris proclaimed, the word crackling through the tense atmosphere. The three kids leaned on a leg apiece of the tripod. At 2300 hours one hot summer's night, Chris began laboriously ratcheting up.

Each hitch required a slow lift of the lever, a careful lowering to a notch, and then a push of a release button. Even Chris seemed to find difficulty using it. But he persisted. As the weight came full on, Terence's timbers began to creak and groan.

Rosemarie in the galley adjoining took another quick look then firmly closed the door. Squeak, grind, croak and groan. Jenny slowly began to lift, her journey sporadic and wavering. Every click of the ratchet up, we were on a knife's edge. It seemed years later when we could see she was half way up. Her massive bulk was poised directly over our starboard main engine.

From time to time we supported whichever of the tripod legs was looking faint.

I instructed my mind to think of nothing but the job in hand. My mind had difficulties. I could see Jeremy gazing down with a set expression.

"Are you sure it will be alright?" Carolyn expressed all our thoughts, as the ponderous process continued, only a slight squeak in her voice.

Chris grinned through his sweat. "Confidence! You must have confidence!" He latched up and down, and raised the deadweight a little more. In the humid night there was perspiration on all our faces. I popped out on some errand.

Suddenly I heard shouts, the slapping of wood, thuds, and confused cries. I rushed back to the saloon.

Terence was a tottering ruin. Molly hung limp and forlorn. The kid's faces displayed various degrees of dismay, terror and concern. There was no sign of Chris.

"What's happened for Crissakes!"

Carolyn pointed down and flapped her hands. "Look," was all she could muster, but I was already half way down the hole.

I saw a face peering out from under the deadweight of Jenny, which was just off our engine. Chris' voice, slightly strained came from beneath the mass. "Oh, goodness. I'm taking all the weight. It's alright for a minute. But could you please try and get the tripod up again?"

We sprang into action, pulling and heaving at the Tripod. Nicholas scrambled down with me to help Chris bear the weight.

"We need to release Molly," Jeremy shouted fiddling with the ratchet.

"Ah," exclaimed Chris's breathless voice from below the heap. "Of course, you don't know how to do it!" In careful tones, from somewhere under Jenny, Chris began instructing Jeremy in the mysteries of the mechanism.

Jeremy began tortuously to try to work Molly's ratchet mechanism. Chris' voice raised a semi-tone. "Ah... ..will you please hurry."

Jeremy worked with desperate anxiety. Carolyn rearranged Terence's legs. Nicholas and I heaved with

Chris. Suddenly there was a blessed 'click-click'. Savior Jeremy had coaxed Molly back to work.

The wire tightened and took the strain. From below us came a heartfelt sigh. Terence held. Molly pulled. Jenny lifted on her way up again. Chris re-emerged seemingly unscathed, uncomplaining, to take charge again.

At some time in the early hours Jenny was settled safe, still, on the saloon floor. The relief was tangible.

How to ease her out of the wheelhouse and over the aft deck to shore was another problem. For another day. For now, we crawled into our beds exhausted for the few hours sleep before dawn.

The following evening after our day's work Chris came again to pronounce on the next stage of Jenny's journey, "It's very simple really." But this time he was right. Molly, with newly appropriate knots, was this time organised to pull horizontally, and did so without difficulties. True the lump still needed some human assistance over bumps and round corners. We all grew muscles we didn't know we'd owned.

We had all been townies. Now we were laboring as hard as any navvies, and for hours any navvy would have gone on strike over. We would drop into bed utterly exhausted. And cheerful.

Quite why the convolutions which accompanied Chris's help should have surprised us is difficult to say. Chris was never one to do things the easy way. We had learned that from his stories and in an earlier experience with him, in the first days of his assistance working on Jernica.

We looked forward to sitting around with a glass after dinner in the wheelhouse after the day's work, listening to his fund of stories.

The kids had already wheedled quite a few out of him.

The first time was when he sat back with his beer, grinned at us and in answer to the kids' promptings said, "What? You mean like when I was a turd burglar in Spain?"

Our laughter was accompanied by raised eyebrows.

He explained, "They built all these houses with drains which were too small. They were always getting blocked. The way the Spaniards had built them you couldn't unblock them with rods or even dynamite! Nobody knew what to do. You can imagine," he said with an even broader grin, "people were getting desperate!"

"So," he went on, after another suspenseful swig at his beer which had the kids fidgeting for the dénouement, "I used to don a diving suit and go in with a shovel!"

We wrinkled our noses. He laughed, "Nobody else would do it. I made a fortune!"

He had also earned a living smuggling expensive cars into Switzerland. This occupation finally landed him in a Swiss jail. We muttered words of condolence.

But Chris was full of enthusiasm. He couldn't say enough in praise of the jail and the jailers. "It was a very friendly place, food was marvelous," he said as though recommending it for a good holiday.

Inevitably, dangerous sports also appealed to Chris. One day we all drove into the mountains behind Nice. The road was carved out of the side of the mountain, to which it clung precariously. Gloomy and overhung menacingly with rocks, in winter the road breaks out at last above the clouds and into the blue skies of the ski slopes which, with blue seas nearby make the Alpes-Maritimes a paradise for sports lovers.

This was summer, and we were heading for a lower peak from which you could jump into space. Or Chris was. We were there strictly to see him do it. He was one of the first hang-gliding enthusiasts.

We parked on a roadside, and the kids helped him unfurl his hang-glider from the roof. We then trudged over a field, coming to a halt at a precipice.

Peering very cautiously over the edge, we could see toy cars winding along a road many hundreds of feet below. A toy village with tiny cows set in green fields shimmered through a haze a long, long way down.

"What a glorious view," said Rosemarie.

Chris was bent over, busily inserting struts into appropriate grooves of his skimpy flying machine.

"He's not here for the beauty. He's here to throw himself off the edge," I said.

To my horror Chris looked up, grinned, and said, "Do you want to have a go?"

"Go on, Dad," said Carolyn, at an age when miracles are no problem to Dads. She was rewarded with a scowl from me.

I said "Er," and was then saved by a French enthusiast who had arrived at the same point for the same hair-raising purpose. We noticed his machine had a harness underneath. Chris's had a seat.

We'd also been puzzled that in answer to our welcoming smiles earlier the Frenchman had been frowning and shaking his head. He now pointed in horror at the assembly of spars and bright red flapping material which Chris was just preparing to launch over the edge of the cliff, with him aboard.

"Qu-est-ce que vous allez faire?" he spluttered.

Chris chuckled, positioning himself underneath his machine ready to propel it to the edge for launch. "I should have thought it's obvious what I'm going to do."

"But ... not with ... with .. that!" exclaimed the Frenchman, evidently horrified.

Chris's answer was a simple nod, before staggering forward under the frame, now catching the breeze.

"Oo-la-la!" said the Frenchman, They really do say it.

Chris didn't quite make it on the first try, or the second, and readjustments were needed. As he prepared again, the Frenchman had time to point out that Chris's sit-in model was one of the first-ever hanggliders. After a number of people had been killed using them, they were now banned. Intrepid fliers who preferred staying alive now launched themselves spread-eagled on a harness with much greater control.

Chris responded with a broad grin, and another heave forward which succeeded in wobbling him and his contraption over the edge. We watched with our hearts even more in our mouths. But a few moments later to our great relief we saw him sailing into view, wheeling and gliding in his killer bird.

Carolyn was quite happy now for me to remain a spectator. So was I.

We drove to the plains below where Christopher had soared down safely. Why, we asked him on the way back, had he hung on to the deadly model? He gave his invariable chuckle and said, "Well, it's more fun."

He also found it more fun to dive without checking the air in his bottle. When Nicholas pointed out it was dangerous, Chris scowled. "There's no point in fussing. That's what the reserve is for."

We were to learn later there were tragic undertones to Chris' devil-may-care attitude to life.

Meanwhile some of the crew's attitudes were subtly changing. We would shower in the evenings. But if we stepped ashore with an ineradicable paint mark or other splodge on our skins or clothes we didn't even notice. Indeed we couldn't understand how people could walk about so neat and tidy.

The kids were growing up almost visibly. I found Carolyn one day lowering the heavy Mercury outboard engine into the dinghy using one of the aft davits. The apparatus looked under strain.

"What are you doing?" I asked anxiously ('bossily', was Carolyn's version). Carolyn replied, "Don't you worry about me. We'll be alright." I demurred. And delayed.

"Go on!" Her tone was a little sharper; she was very self-assured. She was beginning to sound like her mother. I left, hoping that it looked as if I had some urgent business.

Nicholas was so far weaned off books to accompany Chris to workshops to fabricate an exhaust for Jenny.

We used a local workshop owned by Victor. Chris had brought Victor over one evening complete with welding and cutting gear to make the base of the old jenny fit the new.

Middle-aged with powerful shoulders he appeared in filthy vest and sandals, face grimy with dirt after the day's work. He looked like us. He also brought a wide grin, his daughter and assistant, and a shaggy dog which would follow him around, tongue hanging out in the heat.

We soon discovered they all had a taste for gin and tonic; luckily for our stocks, excluding the dog. Victor's skills were widely known in the region. He chose his work according to how he felt and priced it the same way. We were lucky. He liked the English.

He welded a base for the new jenny; and supplied and fixed a pulpit (the high guard-rails) around our bow. It took many days, supervised always by the dog.

Vic would finish on the aft deck late at night. Sometimes his wife and grown daughter would join us. Glasses in hand, the lighthouses across the bay at Garoupe and Antibes winking at us, we would discuss the world and soon sort it out.

He was worried about the future of his business. "The young men want their rights, and high wages. But they don't want to work," he would complain along with every other entrepreneur in the west.

He had other complaints, and they would all end with a sigh and shrug and "C'est la vie," and "stupid dog," as he glanced at his constant companion.

Victor also allowed us to scour his workshop for a stainless steel tube to fabricate a radar mast. Chris was to make it with my assistance. The one we found required shortening. The cutting device was a long-handled guillotine. Chris had a go first. To give him a rest, I took over. I pulled on the handle. It didn't even scratch the metal.

"Try a little harder, Chris said.

I lifted my feet in the air and pulled. There was a tiny slicing noise.

Chris twitched a nose. "Ha. A little harder"

This time I leaped into the air with hands raised aloft on the handle, lifted my feet like a pole-vaulter, and came cracking down on the handle. There was a highly satisfactory sensation of knife going through butter.

"Keep it up," Chris chuckled.

I continued my dervish leaping. Victor's wife came into the workshop to see what the noise was, but left when she saw it was only madmen. I was soon exhausted, but we were nearing the end.

With a final cry I leapt up and bore down. There was a loud cracking. The edge sheared off and I landed with a breath-shattering thump on my back. Chris laughed, and enquired when I would be getting up.

The days sped by, Chris popping in at odd times to begin installing the AC generator. We continued with our chores, always black and grimy.

Our friends wrote to us envying our luck, our lagoons, drinks on the aft deck, hints of nude ladies sunning themselves all around, while they had to sweat away nine till five in the office.

They would have felt better had they seen us the day Rosemarie and I decided to clean the canvas awning over the aft deck. We'd been funking it for some time. It was yellowed and greasy, the result of age and constant sun and salt.

Late one morning, we spread it over a low wall on the quay and began scrubbing in the full sun. We used one cleaner. It had no effect. The sweat pouring off, we used another. It stayed yellow.

We scrubbed some more. The heat rose in waves from the concrete quay and enveloped us from the sky. In this furnace no mad-dog stirred nor person was to be seen. The sun climbed to its apex. We roasted and scrubbed, the sweat stinging and blinding.

The fabric remained yellow. We tried another patent cleaner to mix with our sweat and a miserable grey began to replace the dirty yellow.

I began to pull the fabric out. "Be careful," Rosemarie gasped with the little breath she had left. "It's as fragile as the Dead Sea scrolls."

"I can see that, I am being careful," I wheezed and tugged carefully. A great rending sound filled the air.

We both stood motionless, scrubbing brushes in hand an ancient frieze of slaves at work. We silently surveyed the shredded result of our exhausting labors.

"I think we'll finish the cleaning, and put it back," Rosemarie said finally, with extravagant calm. "What's left of it."

We spent an hour re-attaching the canvas over the aft deck. Rosemarie advised great care. I assured her I was giving it.

I pulled, there was a thin rending and chunks of sky showed through the awning.

Another long silence ensued.

"Let's get it off, I'll sew it." Rosemarie said very deliberately. We started carefully untying. With pursed lips Rosemarie set to with her sewing machine.

A few minutes later, with the yellowing parchment canvas draped all around her like a Thing from a horror movie, the last needle broke on her precious Pfaff sewing machine - a treasure which predated the kids.

Rosemarie slumped down, more or less defeated for the day, a most unusual not to say unique event.

As I was thinking of something soothing to say, but realising that silence might be golden, Carolyn came in and slumped down with an exhausted sigh by her mother.

"How about fitting a little schoolwork in?" I ventured.

Carolyn nearly burst as she stood up, glared, and made for her cabin.

"I get up in the morning! Work all day! Fall into bed at night! It's .. it's .. it's a .... "She stormed, leaving her sentence unfinished, her meaning clear, and her cabin door slammed.

Dinner that night was a quiet, indeed virtually wordless affair.

Dinner was never the end of the day at least for Jeremy. After the plates disappeared, so would he. He re-emerged from his engine room at eleven o'clock, the colour of soot. His white teeth demonstrated a grin.

"I'm down to some lovely brass!"

Dutifully, I descended below to inspect the pipes he'd been scraping for days through layers of rust and paint.

The brass gleamed golden at me. His engines were beginning to look like a modern sculpture. "Tremendous," I said full of admiration. He beamed at the shared pleasure, until I made my mistake.

Jeremy looked like everybody else, exhausted; so naturally I said, "I reckon you can get to bed satisfied now. You've had a long day."

"There's plenty more needs doing," he snapped. He grabbed the tin of metal polish and began again on a piece of pipe not quite up to regulation gloss.

"You'll need something left for tomorrow," I said, managing to prise the tin from his hands and he went grumbling off to waste time sleeping.

AFTER ALL IT'S A BOAT!

As the next morning dawned bright and sunny again I ran through the boat turning the family out of bed.

"What's the fuss?" Rosemarie complained opening an eye.

"This isn't a bloody workhouse," I said. "It's a boat."

"So?"

"So we're going to sea. There's no law against taking a boat to sea."

Our idea had been to concentrate on the work; it would be done; and we'd be off in two weeks. The deadline was long, long past. Clearly it wasn't working out so simply.

Each evening we'd stood on deck and scoured each other with rags dipped in white spirit. We could never entirely remove the stains but had no trouble in removing patches of skin as the howls testified. Nobody enjoyed schoolgirl complexions.

It was clear that we'd be going on like this for many weeks more than we had imagined. It was time for a break. In any case we badly needed practice before we set off on serious cruising. Family drills were required at slipping, weighing and dropping anchor, navigating and of course berthing.

We all attacked the boat with a new spirit of enthusiasm. We cleared up bottles, tins, brushes, rags, tools and other paraphernalia of a ship at work.

Our horizons lifted. Our surroundings looked different. We could see the coach roof over the galley as a sundeck, not as a surface to be scraped, sanded, painted several times and sanded again. The distant Alps were once more a backcloth to cruising bays.

A friend, big Matt, the original of a brawny six- foot Scots skipper, said he'd come along to keep an eye on us. Jeremy started the motors and their thurrumph-thurrumph made the sky seem sunnier.

Carolyn and Rosemarie threw off the aft lines. Jeremy started the winch and stood by it as we moved out, the anchor chain slowly streaming back aboard.

We had one worry. We'd seen many boats with problems weighing anchor as they picked up lines from other boats. We kept our fingers crossed and there was Matt's reassuring Scots burr in the background. "Aye. That's fine. Keep her like that."

But midway out, Jeremy started signaling from the winch. The chain had locked tight as it passed through the hawse pipe on its way below. I left the wheel, and looked over the bow.

"Tight as a drum," said Matt. "Let's get everything above the water." We winched; but then the chain stuck in the hawse pipe. We winched, with stops and starts, for half an hour, with the chain continually jamming in the hawse.

Laboriously, we brought our anchor to the surface, together with a number of other chains.

"One more chain and we'll have everybody's in the harbour," said Jeremy, cheerful at all the experience he was getting. I joggled the engines keeping our rudders and props off the surrounding mooring ropes.

Matt had meanwhile diagnosed the cause of the constant jamming. "Your chain is too large for the hawse pipe," he told us. "A larger chain has been fitted at some time."

We proceeded laboriously, winching chain in, letting it out when it stuck, heaving in again. At last we were clear. Thankfully I steered for the exit. Then suddenly I realised I hadn't seen Nicholas during this long struggle.

"Where's Nicholas?" I shouted to all within earshot.

"He hasn't been bloody reading in the middle of all this, has he?" somebody complained.

A filthy, sweat-streaked face rose slowly out of the forward hatch. It turned slowly in my direction, blinking to see the light. It spoke, saying, "You may remember you asked me to flake the chain."

For more than an hour Nicholas had been doubled over in the black fetid chain locker trying to weave the chain neatly as it came below on its highly erratic journey - and trying to keep head and hands out of harm's way the times the chain locked and had to be let out. This arduous work was necessary to ensure the chain ran freely when we let out the anchor.

Anchor chains pick up all the mud and all kinds of decayed organic matter from the sea-bed - i.e. in a busy marina it is like thick, black, greasy glue, and stinks to high-heaven.

Nicholas was covered in thick black greasy glue and stank to high-heaven.

I mentally garbed myself in sackcloth and ashes as we entered the peace of the open sea.

We enjoyed several hours of practice around the broad bay outside the marina. I discovered there was a delay of about three seconds before a gear shift engaged on our motors, which explained a number of embarrassing moments during berthing and slipping. I'd unconsciously expected the motors to provide the instant response of the thirty foot launch on which I'd done my training.

Soon I began to feel Jernica responding obediently. Carolyn enjoyed the first pleasures of sunbathing on the roof she'd done more than most to sand and paint, and looking over the bow for dolphins.

Jeremy, snow hat on, flaps down, was happy admiring and tending his engines at work, seeing little of the sea.

The time came to set off back to our berth. Back inside the marina I signaled to Jeremy on the winch and the girls with the lines aft to be ready. I dropped my hand and Jeremy let go the anchor.

I put the engines astern and concentrated my attentions aft. Suddenly there was a shout. Rosemarie come trotting in. "Chain's stuck again."

Matt went forward to begin a sequence. Stoop, grip, heave. For ten minutes he kept going, Jeremy watching him like a hawk, as Matt used his broad shoulders to heave the chain from the constricting hawse, a little at a time.

I worked at the engines, keeping our stern off other mooring ropes, as our bow swung around our errant chain.

Matt left the winch to speak to me. "Won't be long," he said, "I reckon we'll have her clear very shortly."

At that moment there were shouts from ahead. Carolyn came aft on the run. Her face was flushed. "Dad Come quickly! Jeremy's caught his hand in the winch."

I felt I'd been struck a heavy blow in the stomach. We had all discussed the need for care on the winch; this is the site of countless accidents, even to the most experienced sailors.

The results could be terrible, a whole limb lost.

Fearsome thoughts jangled through my head as I raced forward. But whatever had happened I was too late. An ashen-faced procession was coming towards me.

Jeremy, his face green, had his right hand cupped in the left. Rosemarie following was bent almost double. Blood was spilling from Jeremy's hand. Dark cascades stained the deck and I remember thinking crazily, 'the decks will have to be washed'.

I took Jeremy around the shoulder to lead him into the wheelhouse. "I'm alright," he grunted. I tried to look at the hand. He was shielding it and wouldn't let go with the good hand. He lay quietly on the wheel-house settee, all traces of colour absent from his face.

Rosemarie followed him in. She remained strange-ly bent over and said, "I've strained my back. I can't stand up." I sent Carolyn, her face tear-stained, for the medical chest. We gently unclasped Jeremy's hands. He looked away as we examined the damage.

His fingers were pulped and bloody and swollen. But he was able to move them slightly, and we couldn't see bone.

"Does it hurt?"

"Not a lot."

We expected the pain to come later after the shock wore off. We gave him some strong pain killers and Rosemarie still crouching bandaged the hand. I learned what had happened. In Matt's absence, the chain had stuck again. Jeremy copied what he had seen. But he didn't have Matt's know-how, or strength. As he lifted the chain out of the hawse the weight came down on the anchor. The chain passed on its way up or down from the hawse over the Gypsy – a cogged wheel. Jeremy's hand had been trapped between chain and cogs. He reached for the winch switch to free his hand.

Instead, it was drawn further into the cogs. He stopped it and shouted, "My hand is caught," powerless to move. Rosemarie turned and saw the family nightmare come true. The anchor weighs eighty kilos i.e, one hundred and eighty pounds. And there was the heavy weight of the chain.

Rosemarie bent and heaved the chain off Jeremy's hand. She had long attended specialists for back trou-ble. Now she could barely move.

Matt looked at the hand and was calmly cheerful. "Look's like it could have been a lot worse. There's a good hospital up the road in Antibes."

The worst moments were the next half hour, when we had still to keep freeing the chain to drop anchor, the while Jeremy lay silent, shielding his pulped hand.

At long last we berthed. Matt and I accompanied Jeremy into the car. As we did so, his knees crumpled momentarily - the only sign of stress he showed throughout.

Antibes' hospital casualty ward was bright and devoid of patients. Jeremy had his head patted by a pretty nurse as we told his story. His hand was bathed and he was anti-tetanused and x-rayed. A doctor returned smiling. "You've broken the bone in one finger," he told Jeremy. "It should heal without much trouble." With a final "You mustn't use your hand. Keep it clean," the doctor disappeared.

The news of a broken bone has never been greeted with such joy, indeed hilarity, as Jeremy arrived back on board. He was showered in happy tears.

Rosemarie, it was now clear, was the major victim. She was bent over, locked solid and in pain; and there was nothing we could do to help. I looked at the two practical ones in the family.

"A fine mess," I said. "We'll have to do things for ourselves now."

A few minutes later I found her still trying to continue to work. As I stopped her I saw tears. They weren't from pain, but from the frustration of not being able to work.

Later I found her in the only position she could maintain, lying down in a crouch. She had placed herself on some canvas on the side deck. With Nicholas standing by, she was varnishing the outside of the wheelhouse. As she finished she called out "Nicholas!"

Nicholas grabbed the canvas on which she was prostrate and gently pulled it forward. She started to varnish the next area.

I thought I would go mad. As I opened my mouth to speak, I saw Jeremy with a rubber glove on his good hand disappearing down the vertical ladder into the engine room. I couldn't believe it.

"Where the hell are you going?" I shouted at the top of his disappearing head.

"Where do you think," he answered, before disappearing.

"For God's sake," I said, peering down, "What are you going to do?"

"I'm in the middle of stripping the paint," his voice floated up. I couldn't believe my ears.

"Stripping! You're mad! If you get rust or stripper on that hand in the state it's in, you'll lose it! Come out immediately!"

"Why? It's covered by the bandage."

"Come bloody out!"

A belligerent face appeared at the bottom of the ladder.

"I'll do it," I said.

"I want to do it."

"Come out!"

Slowly he emerged.

An hour later I was at the top of the ladder again, bawling, "I said come out!"

Rosemarie crouched into view. "He wants to do it. Leave him."

We had to return to the hospital a few days later. The same casualty-room staff greeted us with the same cheerful smiles. Then they caught sight of Jeremy's black, grimy, oil and paint covered bandaged hand.

The smiles disappeared. I was the object of dirty looks.

"Why, M'sieur, are the bandages so dirty?"

"Well," I explained, "you see he's been working in the engine room."

I was surrounded by a hostile, shouting staff. It wouldn't have taken much to have converted them a lynch mob.

What did I mean by making the boy work with his bad hand? Had I no humanity? What was more important, engines or a limb? What sort of person was I? Was it true what they heard about England today? And so on.

I nodded vigorously in agreement, put my arms up in defence, pointed to Jeremy, nodded many more times and said, "Oui oui. But tell him."

They redressed his hand with much muttering and 'oo-la-la's' in my direction.

A few days later Jeremy was watching a crew on a work raft passing beneath our bows. He forgot our stanchions (stainless-steel supports for the guard-rail) had been loosened for repairs. He looked over the side, leaning on the rail.

I saw, and shouted. He fell. By a complete miracle his somersault landed him on his feet on the raft. Not on his head, or maybe worse, his hand. He climbed back aboard with a shaky grin.

His mother appeared at the commotion. We explained what had happened. She lifted up her eyes and said, "Well thank God he's alright."

I agreed, shuddering to think what they would have done to me at the hospital if I'd taken him back with more damage.

I spent a day in the foc'sle hack-sawing with Nicholas at the hawse pipe in which the anchor chain was jamming. It was a labour of love, and we all felt the boat was a better place when the murderous object came free.

Someone had suggested we could replace it with a plastic one. Its main function was to keep out water or rubbish from the anchor chain. It didn't take any strain.

The noise and dust of building were all around us as the marina was still building. The sites were littered with debris. One evening after dark I tripped over a length of discarded plastic pipe on one of these abandoned sites. Jeremy who was with me agreed it was a danger to pedestrians.

We inspected it more closely. Jeremy said," It's the right diameter. All we have to do is cut it shorter."

It was soon installed. There was no way the chain could jam. Our new pipe was not only larger than the chain; given any pressure it would simply shift fractionally.

We couldn't wait to try it. We planned our first real day's cruising and invited the Naert family. The anchor came up without a hitch and there was great relief all round.

Out into the open between seas and skies of matching blue we made our way off the Nice sea-front, and then by the massive but pretty bay of Villefranche, a favourite anchorage for small yachts and the American Med. fleet alike. We were heading for the other side of its easterly prong, Cap Ferrat, into the serene sweep of Scaletta Bay.

It was a perfect setting to begin to discover the joys of a short cruise. We could see the tops of masts in the marina of St. Jean Cap Ferrat. Farther along the coast we could make out more masts at Beaulieu. Our foreground was wooded green hills with a discreet sprinkling of red-roofed villas. The Alps showed mistily.

One or two other sailing and motor yachts rode at anchor. But they were some distance off. We drank in the space and quiet, not surrounded by boats and the noise of work, warm not roasting, rested and at peace.

We dropped anchor and succumbed completely. We draped ourselves around languidly, and opened bottles, not a pot of paint in mind let alone in sight.

It was hot and peaceful as Rosemarie began to prepare lunch. The sea was calm. Relaxation seeped through our mind and bones.

"We've earned one trouble-free day like this," I said "without a care."

As I said it, I was watching the kids all playing together. I saw Clorinda, our French friends' teenage daughter bound along the coach-roof following Carolyn's example.

But she continued bounding, as Carolyn had not done.

Clorinda shouting with laughter skipped and danced merrily onto our "fragile -as-the -Dead-sea-scrolls" canvas roof over the aft deck.

As in a slow-motion film, her feet continued running but she was falling with a rending sound through the canvas over which we had laboured so many hours. As the canvas ripped apart she dropped, still running, onto the deck.

Fearfully, everybody raced to pick her up. To our great relief she was no more than shaken. With everybody gathered around her in concern, she picked herself up and grinned to show she was O.K.

Our fear gradually changed to somewhat hysterical mirth. Any onlooker must have been puzzled. A group of adults and kids were sprawled over the deck with rags of canvas splattered all around them, shaking with laughter.

As we lay about giggling somebody shouted in alarm, "Lookout!"

Slowly, with great dignity, the tall staff proudly carrying the red Ensign subsided to fall with a loud clatter alongside us. Clorinda, it emerged had grabbed at the aerial wire attached to it as she fell.

"It's like an earthquake," somebody commented and that's all it took for everybody to collapse again with laughter.

Minor disasters apart, this taste of freedom made us more impatient to escape from the concrete of the marina to more serious cruising grounds. But Chris was still coming and going finishing off his work.

Day after day working all hours, our two weeks in Baie des Anges had slipped by unseen and it was now two months. Our departure was impossible before jenny came into service. Now it was in, it seemed to have problems working. We could see the summer disappearing.

Then one day I noted in my log, "2217 jenny starts after much coaxing." Few sweeter tones exist than a reluctant engine being wooed into life.

The next line in the log reads, "2217.45 seconds, jenny stops." There came an extraordinary cacophonous clatter from the engine room as jenny expired.

As the noise stopped, Jeremy shot over the top of the engine room ladder. His eyes were wide, his face pale. He gave out a great sigh.

He'd been warned in his first exploratory days in the engine room about diesels running away if oil overflowed into the cylinders.

A friendly skipper had described the process to Jeremy: "The oil takes over from the fuel; the engine races faster and faster; you can't stop it. It blows up: It takes only seconds." It can be stopped only by stuffing rags into the air intake (assuming no automatic cut-off, which we didn't have). That is, if you have the rags handy; and the time." Jeremy had had nightmares about it.

Chris had filled the jenny with oil prior to starting. The dipstick registered nothing. So he poured in more - but still without trace. They ended up pouring in gallons of the stuff. Then they started it up.

Jeremy found breath to explain what happened next. "It had no sooner started than oil began gushing out from absolutely everywhere. The engine raced faster and faster. I was sure it was going to blow up!"

He had stood transfixed, watching his nightmare to life. But Chris tore off the blower cover, and stuffed it full of rags which luckily were to hand. The motor stopped in time.

Jeremy said, "I was never more terrified in all my life!" His eyes were still like saucers to prove it.

But Carolyn ignored Jeremy's brush with eternity for more romantic considerations. "If the jenny's working that means we can leave doesn't it?" she asked excitedly.

"That's only the engine going, we haven't even started on the electrics yet," Jeremy snorted. But in the next days they began to function. We made at least a temporary departure, a little earlier than planned.

One morning Carolyn wandered in, paint brush in hand and asked, "What's that they're putting up on the quay? Right alongside the boat?" I glanced outside and had goose-pimples.

"It's a cement mixer!" I raced off the boat and was never more conscious of our bright new paintwork and varnish, the result of so much sweat and exhaustion.

I approached the would-be cement workmen "No no, non non. What are you doing! Stop!"

They smiled uncertainly and then I was almost knocked over by an enormous truck. It was carrying powdered cement.

"You're not going to drop that lot by the side of us here are you?" I enquired with a feeling of dread, not to say hysteria.

The driver shrugged and went to drive on. I stood my ground. I pointed at his load, made dropping gestures at the ground, pointed at our boat and made sweeping gestures and rolled my eyeballs.

He nodded cheerfully "Yes yes. I drop ze sement."

"Wait," I shouted "Attendez. Faites rien!"

He frowned and shook his head.

"Attendez, attendez," I bellowed and pointed at Jernica and then at distant horizons. "Nous partons. Toute de suite!"

To my relief he turned off his engine and lit a cigarette. The cement mixers (human) now looked quite happy to sit and wait for the rest of the day. But I wasn't chancing it.

"Jeremy," I hollered, "Start the engines! Carolyn, Rosemarie get cleared away. We're going out! Nicholas whip around to the Capitanerie and say we want a different berth when we return."

There was frantic activity on deck. We were luckily due to go out in a few hours' time to pick up an expert for compass swinging – where basically the boat's heading is swung around and the deviation of the compass for any heading, caused by magnetic fields on the boat, is measured to produce a deviation card so that appropriate adjustments can be made on voyage.

In a record fifteen minutes we had cleared everything away and the crew was at action stations. Soon the cement mixer was disappearing astern and we were nosing into the blessed, sunlit peace of the bay.

The professional compass swinger was also on board. (The work was basically a matter of pointing

Jernica's nose at an object on shore on a known bearing, comparing it with the compass reading, and making the necessary corrections.)

When we returned some hours later the compass was corrected and Rosemarie had applied a new covering to one of our bulkheads.

We had a lively conversation with the Capitainerie. They were desolé, mais the marina had to be completed. That was not unreasonable.

We concurred. But being covered in cement, we argued in the appropriate loud voice and much shaking of head, ne vas pas. Reluctantly they agreed. We went to a different, temporary berth, safe from the workings of workmen.

I was awoken next morning by tapping sounds. They were followed by a great blow on the hull which resounded through the boat, waking everybody.

I raced aloft then raced down again to haul on a pair of shorts, and finally made the deck. It was 0730 and we were berthed on this occasion alongside the quay. A workman was poised in the (literally) few inches between quay and hull. He held a hammer in his hand and was contemplating the gap with some trepidation.

I saw in a moment he had been trying to hammer in a mooring ring just below the quay. The pin of the ring he was supposed to hammer was a couple of inches longer than the distance to our hull. He had still tried to hammer it. The inevitable result was a large welt in my paintwork

"Look!" I pointed. He first withdrew his hammer, and then himself. From a safe distance he looked at the dent and shook his head. "No no, not me."

"What's this then?" I dragged the end of my finger over the rippled paint. It flaked away effortlessly.

"Was not me. Was already there," he shouted at the top of his voice, to emphasise his innocence. I dragged an official out of the Capitainerie who passed the workmen the message that bashing our hull was not an essential item in the day's routine.

As he moved off a bulldozer started up ten yards away. We looked at it wearily.

"That's it," I said to the family. "Whatever we haven't got now we'll find or do en-route. Give it a day or two for the loose ends. Then we're off."

The gremlin was listening and laughing. That evening the fuel pipe to the generator fell off flooding the engine room bilges.

An English electrical engineer, Brian Simms, was luckily at hand and was able to fix this and other pipes and he also eliminated a mystery short circuit, so giving us a bonus for the faulty fuel pipe work.

I went to see Victor at lunch time next day. As usual I was offered his brawny forearm in greeting instead of the standard black hand. He wouldn't talk before I'd drunk an enormous glass of local wine.

"Victor," I said "We're going. Let's have your bill." I'd asked him for it before but he hadn't given it to me. Now I emphasised, "We're off tomorrow!"

He gestured to a friend sitting there. "Isn't that wonderful! He could leave, but he comes and insists he must pay the bill." I laughed at the joke.

"How much, Victor?" I asked.

He said, "Nothing. You pay nothing."

I couldn't believe it was other than a laborious joke. But after a great deal more arm waving and shrugging it was clear he was quite serious.

I pointed out that not least such exceptional generosity would make it difficult if not impossible to ask him to do work for us again.

"We don't want to lose the best workman on the coast, "I pointed out.

I couldn't move him. He really wouldn't let us pay and there was no adequate way to express my thanks except, as he indicated towards the bottles, by joining him in a few more glasses.

"C'est la vie," was all he said. When I drifted back to the boat later with the news, we all agreed that Victor was an outstanding aspect of our vie.

We left next morning. Our cruising life had started. As we headed for the exit, we felt our spirits soaring as high as the day we first stepped on board to live. We didn't know what lay ahead. But we already knew that, "C'est la vie," was for us.

SCREWDRIVERING TO
LE LAVANDOU

A boat is often described as a hole in the water into which you pour money.

It is perhaps less appreciated that it is also a black hole of time. However long a period and large a cost is estimated for work on board, it will, without fail, suck in your effort and money for very much longer.

We had learnt this lesson. We had come to Baie des Anges for two weeks of work. We had stayed two months.

It was July 4th, our own Independence Day. We were on our way out of the marina. The sky was agreeably blue, as it is inclined to be in July in the Med.

Having stowed fenders and ropes the girls settled themselves decorously on deck, paint and varnish at last forgotten. We all said a thankful "at last," as we headed for the exit. We relaxed.

The port engine conked. We'd never had a moment's trouble with it before.

"Jeremy!" I called, starting up again.

His anxious face appeared in the engine-room hatch, "What happened?" he asked.

"You're the guv'nor down there," I said. "I was hoping you'd tell me." The engine started and conked again.

It was happening as I maneuvered around some sharp corners and mooring lines.

Jeremy soon diagnosed that the revs were too low at idling speed. A final tune-up by a helpful skipper the night before had obviously proved too much for it. Jeremy, a screwdriver, and five minutes corrected the problem.

We motored out into the bay. More grateful sighs.

Jeremy looking at the dials ordered, "Stop engines!" in my ear.

The girls and Nicholas poked their heads into the wheelhouse as the engines faded. Jeremy shot below.

He was soon back with a sheepish expression, having sorted the problem told him by the dials.

Preparing for take-off he'd spent days reading the GM instruction manual, checking every item, changing oil, and filters. Having flushed out the old water in the engine heat-exchangers he'd filled up with fresh. But he hadn't noticed an airlock which had caused the engine to overheat.

Carolyn patted the guilt-stricken engineer on the head and said, "You see? He's human."

Our course was westwards along the coastline towards the Isles d'Hyeres, a group of islands just to the east of Toulon. We'd been told they were attractive cruising grounds. We passed the familiar outline of St. Raphael, and before long were approaching the Gulf of St. Tropez.

I was attending the chart table. Nicholas was at the wheel, the girls sunning. The crew of Jernica was as serene as the weather as Jeremy said in my ear, "There's water coming into Carolyn's cabin."

The starboard propeller shaft ran under Carolyn's cabin. As we entered, we could hear loud sploshing noises. Carolyn found it more aesthetically satisfying to strew her clothes around the floor than into her wardrobe, but we swept the litter onto her bunk and raised the floorboards.

A great frothing and surging of water greeted our eyes. The bilge was almost totally filled with water. The shaft was submerged. A great spout of water seemed to be welling up.

I said aghast, "Look at that!" which even at the time I realised had to rank as the most irrelevant comment ever made by the skipper of a sinking boat.

Jeremy's habit when faced with any working problem was to look at it. It doesn't sound much. But there were times we thought he had X-ray eyes. Sometimes he would look, and say nothing, however prompted. He wouldn't speak until he'd reached a conclusion.

Jeremy looked at the bubbling water.

"It's possible the spurting's caused only by the speed of the shaft going round," said Jeremy, brow creased, after a few moments more study.

The water seemed to be rising. "Looks like a leak to me," I said. I hastened back to the wheelhouse but

Jeremy was way ahead of me en route to the engine room and the bilge pumps.

Our course was due to take us seven miles offshore. I could imagine the water overflowing into the cabin and then spreading.

The girls and Nicholas had caught the scent of scurrying and were waiting for more news. "We might have to put into St. Tropez," I told them.

"Why? asked Rosemarie, not unreasonably

"It's a nice place and there's a little water under Carolyn's floor," I said.

As I gave Nicholas the new compass heading, Rosemarie said, "You mean there's a leak?"

"Probably not," I hurrumphed, "but we won't take any chances."

Meanwhile there'd come the rumble of bilge pumps working and Jeremy scampered past again.

"I'm on the new bearing now," Nicholas reported.

Jeremy returned to the wheelhouse. "There isn't any leak," he said in relief. "It was after all the shaft turning in the water which caused the spurting. It's OK, come and look."

He marched me to the cabin. The bilge was pumped out dry. The shaft was spinning stainless steel bright. A slow but regular drip of water was visible from a gland. Jeremy explained the function of the drip was to cool the bearing. We would need to pump out the shaft bilges from time to time to avoid a buildup of water.

I returned to the questioning faces in the wheelhouse. "It's O.K. I thought we might have a bad leak. The bilges just needed pumping."

I was feeling rather pleased with the way I'd handled the situation. No panic among the crew, no life rafts launched, course set for the nearest port, dead-reckoning of our position maintained on the chart. Perfect.

Rosemarie started laughing. "We could tell something was wrong."

"How?" I asked.

The answer came from Carolyn. She stopped her fit of the giggles long enough to say, "I love it when Dad tries to sound all calm and collected."

I mustered my dignity and turning to Nicholas gave him the bearing to resume our course.

"I'm already on it," he said laconically.

We were still afloat a couple of hours later, cruising along the north coast of the Isle de Levant, the first of the islands in the group. We were headed for the next island, Port Cros, and its anchorage of Port Man.

As we approached, the bay looked crowded with yachts of all shapes and sizes riding at anchor; but as we entered space seemed to open up. We dropped anchor and Rosemarie appeared with tea. Jeremy at last allowed his engines to be switched off having insisted on a suitable cooling-off period. We gathered to sit on the foredeck in the silence.

The bay was heavy with shrubs and woods. The air was fragrant. The afternoon sun washed a soft luminescence over the sea, tinted with the colours of the boats at rest around us. There was a faint clink of glass and the occasional sound of laughter from figures reclining on neighbouring yachts.

The spell was broken by the snap of the bathing ladder being fixed in place. We were soon swimming in the water, warm and silky.

My course happened by merest chance to lead past a small sailing boat with a nude lady aboard. As I swam past and wished her a good afternoon Carolyn's voice gurgled in my ear, "Trust you."

I pointed out the need for yacht persons to be polite to their neighbours, and for crews not to play gooseberry on their skipper.

Jeremy had forsaken his engine room and was now jumping and diving non-stop from the coach roof into the sea. It was a remarkable display of energy for a grizzled old first engineer.

I was surprised to see Nicholas swim by with a cheerful grin and no book. And when Rosemarie splashed along having decided there wasn't anything she must cook, sew, clean make or wash, I knew that Jernica was beginning to weave magic around us.

We showered on a few cupfuls of water. We carried limited supplies, like every boat. We'd learned early to become fanatical guardians of our water - and energy - in our case gas. (On a short trip back to London I couldn't bear the waste of water and gas when a friend filled a kettle to the brim for two cups of tea. So I emptied it two-thirds. It was pure habit. I nearly got thrown out. After all, it was her kitchen.)

That first evening at anchor, eating dinner late on the aft deck in the soft light and air, to the murmurings of the boats around us, we felt we'd taken an enchanted step inside our new existence.

As twilight faded, our seats became stalls in the marine ballet. As the sea breeze gave way to a gentle ruffling from the land, the boats all bobbed and turned at their anchors to face their new master for the night, and for each little shift in the direction of the breeze the boats would form new ranks, our neighbours departing, distant boats sailing nearer, for our examination.

Our first night at anchor was quiet. But there were unfamiliar sounds - creaking chain and poppling water. I arose several times from bed to make sure we were still floating peaceably. I was rewarded with a view of stars forming an unbelievably incandescent roof, and the silhouettes of yachts like friendly watchmen around us.

Across the channel from our anchorage was the nudist colony on the Isle du Levant. Boats were in the habit of anchoring off the shore with binoculars at a premium. We discussed this remarkable practice and then went on to consider our next port of call.

"We know where you think we ought to go," said most of the family.

"Port Cros," I declaimed, enjoying a rare moment of one-upmanship.

We'd been told it was like a Caribbean lagoon. But two people's views on a place are as likely to coincide as their tastes in drink; and with similar results. It will leave one lightheaded and the other cold sober.

The entrance to Port Cros is a circular bay. We saw lushly wooded hills descending steeply to the sea. Villa roofs showed discreetly here and there. There were palm trees on the foreshore, some wooden jetties, two or three shack-like shops, and some restaurants.

It did look like a Caribbean lagoon. A cat and a donkey were parked side by side under a palm tree, gravely watching our entrance. They looked so much like a friendly reception committee that we waved and called out to them; they didn't wave back.

That night we experienced our first short swell while at anchor. I was soon up and about seeking the source of anxiety-inducing noises. Two of them defied me until well into the early hours. Finally I tracked them down.

The anchor was not dropping off, nor were other boats boring holes into our sides. But a swinging frying pan was scraping the galley walls and a crash helmet in a cupboard was rocking from side to side.

My subsequent night excursions on similar exercises were greeted with mumbled, "Go to sleep. The frying pan's not going to sink us," from the other, warm side of the bed.

But Jeremy's vision of life on a boat as a mere schoolboy swimming and sunning was doomed to an early demise. Idyllic surroundings or not, he was soon back down the engine room. Hose fittings were molting off the generator; and the outboard motor for the dinghy would proceed only in fits and starts despite all of Jeremy's attentions.

Jeremy and I crossed to the port of Le Lavandou, eight miles away, in the dinghy. We kept the outboard going by keeping our fingers crossed, and squeezing the little black hand-pump on the fuel feed line.

Safely arrived, we began what subsequently became for weeks a continual and dreary task; trying to find an agent prepared to service our ailing outboard. They were all too busy, as France prepared for the annual holiday scramble on July fourteenth.

We returned with new pipes for the generator. Jeremy fixed it, covered himself in oil, and reported later that a new leak had started. Even Jeremy began to look fed up. The generator just had to work. Without it, batteries would die and our boat's systems with them.

It was clear that our second-hand generator was not the greatest-buy ever.

We needed to cross in the dinghy once more for parts to fix the new leak.

At this moment the handle to the outboard decided to break off. We wouldn't be able to steer the dinghy - even if the engine worked.

Jeremy sat looking at the deficient outboard. A little later he said, "We can go."

"But how? I asked.

"We can screwdriver over," he declared. He inserted a large screwdriver through an aperture into a notch of the engine. "Look!" The screwdriver was now a steering and throttle mechanism.

I looked out at the channel where white horses were beginning to prance on the waves, and laughed.

I said "You don't think I'm going to cross eight miles over that chop on a bloody screwdriver?"

"It'll be alright," he said, "but we'll have to hand-pump the fuel all the way over, as well.

"That settles it. It's crazy, we're not going!"

A few minutes later we were on our way. It was bumpy and hairy, and crazy, as Jeremy tried to steer to catch the crests of the sea building up, and to keep the right throttle adjustments with the large old screwdriver.

I had a go. The screwdriver kept bouncing out of its notch and the dinghy lurched and leaned at all angles.

The return journey a few windier hours later was worse. I couldn't sit next day my bottom was so sore from bumping, and Jeremy even confessed to a sore arm. At least we'd brought back more pipes and fittings. We'd also found more outboard agents, all still too busy to attend to our motor.

Next day, with kind permission of the generator, which was working for a change, we were able to walk and swim and behave like a cruising boat again - and to enjoy the entertainment which is always likely to be in the offing from other boats.

A tiny sailing yacht put into the lagoon. A wizened old man dressed head to toe in whites, topped by an enormous sombrero was in the bows; a slim lady in a white ankle-length dress was at the outboard controls. Her face was also hidden under a sombrero. She could have been any age.

In the setting of the lagoon they were unreal, ethereal, pure Gaugin.

His eyes were fixed on the quay they were approaching. He shouted to his lady at the helm to turn left.

"A gauche! A gauche!" his cry rang out.

She remained unmoving, in a frieze. Aesthetically her lack of movement seemed fitting, as though motion would have spoiled the serenity of the picture they created.

On the other hand they were heading straight for a passenger boat moored at the jetty.

He turned towards her. "A gauche! A gauche!" he screamed at the top of his voice.

She retained a dignified, and we guessed, terrified immobility. They were only a few feet from the hull of the ferry, on a collision course.

The man in white clapped his hand to his head, then began jumping up and down gesticulating at the lady and screaming "A gauche! A gauche!" He was so agitated he barely maintained his balance.

At the last moment she moved a thin arm, and the yacht turned, away from the ferry. And away from the jetty they'd been heading for.

By now faces were peering down from the ferry, and from every deck in the harbour as once more the old gentleman jumped up and down, beside himself with rage, shrieking "A gauche! A gauche!"

This last was too much for all the onlookers. From all points came the cry, "A gauche! A gauche!"

He decided to wait no longer. Scrambling aft he snatched the controls from the hands of his motionless partner, and turned left. Then he turned to the countless watchers, and as in a theatre, gestured to them, and at the lady, miming clearly "See what I have to put up with!"

All under control, he handed her back the helm with a flourish.

As he did so he realised they were now about to crash into the quay. He turned, jumped up and down and shouted instructions again.

But his voice was drowned by shouts of, "A gauche! A gauche!" from all around the harbour.

The lady this time reacted to the shrieking and fiddled with the controls. There was a roar of engine and their yacht leapt towards the quay even faster.

The skipper jumped, screamed and clapped his hands on his head and the lagoon rung again with "A gauche!"

The many bystanders on the quay darted forward and grabbed the pulpit of the little yacht to swing it off before the hull could crash the quay.

As the old man finally switched off his engine, with more gestures, there came a generous round of applause from all around the harbour.

On one of our visits to Le Lavandou we'd called in on Tim and Anne at the neighbouring marina of Borme les Mimosas. We'd found Anne earlier as she was a teacher and Carolyn needed help with her biology. The couple were running a boat business in the marina.

They came motoring over in one of their "Fjiords", a small but luxurious Norwegian motor launch. Anne was our first topless lady guest and Tim our first nude bather. In that setting clothes did indeed seem more bizarre than bodies.

Jeremy now subjected the generator to a minute examination. We decided we must put into Borme to find materials and engineering support. Rosemarie agreed enthusiastically. In between painting and cooking and varnishing she'd bought canvas, as well as new curtains and materials for bench seats and deck chairs. She was also making dresses for herself and Carolyn.

We had been shocked by spare-part prices. Rosemarie knew we wouldn't get too many bought clothes. With all her activity the Pfaff sewing machine's bobbin, badly overworked and exploited after twenty years of faithful service, had broken down.

It was one of the few times we'd seen Rosemarie discouraged. This major disaster no less than the jenny demanded an early return to port.

At Borme we just about avoided berhing with the gangway resting on a quayside restaurant table. It was either a question of us moving to another marina (we seemed to be in about the last slot available) or the waiter moving his table one centimeter so that we could get the gangway down. We persisted and the waiter finally realised our gangway might not improve his Coq au Vin, and grumpily moved his table.

Thereafter our activities on board were part of the diners' entertainment. They would have one eye on the soup and the other cocked to watch our activities. We felt like the inmates of a zoo, only we hoped we were better looking.

Lolling on the aft deck being admired from shore is of course some people's idea of the ideal summer cruise. One advantage is you're sort of boating, but don't get seasick, although glass in hand you may well get half-seas over. St. Tropez is full of such peacocks. The crews of sailboats are apt to view all motor yachts through that lens – in a word or three as 'a gin palace'. But the pace and depth of our work aboard should have left nobody in doubt we weren't that sort of boat or that sort of crew.

As we berthed at Borme we had been handed a leaflet saying "Demandez Mike" for all kinds of shipboard jobs. So we demanded him. He turned out to be a cheerful native of Portsmouth and lived on a boat with his wife and child. His work was as reliable no-frills as one would expect from Pompey; England had lost him from a sense of frustration. The best skilled workers in many Mediterranean ports, we were to find, were Britons who simply wanted to do the work they enjoyed in their own way.

For several days Demandez Mike worked in the engine room gloom with Jeremy. He was dirty but happy as joints, seals, and cocks for the jenny were refurbished. And we began to learn the lesson that it is easier for the engineer to pass through the eye of a needle than to find a shop with the right spares.

Jeremy learned from Mike the virtues of imaginative improvisation. Rosemarie meanwhile was doing her own kind of improvising. Failing to find a Pfaff agent, she had pounced on a hand-sewing machine owned by Madame Demandez Mike and spent her days furiously whirling the handle; or better grabbing any passing crew and getting them to do the whirling.

The day came when Jeremy pronounced jenny fit for active service. We were ready to put to sea again. We started with a lunchtime anchorage in Port Man again.

We'd been anchored quietly a few hours when a smart Belgian yacht arrived. The owner, resplendent in a hat more decorated than any Admiral of the Fleet's, dropped his anchor and the second it was down retired to the aft deck for cocktails, which suggested that he wasn't an Admiral or even an Ordinary Seaman for it is elementary to stay by your anchor long enough to be sure it has held.

Minutes later we heard a loud squawk. Carolyn was pushing his pulpit off our bow. We rushed forward to add muscle. We pushed them off, and they swung round and the ladies and gentleman on their aft deck slowly came into view. They froze glasses to lips, mouths open. One lady put her glass down, looked at the bogus Admiral, and asked him indignantly, "How on earth did they manage to bump into us?"

Rosemarie and I vied for the privilege of adding a few words in their further education. Admiral Hat finally downed his glass, muttered a few words to Madame about the English, upped anchor and departed. We noticed that his pulpit, designed like the hat for decoration rather than protection, was a trifle bent and so honour was satisfied.

We sighed, spread ourselves around the deck in the sun and relaxed. Then a wizened, frowning face popped up out of the engine room. "It's losing oil fast," said Jeremy.

"The bloody generator?"

"What else?"

"O.K." I said, "Port Grimaud. It's big. Lots of yachts. There're bound to be lots of engineers."

Grimaud was about three hours to the east. We took off, and the Mediterranean showed us her fickle face for the first time. An hour out of Grimaud the skies turned dark and threatening. An oily swell was moving on the water.

We entered Grimaud to our first storm. With lightning raking black skies and rain sheeting down Nicholas played Wagner's Tannhauser at full blast on his cassette-player.

So we entered the port with a certain amount of theatre; Wagner and thundering skies alike howling Gotterdammerung but Jernica not giving a damn, as she steered serenely through it.

We'd liked Grimaud from land. We liked it more from the sea. We never found a marina which managed completely to shrug off its artificial origins. Grimaud succeeded more than most. A touch of Venice, built on a wasteland. Houses skillfully reproduced in pink and yellow terraces to look like the real old thing.

Elegant bridges over the canal network; new curved vistas around each corner. Above all an absence of the rectangular high-rise boxes which are the assassins of architectural character. On land we found an integrated pattern of piazzas, markets, shops and a church to breathe a fair resemblance of a centuries-old harbour.

We berthed near the church with a wide lagoon before us. Next day we began our search for engineers. We began to learn about the great phantom of the Mediterranean - the Tomorrow Engineer.

He says, "I'll come tomorrow." We give him heartfelt thanks. He doesn't come.

"Where are you? You said you'd come." "Tomorrow, Tomorrow"

Next week, still waiting. "Tomorrow, I told you. Don't worry."

Ten days later, still sitting in port, "if you can't bloody come, tell us. Then we can arrange something else."

"Please not to swear. It is not nice. Don't worry. I'll come tomorrow. Definitely." We ended up with our non-Mediterranean engineer, Demandez Mike again, dragging him over from Borme.

Everybody got busily to work again on the boat. One day we berthed alongside the quay by the Capitainerie building at the entrance to Grimaud, having taken a day out from engineers, phantom or otherwise.

When it was time to move off, small yachts were berthed hard on our bow, and stern. Fingers of the dreaded Mistral were pushing us firmly onto the quay. I used the mooring lines and a large fender on the bow to set Jernica's stern out from the quay and into the wind to give us room before going forward.

It was the first time I'd tried to "spring" the boat off in this way. At the right moment, as I thought, we let go the spring and continued aft. But I hadn't pointed her stern sharply enough into the wind. Instead of continuing out into mid-channel, Jernica, shoved by the wind, began to swing back fast towards the small yacht by our stern. But if I throttled down the wind would shake us even more sharply in its teeth – and into the yacht.

The controlled walk of the lookout crew members from the stern to the wheelhouse became a frantic gallop. Discrete, dignified murmurs, which I had tried to instill in the crew as the appropriate method of communication between deck and wheel at moments of stress, became instead strangled cries of "Aaaarrgghh! We're going to hit that yacht!"

Truth to tell I required no instruction. My own view showed sharply enough the mistakes I was making; it also gave me a clear, if fleeting picture of the owner of the yacht, transfixed in terror, his luncheon sandwich poised motionless before his open mouth, as our steel stern roared towards him.

He didn't realise my own terror was greater. I made adjustments on the wheel and throttles and somehow the yacht and sandwich lunch were safe. There carne a loud scraping noise from our portside. I had the dubious satisfaction of knowing it was only our own hull being scraped along the quay.

By now the most sang-froid member of my crew was now experiencing some difficulty in not tearing her hair out. However, as I pointed out later, we also missed the yachts moored just forward of our grinding bow.

When we finally reached our berth we examined the badly scraped hull. The crew was not in the habit of seeing Jernica in a condition less than perfection. I obviously looked in need of comforting for Carolyn patted me on the back and said, "It looks a mess but it's only superficial. Leave it to me. I'll fix it, you go and make a cup of tea."

When Carolyn had finished filling and painting, the hull looked like new. So I learned that there was one more job our crew could manage as well as any pro at the same time as I learned to make sure our stern was far enough out before moving off when a wind was blowing us on.

Otherwise it was workaday as usual. From his reading of the boat's Authorised Version of the Bible, otherwise known as the GM Workshop Manual, Jeremy was sure that the air-boxes on the engines needed cleaning out.

A number of visiting experts had assured him it wasn't necessary. The lack of flow from the air pipes which he had detected could be ignored, they said. Jeremy wasn't prepared to ignore anything.

One morning while everybody was about their business, Rosemarie suddenly cried, "My God!" We all rushed to the alert. We saw a strange, stricken figure slowly rising from the engine room. It was covered in black sludge. Eyes peered out in a state of shock.

We more or less carried this creature into the shower, so that no slimy trail would affect our nice clean boat. Rosemarie scrubbed it down and Jeremy emerged.

He told us his story in a quavering voice.

He'd opened the partition in the engine to clean the air-box windows. He had had to dip his arm in and start scraping around. As he did so, a stream of thick, black prehistoric goo began to creep out of the box and ooze past him. He tried to stop it, and clean up. But it infiltrated past. The more frantically he tried to clean the more he spread the ghastly sludge all across his pin-bright engine room.

Ignoring all his frenzied efforts, it spread over the floor, into the bilges, and finally covered him from head to foot.

For once Jeremy was out for the count. I descended below to attack this slimy enemy and begin to restore the engine room to its pristine state. We couldn't afford to have the engineer quit.

We spoke later to a professional GM engineer. If the air boxes hadn't been cleaned the engines would certainly have stalled some time later in our passagemaking, he assured us.

A grin was restored to Jeremy's face next day. "Well?" He showed me a control handle for the Mercury he'd fabricated from a bolt. So I knew our engineer was staying.

Demandez Mike and Jeremy now made a final assault on the jenny, and we hoped it might not expire on us, as a doctor might have hoped his most sickly patient would stay alive.

During our stay in Grimaud, the Mistral wind, fierce and biting had regularly been showing its fangs. With the jenny patched up again we looked impatiently at the skies for signs of improvement so that our life of true cruising could begin.

ANYBODY SEE GROUP
FLASHING TWO?

We put into Cogolin marina, adjacent to Grimaud, for a change of scenery while waiting for better weather. Of course the Mistral never lasted for long in summer, people said.

The wind didn't care what people said. It just went on blowing - days, a week, more. Cogolin seemed to be filled mostly with Belgian boats, though with scarcely a Belgian body in sight. We all agreed it was boring. We might have been excited if we'd known we'd tied up alongside film star Romy Schneider's yacht, but we didn't know until she'd left.

We felt very frustrated, but we weren't going to fool about with Mistrals. Our tedium was relieved by Lionel, a Channel Islander whose boat had been alongside ours in Grimaud.

He visited us with his wife Enid and a great fund of stories. He'd once visited Spain on a friend's yacht. They had to put into a port to look for another friend. Lionel, on the bow, reported to his companion on the wheel that there was nowhere to tie up.

"Over there," said his friend, pointing.

Lionel looked. "But that's the commercial quay," he pointed out. "Yachts aren't allowed there."

"We'll only be a few minutes," said his friend, nosing towards the quay. As they approached the quay, Lionel made ready with the lines, but saw a policeman gesticulating furiously.

"Don't worry," his skipper called out. "If he says anything, all you've got to do is shout back 'No comprendee '"

They approached the quay with the Spanish policeman wildly waving them off. Lionel flung the bow lines ashore shouting, "No comprendee! No comprendee!"

In a rage, the policeman picked up the line. He shouted "You comprendee - FUCK OFF!" The line came whirling back aboard as the policeman pulled out his gun.

Lionel commented, "I've never been on a boat which left a port so fast."

We said we weren't surprised and sympathised with each other that the good old days when the English could hide behind their well-known ignorance of others' languages were fast fading.

We were having our own expletive-deleted problems with the continuing heavy weather.

Rough seas and Mistral was the forecast next day - but not quite so strong. The following morning further improvement was promised. Our spirits lifted.

We began our preparations for a voyage to Corsica. Carolyn asked, (again) "How long will we be at sea?"

I said "Ten hours."

I wasn't there when Columbus mentioned to his crew they'd be journeying over the edge of the world, but the results couldn't have been far different.

Carclyn looked at me open-eyed and repeated, "Ten hours!"

We'd decided on a night passage. My training and general reading were fairly unanimous on this point; a dawn landfall by a light winking a known sequence is easier to identify than a hazy coastline. Then you head into harbour in growing daylight. That's what the book says.

We were making for Calvi on the north-west coast of Corsica, the shortest route from the French coast. A major lighthouse, Revellata, was conveniently placed, only two miles south of Calvi.

I turned to the Admiralty List of Lights. Revellata's sequence was a group of two white flashes every 15 seconds, visible from 27 miles. On the chart I stepped 27 miles along our track off Corsica and wrote "See Revellata" on the chart.

If we left at nine in the evening we'd be looking for the beckoning light at about four-thirty in the morning. I also noted the lights sequence of the citadel at Calvi; and those at Cap Corse.

Nicholas, who'd been looking over my shoulder started to chuckle and called out, "Get the life-jackets ready. Our navigator's noting the lights at Cap Corse!"

"So?" Carolyn enquired, open-eyed.

"It's forty miles north of Calvi," laughed Nicholas. I laughed too, to hide my nervousness and the fact that I also knew the Cap was 40 miles north and that at least if that's where we landed up, I'd know.

I checked where to take fixes going out, to monitor any funny stuff on the compass, but luckily Nicholas didn't get hold of that for family publication.

The sun slipped slowly down its blue cloth. It lost its fire and turned bronze. We were all excited and tense for our first night passage.

Carolyn had secured the dinghy to the stainless-steel davits over the stern; Rosemarie was busily securing everything below, including the contents of cupboard, loose pots and pans, books. Jeremy was attending the pre-start-up rituals of the engines.

We reflected that if there was any engine trouble mid-passage all eyes would turn to him. For a fourteen-year old it would be a night to remember.

Nicholas contorted himself around the lazarette giving a turn to the grease-cups for the steering gear.

Rosemarie conjured dinner out of the melee but we were too excited to enjoy it. The sun, normally so quick to set in fine weather was now fighting a perverse battle to stay above the horizon. But Copernicus was right after all, and it finally had no choice but to slip below the horizon.

"Everything O.K. below Jeremy?" I asked. His smile was happy, maybe a little strained. "I think so."

I had good kids.

"Let's start the engines." I switched on navigation lights, and radar. At 2100 we slipped by the entrance lights of Marina de Cogolin and out into the Gulf of St. Tropez. There was not much of a sea and we were soon making our cruising speed of ten knots at 1800 revs.

The twilight began to vanish about us as we stood on deck in a mood of quiet excitement. We made our way through the Gulf. To starboard a confusion of lights beckoned to us to come and join the fun in the harbour of St. Tropez, but we were not to be lured. Jernica and her crew headed for the open sea.

As we passed the Rabiou shoal and into the open sea it became dark. And then very dark. Nobody in the books had mentioned how very dark it can be at sea at night without a moon. We could see no other boat's lights. We couldn't see the sea. The compass was our guide, with the radar telling us there was no other craft to hit.

I set course for Calvi and we gathered on the aft deck to watch the land slip away. First St. Tropez and the other coastal lights faded, then the lights signaling from the two Gulf rock banks slowly became indiscernible. It was black all around us. There was only the sound of our engines and the sizzling of sea against the bow.

We felt very small on a very large Earth.

We'd fixed red lights over the steering position and chart table. Together with the luminescence from the radar screen, it spread a warm, comforting glow.

Rosemarie produced sandwiches and hot drinks. There was a slight swell but Jernica was moving easily. I hadn't organised a watch. The family had decided to do what they felt like doing. There were enough of us for this free and easy approach.

The helmsman - Nicholas or Carolyn- was quite busy. He or she had to steer, keep an eye on the engine gauges and maintain a look-out both visually and by radar. I was keeping the chart updated and keeping an eye on the helm.

Jeremy was busy double-checking gauges and he descended to commune personally with his beloved nuts and bolts every half an hour.

It was some time after midnight with Carolyn at the wheel. She was working harder. She said anxiously, "It's more difficult to hold the course. She's swinging about a lot."

Half an hour later, Rosemarie said, "We seem to be moving about quite a bit," in a voice which indicated the skipper ought to be doing better.

I'd already stuck my head out a number of times to try and work out what the sea was getting up to. But I was learning that without a moon on the sea at night you can't see a thing. There was no wind to explain our lurching and bumping.

Carolyn a little later left the wheel for a horizontal position on the aft deck bench seat. This was her post when feeling queasy. I actually held the record of being the worst family sailor. When we'd chartered I was the only one sick apart from the cook/delivery skipper on the roughish channel crossing.

Now as I leaned over my chart table I hoped I wouldn't let the side down again and had a nasty feeling

I would. The roll angle increased. At 0200 I recorded in the log, "Rough Seas".

Nicholas now retired from his spell at the wheel. Jeremy and I took over wheel and lookout and gauge watching.

At 0225 I recorded "Violent Motion. Stuff flying about. Speed reduced to 1500 revs." The crew was now in fairly fixed positions - either flat on their backs, hanging onto the wheel, or bent over chart table.

We were caught in a strange sea. Jernica would be going steadily and then suddenly lurch from side to side; then she would plough on before jumping like a fish from the water, crunching heavily down again into the sea. She would then continue quietly and casually before the next mighty lurch and leap.

Strange noises or rather crashes were taking place at intervals within the boat. No matter how hard I looked I couldn't make out what was hitting us. It was clear we had beam seas; but why so violent, with a complete absence of wind?

After one especially violent leap and lurch I suggested putting back to San Remo which would have put beam seas on our stern. The recumbent figures weren't as dead as they looked. They mustered enough energy to mumble me down.

Nobody was going back to all that hanging around, waiting again for the weather to calm. The interior of the boat was beginning to resemble an earthquake area. At the first clatter Rosemarie had rushed below.

"All the books have been flung on the floor," she groaned. At the next crash she staggered through to the galley.

She found custard powder, marmalade, and other glutinous materials strewn liberally over the floor but didn't bother to tell us at the time. Coming back she trod on a book and an orange underneath it burst, spraying all over the floor.

The calm waters of St. Tropez had caught us with our inexperienced trousers down. We hadn't battened down tightly enough.

Carolyn was viewing more serious trouble, aft. Lying down, staring astern, she saw the dinghy begin to swing from side to side in the davits. The diagonal supporting ropes were under increasing strain. The swinging became more violent. Then one rope snapped, followed swiftly by the other.

The dinghy which we'd left loaded with the heavy outboard was now attached only by vertical wires. Helplessly Carolyn watched as the dinghy careered viciously from side to side.

The davits seemed to be holding though; and nothing seemed very important to her anyway because, as she told us later, "I was so sick I thought I was going to die. I kept thinking 'it'll be alright if morning comes.' So I kept shutting my eyes. But when I opened them again it was still dark."

Jernica's equipment did not include the means of telling us our speed, or distance we'd travelled. We had only the rev. counter. We knew that at 1800 revs we made eleven knots, but what was our speed

now at about 1400? I made a quick pro-rata calculation, crossed my fingers and recommenced the dead
reckoning.

I took the wheel from Jeremy. We were now the
only two vertical crew members. It was past three in
the morning.

"You'd better get a couple hours of sleep," I said.
He protested.

"Clear off. Then I can take a rest when you return,
"I said. When he still looked reluctant I said, "I'll even
keep an eye on your engines."

That did it. He departed, but not before saying,
"Don't forget to clean up the oil leak." My heart sunk a
little lower. An oil seal on the port engine dynamo was
leaking and he'd been cleaning it up regularly.

We crashed on. I climbed gingerly down into the
engine-room from time to time, very reluctantly, as
the effect of lurching and leaping was much worse
there. I ran an eye over the engines, but I was there
primarily to wipe up the oil, because I knew that if
he saw a smear on his return I might as well resign as
skipper.

Within the hour Jeremy was back, first inspecting
the engine room, giving a grunt, and taking the wheel.
I went below for my hour. When I returned Rosemarie
was wobbling around on hands and knees amidst the
debris on the floors, trying to secure the horse after it
had kicked the stable down.

At some point when all the family bodies in various
inert shapes were lying about the wheelhouse I had a
look at the chart.

In the jovial tones of a doctor encouraging a terminal patient I said, "We should be seeing the Revellata light soon."

My morale-boosting was short-lived. I immediately followed up by announcing, "Oops! I am going to be sick.."

Desperately, I realised I wasn't going to be merely sick. I was going to do it all over the wheelhouse floor.

At that moment the patron saint of novitiate sailors looked down from heaven (or up from his locker) and gave a forgiving smile. As I'd collapsed there'd been another violent roll. The motion sent something literally skittering into my hand. It was a fruit bowl, large, deep and for the moment, of course gratifyingly empty.

With heartfelt thanks I clutched it to me, and employed it to good purpose, one never imagined by its makers.

Through such beneficent intervention I salvaged some honour, and earned the only good laugh of the night.

Rosemarie went aft to see Carolyn and found her leaning over the rail, also being sick. The rolling was such that the scuppers were disappearing into the water. Rosemarie was terrified. She grabbed hold of Carolyn's belt expecting at any moment to see her disappear over the side.

These incidents marked the nadir of a long night on a black sea. I lay on the floor, recovering, but not daring to move for fear of further disgracing myself. Jeremy sat rocklike at the wheel. He had given up visits to the engine although maintaining an eagle eye on the dials. He also had a grandstand view of our heaving bows.

The breaking seas were becoming visible. Jeremy at the wheel could give warning of the big ones.

"Here it comes." He would wrap himself around the wheel, while we all hung on tighter.

I checked my watch again. Anybody see Revellata?" I called hopefully from my horizontal position. "Anybody see group flashing two every fifteen seconds?"

The thought of seeing land brought new life to the stricken crew. Nicholas propped himself up to look around. Carolyn crawled in to enquire what the shouting was about and then began scanning the horizon. Nobody could see anything.

Rising to my feet I joined the look-outs. We could see nothing.

Carolyn cried in frustration, "Oh! Where the hell is group flashing two!"

We were at least cheered by a faint natural light creeping above the eastern horizon.

Soon we could see our tormentor. The weeks of wind had created a massive short swell. It was directly on our beam, moving against us in great towering heaving surges. The bigger ones had foaming crests, which had served as warnings for the helm.

We wondered how Jernica had managed her many periods of stable progress. Nicholas said, "Blimey!" Much later he confessed that at this moment he felt frightened. We all were.

Carolyn appeared. "Quick! The dinghy! I think it's breaking away!"

I went out on the aft deck. The pounding had completed its work. The large stainless-steel bolts holding the davits firm to the deck had sheared. They now swung drunkenly from side to side.

The dinghy, suspended by cabled wires from the davits and suspended over the seas breaking aft was thrashing from side to side.

Would the wires hold? The dinghy could break loose at any moment.

I said, "If we could get another line into the dinghy I can see how to control the worst of the swinging. But how do we get in it?"

Rosemarie flung a rope at me. "Tie a bowline around yourself and I'll hang on to it."

Jeremy was on the wheel. Nicholas with all the knowhow and sang-froid of an old-salt shouted at him, "turn into the sea and slow down." The rookie crew was doing well.

I tied the bowline around me. The ship's motion became easier as Nicholas turned Jernica's shoulder into the swell. I timed my leap, sprawled into the dinghy, and had soon secured it tightly enough to dampen the wild swinging and threat of breaking away.

I reorganised our course. We'd get off this direct but deadly course. We'd do a long leg putting the swell behind us and stopping the pounding; then we'd turn at a point we could put the boat's shoulder into it, which would also make for a happier ride.

"We ought to land up more or less in the right place, but it'll put us even more behind time," I told the fatigued crew. Everybody was quite happy to swap time against the continual pounding.

Luckily nobody asked how much more time, because I wasn't sure. I had qualms about the accuracy of my dead reckoning. I reckoned the tracks I was now drawing on the chart could be a long way out.

We turned, putting the swell astern. It was the same sea, but magically soothed. Jernica rode easily. In moments, the exhausted crew was sleeping peacefully.

Daylight was brighter in the sky, but there was no sign of land. I turned my attentions hopefully to the radar.

Our original ETA at Calvi had been 0615. At that time I turned Jernica to head directly for Calvi. But our sixteen mile radar showed no trace of land.

I continued to search for the first tell-tale shadows on the fringe of the screen. There was no sign of land either by eye. There was only sea. The slowings, stops, starts and changes of course had evidently been too much for us. We were at least two hours behind our original ETA. And not a whisper of land.

I thought, 'Other people land a few miles out. You're the first navigator who can't even hit Corsica!' With a sinking stomach which had nothing to do with the swell I resumed my vigil before the screen, thinking of my crew sleeping, innocent and trusting.

But then I saw the shadow; and at 0645 noted in the log "Radar 16 miles land". I knew then how Columbus' crew felt on sighting America. But the flood of relief was short-lived. Land - but where?

Such were my inexperience and doubts after that frantic night I considered whether it was even Corsica. Still no land was visible with the naked eye. As the image grew stronger on the screen I looked more closely at the chart. It was becoming evident we were heading for a small peninsula.

Suddenly, as I raised my head from the screen, hills burst out of a thick mist. Seconds later I saw a light blinking, piercing the gloom. I counted the flashes - two. Then the interval - fifteen seconds.

We closed the light. Painted boldly across the lighthouse on the edge of the cliff was a beautiful word - "Revellata". A couple of miles beyond, the craggy citadel of Calvi sat solid atop the hills, beckoning to us.

I wrote in the log, "Revellata 0745."

Jernica's bows came round under the citadel and into a new sea, with still waters. Yachts were riding quietly at anchor in the sweep of a bay mirrored in a sea of coloured glass. Other boats were moored at the quay. No person was in sight.

Beneath the fort nestled the port. She was an old beauty, a huddle of small buildings, friendly in their soft, warm colours of old-gold walls and ochre tiles, and seemingly unspoiled by modern intrusions. Mountains cloaked in green with rocky peaks swept around the miles of bay.

I had time now to reflect that the weeks-long Mistral had clearly heaped up the monstrous swell which had lain in wait for us; and that weather forecasts which omit mention of swell are as useful as three-legged guard dogs.

A voice hailed me from a sailing yacht which had been closing us. 'A weather-beaten face enquired "Where are we?"

"Calvi", I said.

"Ah. Calvi! It was a foul night out there wasn't it? We were headed 20 miles south. This'll do, "he said, and waved cheerfully and moved off.

I had a small moment of satisfaction. Sailing boat crews call diesel yachts 'stink boats', and assume the crews are all boy racers who look to put their foot on a brake when they're coming into a port. Well, not my lot.

I went the round of the dead bodies. "Wake up. We're in Calvi."

One by one my bleary-eyed and bedraggled crew came on deck to admire the beauty, and drink in the silence.

We chose our spot and anchored. Below, all was quiet and still. But it looked as though someone had thrown a bomb.

Rosemarie took a long, slow look at the strewn wheelhouse floor, at the galley covered in mounds of flour and marmalade and assorted goo, and said, "It can wait. Let's all go to bed."

Somebody said, 'We'd better hose her down first.' We did.

As Rosemarie finally went off with red eyes and grubby hands followed by the others, Jeremy said, "Pity we didn't see Revellata's light."

I said, "I saw it."

Lust At Tea-Time

Later that day we moved over to the quay and hosed Jernica down with a thoroughness to cleanse not only the boat but the last vestiges of the journey out of our minds.

That night – at 23.20 indeed, it was so striking I logged it - the fragrant scent of pines suddenly filled the air as we were seated on deck under the stars. The land breeze had taken over and we slept in a sweet heaven.

We hung around for several days, the Mistral back to plague us. The kids hired mopeds to see the countryside but saw rather more of each others' backsides as their steeds broke down and they spent their time towing each other along.

On one of these mornings Carolyn came running aboard from the quay red in the face and screeching, "What're they doing! My paintwork!"

We could hear engines thumping alongside. We all raced on deck to look aft. A shabby Spanish boat alongside us had begun blowing black clouds of pure soot from its exhausts. It was blowing over our hull and decks and through the cabin windows.

Their skipper, uniformed in a grubby vest, was on deck looking down at the vast pollutant clouds frothing from his exhausts, smiling and nodding.

I hailed him through the smog. "Look what you're doing," I bawled. "We're getting smothered! Stop it."

He nodded at us, still grinning.

The skipper's form was now wreathed in the black clouds booming out from his engines. He shouted back, "Yes! Is good! I must to clear the engines!"

Rosemarie appeared, aghast. "There's soot all over the beds. Do something!"

"It'll be smothering my engine room!" Jeremy hurled himself desperately for the hatchway to his lovingly cared-for workplace where he was soon banging the portholes closed.

The Spanish skipper remained mesmerised with admiration at his soot clouds and deaf to our pleas. I pounded over to the Capitainerie. The two officials in the small quayside office listened, and seemed concerned.

"Well?" Rosemarie enquired on my return.

"I've fixed the bastard," I said. "I pointed out he's polluting the bay as well as us. There's a law against it."

Indeed a thick film of soot now extended over a wide area of sea. I was pleased to see the Port Captain striding towards us about half an hour later. I called Rosemarie on deck. The official stopped and started yelling at us.

We both worked out that he was complaining that we shouldn't be complaining about such reasonable activities.

We spent half a day cleaning the insides and outsides of the boat and even James Bond might have been surprised at the fiendish ingenuity of the kids' suggestions in the event that the soot assault started anew.

Fortunately for the good health of the captain and his soot-propulsion boat, it didn't.

The bay lost a little more of its undoubted glamour at 0630 a morning later. We were rudely awakened by a strange caterwauling. It sounded like a juke box playing at full throttle, its speakers badly distorting; but that was impossible at dawn.

Everybody staggered on deck to find all the aft decks along the quay similarly occupied by bleary, pyjama'd unbelievers. It was true though.

We were listening to a juke-box, shatteringly distraught under the load of its wattage. Four very large and very thuggish-looking men were seated outside the quayside cafe drinking, nodding, and tapping their feet appreciatively to the music. Meanwhile they were staring challengingly at the marina disarray confronting them.

A Frenchman on the neighbouring boat told us these were heavies from a local nightclub, entertaining two Paris friends of the same profession.

We turned our faces to find the breeze. None. The air and sea were calm.

Rosemarie said drily, "The advantage of a boat is you don't have to stay anywhere you're not welcome."

The opinion was widely shared. We were the last to move out, at 0730, from a totally deserted quay.

As we moved happily into the sea-lanes, we discovered the strong westerly swell continuing; and we learned it was a regular feature of the Corsican seas in summer.

As we cruised southwards it thwarted our plans for anchoring in several bays. But I gained a certain pleasure from actually being able to see it and learning how to steer to minimise the effects.

We had a comfortable ride, and by evening we had berthed in Ajaccio, halfway down the coast and the capital of the island.

It was a severe disappointment after Calvi. The citadel was submerged under concrete rectangles, flats, hotels and office blocks. From the port, these hideous constructions blotted out not only the old town but even the surrounding hills.

Squashed in the harbour, our depression was completed by a quayside chandler charging prices outrageous even by Mediterranean standards.

The town was busy, and had good shops and restaurants. But we didn't like the place and decided to part next morning.

"Perhaps we should give it another day here?" Rosemarie ventured as Nicholas sauntered into the wheelhouse.

"Great news," he said. "'Arnerus is just berthing alongside us."

If he had said a bomb had been planted it would have had the same effect. This was the Spanish soot machine we had thought to see the last of forever at Calvi.

We departed next morning very early indeed. We poked our bows into Propriano further down the coast but couldn't find a berth. We finally dropped anchor for the day in the well-sheltered bay of Campo Moro. Sea and wind were getting up and there were gale warnings.

After the concrete of Ajaccio this wide bay with sandy beaches under gentle green hills was very welcoming. A few other sailing and motor yachts shared the spacious mooring.

Our first gale when at anchor blew that night. When I rose in the early hours to inspect our anchor and our neighbours' positions I found Carolyn and Rosemarie already taking an anxious look around. Most people in normal life listen to the weather forecast to learn if it's going to rain. With a boat, it's the wind that's the problem.

The wind eased next day and we walked to the old Venetian tower on the point for a magnificent view over the anchorage and out to a calming sea. That evening we had our first meal ashore while at anchor. Generally, the cost of feeding five at French prices had meant little respite from the stove for Rosemarie. But here was a small restaurant on the beach run by a local fisherman. In this setting it was too good to miss.

The light was fading when we rode ashore in the dinghy and walked along the beach to the restaurant. We ate some excellent veal with good local wine, looking out to Jernica lying peaceably among the other boats, until daylight faded and anchor lights twinkled their positions.

Much later we walked back over the sand, the air warm, water lapping our feet. The moon was casting mysterious shadows around us and soft lights in the water. We arrived at our beached dinghy in a relaxed and boisterous mood.

The beach shelved steeply; over this shelf the aftermath of the gale was sending a short curl of breaking wave. We knew it wasn't quite as innocuous as it looked.

We stripped down to our trunks and, well rehearsed, waded out to push the nose of the dinghy firmly into the breakers. Broadside, we'd be turned over.

We timed our moment. Then we all leaped into the dinghy, Nicholas on the oars started pulling furiously to keep our nose straight while Jeremy was starting the engine.

We'd done it just right. But we needed the motor going if we were going to stay right side up. "Get cracking," I snapped. The engine roared. "Well done," I shouted, as we began to make some way.

And then we all noticed a figure transfixed, gazing at us forlornly from the receding shore. It was Rosemarie. She'd organised bathing trunks for everybody except herself. As we'd all stripped and scrummed out with the boat, she'd stood wondering what to do.

Jeremy stopped the outboard. Nicholas took up furious rowing again. We began to turn broadside.

"Somebody get that silly cow into the boat!" I bawled, years of loving, not to say heroic service, counting for nothing in the perils of the moment.

We paddled, Rosemarie waded, Nicholas and Jeremy grabbed, and Rosemarie was hauled aboard soaked through. The screaming and falling about with laughter in the dinghy was such that we nearly turned broadside again and I had to ban such hilarity until we'd finally made it back to Jernica.

The next day we made for Bonifacio at the southern end of Corsica. We'd been told it was like St. Tropez.

Any resemblance was superficial. The harbour was rectangular with boats moored stern to, backing onto rows of restaurants and boutiques. It all had a sad rundown look.

On board Jeremy's long face announced more troubles with jenny. The fresh water pump was pouring more out than in; and the salt-water pump was faulty, in case we thought life was too simple.

We visited the local agent. We asked for the special impeller we needed for the salt-water pump. He produced it. A Knight Templar wouldn't have looked more amazed than Jeremy did, if he'd been handed the Holy Grail. We'd been unable to find any impeller after scouring the south coast of France. Such delights give the cruising man his day.

Jeremy fixed the fresh water pump. We were free to leave; and we were looking forward eagerly to taking Jernica to fresh cruising grounds - Italy.

A more cheerful crew departing Bonifacio bound across the short strait for Sardinia would have been hard to find. For one thing, against all expectations we had beaten the humorist who organised many main anchoring positions in Bonifacio at right angles to each other.

We had passed an evening perched on the fore-deck watching skippers trying by plea and threat to prevent new arrivals dropping across their cables; and the mornings watching more enraged skippers trying to untangle the spaghetti network of chains brought up by their own anchors.

We viewed with mixed feelings. It was entertaining, but we knew our time was nigh.

I'd actually taken a chance on the weather and dropped a very short anchor on arrival. But we were all surprised and no little delighted when on departure we weighed no more than our own anchor.

Our good cheer as we made our way along the harbour channel was also due to the fact we were bound for Italian waters. We were a family of Italophiles having spent frequent holidays there in landlubber days. We were making for Sardinia.

Safely headed out of Bonifacio Jeremy descended to visit the engines. Before disappearing he paused. I waited to hear what the problem was. But he grinned and said, "I'm really looking forward to good spaghetti."

This announcement demonstrated the strength of our expectations as normally Jeremy would not allow mere gastronomy to intervene between him and a visit to his noble machinery.

We had indeed suffered from the French habit of putting to the grill all food on cheap menus. The French reputation for gastronomy is made at Tour d'Argent and its like and lately we hadn't had the pleasure. It couldn't be spaghetti grille, so we reckoned our trattoria visits would be different, at least.

And somehow, too, we felt the weather would improve. The Mistral was still dogging our steps in a bad summer. Italy we were sure would change our luck.

We were heading for the island and port of La Maddalena on the north-east tip of Sardinia. The sea was calm. We had soon left Corsica behind and crossing the short straits separating France and Italy we weaved our way between the few small islands off the Sardinian coast to head into Maddalena.

The Italianate structures of the public buildings and pastel colours of the houses huddling close together on the low hill were a warming sight. Brightly painted fishing boats were berthed alongside the relatively few yachts.

The entrance was wide and easy for access and maneuver. Rosemarie and Carolyn performed their mother and daughter duo with the mooring lines aft. It was siesta time so their bikini'd perambulations didn't cause more than a small traffic jam.

Nicholas took time off from Tacitus to attend the anchor and Jernica was soon safely secure. Our "Q" flag was fluttering for the first time, to signal we'd come from another country, requiring Customs clearance.

We relaxed contentedly on deck in warm Italian air. Rosemarie looked like the original Cheshire cat, except she was sipping Cinzano, produced especially for the occasion for memories of old. We loved Italy.

We were hailed from the shore. "Aqua?" a voice called. Obviously, our luck was in. Water was our first priority. Good old Italy. "Si, si," I shouted back in fluent Italian.

There was something a trifle strange about the signore now handling the hose aboard. His gait and speech seemed somehow uncoordinated. But we reflected it would be, after all, intelligent to give such a simple job to somebody who maybe couldn't handle a more demanding task.

The hose, soon aboard, delivered water at little more than a dribble. But we weren't in any hurry. As the afternoon wore on, more people appeared on the quay. Suddenly we heard a stream of high pitched Italian.

We identified the source of the noise. A man was standing at the bottom of our gangway. A white hat denoted he was some kind of official. His cheeks were flushed and when it seemed he might burst we knew he was some kind of official.

We gathered cautiously on the aft deck. "Can you speak English please," I enquired, not bothering about my fluent Italian. For reply he screamed a little louder, pointed at the hose-pipe and waved his hands furiously.

"I think," Rosemarie muttered, "That this is the official water man."

"Well? What does he want?"

She studied his gestures and apoplectic mouthings a few more moments before nodding sweetly at him and saying to me. "He wants the hose back."

Rosemarie was right as usual but the information came a little late. Before I could do or say anything the enraged official grabbed the offending pipe and heaved.

Precious water spilled over the quay. We were mystified. A sailing yacht with some Italian youngsters aboard had meanwhile berthed next to us.

One of the boys was talking to Carolyn. I turned hopefully to this linguist. "Will you kindly ask the gentleman in the white hat what we have to do to get the water back?"

The young man spoke to white hat then turned back to us grinning. "He says you have to ask him for the water. The other man's nothing to do with it."

I said, "Please tell him we're very sorry but we had no idea the other man wasn't official. And may we have some water, please."

The young Italian passed on the message. The effect was electrifying. White hat shouted, waved, jumped up and down and stormed off. So that there would be no doubts, he carried the hose pipe with him.

We decided to give white hat up as an incurable case of apoplexy. Nobody had appeared from Customs. A friendly fisherman had already told us that we could, if we wished, sit aboard waiting for Customs but we were likely to grow old; he pointed out where we could find them.

The officials were young, and friendly. We filled in various forms. Another one was inserted in their typewriter.

"Ah, how long will you be staying in Sardinia?" the one at the typewriter enquired, his fingers poised over the keys.

"It depends," I said. "If the weather in your beautiful country is fine we shall stay maybe for weeks. We might go round the whole island. If not ... ," I gave my Mediterranean shrug.

"But how long will you be staying?" he repeated.

"As I was saying," I repeated in my turn, "it all depends on the weather. We don't have any particular timetable. Could be two, three weeks, or days."

"Yes," he said, "but how long will you actually stay?" He was patient with me, happy to smile at Rosemarie. I always took Rosemarie to Med form-filling sessions even when she thought she had more important things to do.

Form filling is an endemic disease of the Mediterranean. The important thing is to give an answer that makes the filler happy, even if it makes little, or indeed, no sense.

"Two weeks," I said cheerfully.

He nodded, satisfied at last, and pounded the answer onto the form. As he dragged the form out and I signed I asked, "Why did you want an exact time?"

He seemed to hesitate before passing me a duplicated sheet. It was in English. "Harbour-Master's Warning," I read. "After the Coming into Force of Italian Laws Concerning Anchorage Dues for Pleasure Boats all Foreign Boats must Pay the following Tariff."

"What is it?" Rosemarie whispered seeing my heavy frown. She'd been sitting quietly through the previous performance.

"Hang on," I read on. I knew that foreign boats in Italy had to have a "Constituto", or ship's passport, and that a small fee was charged for it. Perhaps that's all this was?

But then I must have uttered a family-type squawk for Rosemarie sat up and asked, "What's wrong?"

"Do I read this right?" I asked. "One-hundred-and-fifty lire per ton per day?" I was sure the Customs men squirmed uncomfortably at this moment. One of them nodded.

I performed a rapid calculation. My answer of 'two weeks' now officially enshrined in quadruplicate would cost us £5 a day. It wasn't for harbour services, or charges. It was a straight tax for the pleasure of being in Italian waters. The young customs officials looked at their finger-nails while I passed on the news to Rosemarie.

As we stepped outside my wife said, "Do you mean to say that if we're at sea in Italian waters, being violently sick over the side, it'll be costing us five bloody pounds a day?"

We had wanted to visit the neighbouring island of Caprera where Garibaldi had lived. Instead, 'push-on' became our watchword.

Early next morning, we pushed on southwards, down the Sardinian coast. In Mucchi Bianchi bay in the Arzachena Gulf we realised what we might be missing in 'pushing-on'. The small cove was green with shrubs and trees; the water was clean and blue.

It was a lovely bay, and looked romantic under a full moon at night. We were enjoying a drink with David and Pamela, owners of "Jabberwocky" a Moody sailing boat anchored nearby. We asked, and they said "Yes" they had met "Slithy Tove".

We were still enjoying their company at midnight. It was rapturous until I said, "There goes another fiver."

Next morning we pushed on again, to Porto Cervo, the Aga Kahn's famous multi-million marina development. We quite happily forbore the pleasure of berthing at a quay at an enormous price, plus extras, and dropped anchor.

Ashore we found the shopping area pleasant as long as one didn't mind crowds and high prices. But we found nothing to persuade us to stay.

That was achieved by the Mistral which was seeking us out here too. Its tentacles are long. We had a couple of uncomfortable nights rattling about on our anchor. I was up at nights, wandering about. There is always one unfamiliar squeak. One night it might not be frying pans.

The wind was chill enough for us to don our first winter woollies of the summer. But the wind stopped finally, as even the Mistral does sometimes.

We put out. As usual we tuned our VHF radio into the open broadcast channel on which boats locally communicate with each other. Ears were always kept cocked to find a familiar name which has turned up in the neighbourhood. Everybody's conversation is of course broadcast to anybody tuned in.

A lady who appeared to be Greek was having a long conversation in English with somebody else who appeared to be French about somebody else who needed kosher meals aboard.

When they'd sorted out what sausages to buy, the next voice we heard was Chris, our friend and workaholic from Baie des Anges.

We were all gathered around the VHF waiting in some excitement for his conversation to finish. We called him up.

"Jernica Jernica, calling Thomassina. Over."

After a few moments, to our broad grins, "Thomassina Thomassina, come in Jernica. Over."

Chris had been at Porto Cervo and was now departing on an opposite course to our own. I discussed with him the chances of meeting but it wasn't possible.

We could hear the chuckle. "You know I hit a rock on the approach to Cervo?"

"No. Much damage?" We could imagine Chris working out how close he could get.

Laughter. "We had to slip her. But she's O.K." now."

He asked after our health, and then: "Is Rosemarie there?" We heard Chris' chuckle.

"Yes, sure."

"Give her my love."

"Will do."

"You know, I lusted after Rosemarie. I really did."

"Ah," said I. Help! How many hundreds of listeners? Rosemarie had a rather bemused look. The kids were at an age when they didn't quite know what expressions to put on their faces as his words rang through our wheelhouse - and everybody else's.

"I haven't lusted after anybody in the same way."

Peak listening? Alternative frequencies being used to urge friends on neighbouring yachts to tune in quick? Don't miss it.

"Sorry Chris. You'll have to wait. There's a lot of others feel the same way."

Chuckles. "I'm not surprised."

Chris was one to live on the edge, even when doing the simplest thing like using a radio.

We were to hear later how Chris pushed over the edge for the last time. His yacht was berthed at St. Tropez. He had been dining late at night with friends on the other side of the Gulf. They began to walk to their cars to return. On a clear night the lights on the other side of a bay miles wide can look close.

Chris knew better of course after all his time with the sea. But there had been an argument about Shelley drowning off Spezia in Italy. Chris declared it was sissy not to have been able to do that swim.

He suddenly announced he would swim back. He was immensely strong, and his friends were unable to stop him. His body was washed up a few days later.

It was terrible news for everybody who knew him; but it was not a surprise.

That low moment was to come. For now we only had the high of Chris's further outrageous behaviour. Quite proud of having a siren on board, we journeyed south.

We found a deserted lagoon hidden behind a small island in the south-east corner of the Marinella Gulf. Our only company was a few cows on the nearby beach.

The still waters and warm sweet air encouraged Jeremy and Carolyn to their first night on deck in sleeping bags. With the star-filled heavens for a roof they wondered how they'd ever done anything else.

Before we knew it we were eighty miles on down the east coast, taking advantage of fair seas. We stopped for the night at the only available port, Arbatrax.

We liked it. Simple, large, very natural and un-spoiled, if no great beauty. On the high sea wall, the crews of visiting boats had been encouraged to paint colourful ship's emblems and mottos, and it struck a friendly, welcoming note.

Rosemarie rated the cheap supermarket just up the hill as another friendly gesture. As we entered the port, Nicholas had asked, "May I berth her?"

"No, no," said Rosemarie looking around fearful-ly, and no doubt with memories of my first go in Baie des Anges seared into her soul. He took over. With me barking instructions and him ignoring them, he slot-ted her into her berth smoothly, without a hitch. We had a cup of tea.

Next day, in calm sunny weather we rounded the south coast and put into Cagliari, the capital. At the eastern end of the harbour, we found a new marina. But it seemed exposed and isolated, so we berthed at the inner harbour, by the Capitainerie.

We were within minutes of shops and department stores. Long arcades of cafes fronted the port. On later shopping forays, we felt it didn't offer the excitement of a large town, or the intimacy of a smaller.

We berthed midst navy and fishing boats, the former providing a bunch of smiling navy cadets making themselves helpful as they improved their English with Carolyn.

We needed fuel. The navy told me the man who arranged it could be found in the local cafe. I tracked him down. He was large, balding, in uniform vest. I told him what we needed and asked the price.

"How many gross tons are you?"

I told him sixty, at which he looked very sad. "Fuel is tax-free for boats over seventy tons," he said.

"That's surprising," I said. "In Porto Cervo we were told we qualified for tax-free goods if we were over fifty tons."

He put his glass down to give time for serious thought.

"Oh well," he said at last, "that's Porto Cervo."

The price he quoted us was so high it encouraged me to go on arguing that I was certain we must be entitled to fuel duty-free.

He shrugged. He controlled the supply of diesel. In effect, we could pay his price, or use the dinghy's oars for the next part of our journey.

Back on board, Rosemarie said she wouldn't row.

"Well then, I said, "we've got no alternative. We'll have to pay."

The bowser arrived next morning. To my surprise, our man first boarded with customs forms which I had to sign even though the fuel was not, I was told, tax-free. This wasn't explained. The driver prepared to pump the fuel.

"Where's the meter?" I enquired.

"Meter?" He looked at me in puzzlement. "There isn't one."

"How are we supposed to know when we've had our fifteen hundred litres?"

He smiled patiently. "You don't worry. We filled with fifteen hundred litres at the depot. So when the pump stops, you'll know you've had it."

"We've had it alright," said Nicholas behind me.

The driver started his motor and in due course, not surprisingly, the pump stopped. The entrepreneur came forward for his money. I paid him.

He smiled at me as he had every right to do. "Another fifty thousand lire, per favore."

I smiled in turn, because I thought this was funny.

"I'm sorry," I replied. "I didn't quite understand. I thought you said you wanted fifty thousand more?"

"Si."

"What for?"

During our first negotiation I'd checked several times that the price he was quoting was all inclusive. He had assured me it was.

Now he said, "You must pay for the transport. It had to come a long way."

"From where? Rome?"

"Non, no from over there." He pointed to the fuel pumps nearby, on the dockside.

There was a long and noisy altercation which had a number of bystanders nodding their heads in appreciation at the volume rather than the quality of our discussion.

I didn't pay. He stopped smiling.

Over dinner that night we commiserated with Claude, a Frenchman who had also dealt with our oil entrepreneur that day. He was with his son on board his yacht "Clamorgan" having left business to become a writer. Alongside him was another French sailing boat with three young men aboard escaping from business ulcers.

This wasn't by any means our first such encounter with the motives which can propel families and individuals to leave the comforts of home for the open seas. Some of the factors which had prodded us out of town clearly knew no national boundaries.

One evening we decided to ignore the daily gale warnings which had been, once more, holding us back; for the seas were remaining obstinately calm. We would leave next day for Sicily.

But in the middle of the night I awoke to a strong smell of fuel. I found the engine room awash. Two of the joints on the jenny were leaking profusely. We staunched one with a jubilee clip. In the morning Jeremy tackled the other, on the fuel supply line.

He gave a final, strong, turn and as the joint tightened he lost his balance, and lurched sideways. As he stumbled around, his head hit a water pump Chris had installed.

"Oh no!" cried poor Jeremy. For he had stopped the fuel leak; but there was now a great cascade of water pouring from the pump. We didn't take off for anywhere that day. Carolyn kept the young Italian navy busy buying washers and joints to our order. We didn't need to reward them; or rather Carolyn accompanied her favourite to the local cafe for an ice cream.

By evening Jeremy declared us leak-free, provided we didn't ask for it in writing. We could enjoy again, for how many moments we couldn't tell, the simple joy of nuts and bolts holding quietly together.

We spent the following night in Carbonara Bay - a broad and attractive expanse of sheltered water in the south-east corner of Sardinia.

At three the following morning we departed Sardinia for the sixteen hours trip to Sicily. It would be our first longish sea crossing since our original bone-shaking trip to Corsica.

At least this wouldn't be a night crossing. I was now prepared to swap the classic delights of precise identification at dawn for the simple pleasure of seeing what might be clobbering us during the day.

We set a south-easterly course in calm weather and happily it stayed that way for the greater part of the journey. There was some excitement half-way across when Carolyn sighted our first Dolphin enjoying a free ride in our bow wave.

We all rushed to see this friendly creature. We grinned down at him and he grinned up at us. I ran for my camera. But he must have been camera shy for he disappeared. We all felt quite upset that held left us after such a short acquaintance, as though we were somehow to blame.

Hours later we sighted Marettimo, the most westerly of the Egadi Islands off N-W Sicily; and then the next one on, Favignana. Weld been recommended to stay there.

A couple of hydrofoils beat us into the port. Some boats berthed there bounced in their wash like yo-yos, heaving about and tugging and pulling at their mooring lines.

An instant crew meeting decided to head on for Trapani, a commercial port on the western coast of Sicily.

We headed slowly into a very large harbour, which would account for its commercial importance; and very, very pungent, which may have accounted for the fact there was only one other yacht to be seen.

We came to rest stern-to on the north quay. The gangway was no sooner lowered than a man pushed his way up it. In his late fifties he had small eyes, a sharp nose, thinning slicked hair and yellow teeth. He tried to push on to the deck.

I enjoyed seeing the Godfather at the cinema but not on our boat.

"You want wine, beer, coke, water? You leave it all to me," he rasped still pushing forward; and then perhaps because I looked doubtful he reeled off a list of other desirable items.

I told him we didn't really need anything. He looked shocked.

"Water? Don't you want water?"

"We can always use some water" I said incautiously. But Godfather Part III could sense this was his big day.

"Wine. We have good wine in Sicily." I was intrigued.

"What wine do you have exactly?" and as soon as I'd spoken I realised I had about as much sense as a virgin asking Cassanova if sex was good for you.

He displayed the full range of his yellow teeth.

"For you, I have some marvellous wine. The best. I will bring you some."

"Thanks. We'll try a bottle."

"A bottle? No, no. I'll bring you a case."

"We'd like to try a bottle first," I said.

His voice became growly, like a tractor with tonsillitis. Like a Mafiosi in a film. "What you want to try it for, only one bottle? They sell this wine in England, in America, all round the world. I've only got cases. You expect me to go all the way up to the village and bring back a single bottle?" He spat and I was surprised he bothered to aim into the sea, instead of over the deck.

I said, "We'd like to taste a bottle before we bought a case - even if it was the finest French wine."

He poked his face an inch from mine as though I'd insulted not merely his vineyards but also his mother. Perhaps his mother made the wine.

"It's better than French wine, everybody knows that," he said fiercely.

"Can you arrange some fuel for us?" I asked in a flash of inspiration. We actually did need fuel. And as I'd thought, Godfather allowed his thoughts to move onto this higher and indubitably more profitable plane.

He explained that this was very difficult. But through his contacts and as a special favour he might be able to get me some tax-free and quoted a price per litre.

I said that this was very interesting - and indeed it was as the price was more even than we'd paid in Cagliari. I said I thought we could wait before we filled up again.

He went away with a promise to return. The family discussed emergency measures to prevent the latter contingency. Nicholas suggested a stray half-brick might be needed.

Half an hour after his departure, a voice hailed us from the quay. We looked out and beheld a rusty tank held onto a beat-up motor chassis by a couple of dog-eared straps.

The driver peered out, grinning. "You're the boat that wants water?" he shouted. I could hear horror-struck noises behind me.

"No. Not us," I called back hurriedly. And in case he hadn't understood shouted again, "No us!"

"That's Dad's fluent Italian," commented Carolyn.

Anticipating further argument we all speedily withdrew our heads from sight, peering out while the driver and his mate first shouted to us, then to each other, until they gave up and departed.

Just after eight next morning an official arrived to move us on. "You're on the fuel quay," he said, "and a boat is coming in to fill up."

This I thought was a stroke of luck, "This is the fuel quay? Marvellous! We'd like some!"

He smiled tolerantly, "Not for you," he said. "For boats."

I was about to argue the logic of this remark when we viewed a hydrofoil hurtling towards us at thirty knots.

"Get the fenders. Quick!" Carolyn shrieked as our sailor responsible for such matters. We threw ourselves about. At two metre's distance the foil's engines stopped; fortunately. In a couple of feet more it settled into the water as lightly as a ballet dancer taking a bow.

A good-looking figure (I was assured) resplendent in gold-braided Captain's uniform advanced onto the foil's foredeck.

He addressed the bikini-clad girls who were transfixed holding their fenders.

"Don't worry," he called over with a broad smile. "You can leave everything to me."

He began commanding the quayside onlookers. In moments our aft lines had been let out, and he inserted the hydrofoil neatly between Jernica and the quay.

The scene was spoiled only by the late appearance of Godfather who strutted about shouting, to demonstrate his organising genius although clearly nobody was taking any notice of him.

I thanked the captain for his courtesy. Rosemarie complimented him on his command of English. She also pointed out how frustrating it was for us to be berthed on the fuel quay without being able to get any.

The captain drew himself up outraged and shouted anew to the men on shore. Within seconds, customs forms for fuel were actually thrust at us from shore. Equally magically I found a pen and signed while the captain beamed.

We took on fuel duty free at half the price of Cagliari. The captain and the girls beamed in equal delight.

We could leave. We began to raise the gangway. Godfather appeared and grated out demands for duty-free cigarettes, "for all I've done for you!"

The gangway was up by this time, we were under way, and I said, in case he could hear, that it was illegal. Godfather's stream of Italian followed us out.

"What's he saying," Jeremy asked curiously.

"Bon voyage," I said hopefully but spent a little time worrying about our kneecaps at the next Sicilian port.

We had wanted to visit the Liparis, the islands north-east of Sicily which we'd heard were very attractive. But our two weeks' tax-paid were up and we weren't pre-pared to pay more. So we headed for Empodocle on the south coast of Sicily and a jumping-off point for Malta.

We'd been told the commercial port was dirty. As we made our way in it was apparent the sea inside the port was covered with oil. Otherwise, the outer harbour was spacious, and deserted. It was all rather depressing. With nothing better to do, in the evening we all walked into what we imagined was the dead, commercial port.

We turned a corner - and it was extraordinary - like a curtain going up in a theatre.

The streets behind the port were a brightly lit stage in which hundreds of holidaying Italians were prom-enading. They were gay, vivacious, and elegant, laugh-ing, eating ice-creams and watching each other.

They were the Italians we knew and had hoped to be among. We made the most of this unexpected pleasure, sharing their vibrant company, food and ice-cream stalls, and exchanging a few words. A different world from the waterfront operators.

But next day we had to leave, or pay more taxes. And so we headed south for Malta.

What Daddy Doing?

We left Empodocle early next morning. The tax penalty meant we'd foregone (and much regretted it later) visiting the nearby Greek temples of Agrigento, some of the best preserved to be found.

There was the inevitable swell. There had been very few days free of wind this summer. A few miles out thunder began to sound and lightning ranged the sky.

We had a ten-hour journey ahead. The swell was no more than a nuisance. But half way across the Malta channel a dreaded moment arrived.

Carolyn was steering. Suddenly the port engine began to fade.

I said "Stop mucking about Carolyn."

She squawked, "I haven't done anything!"

She was looking petrified at the controls under her hand. Jeremy appeared by her side to shove the port throttle forward. The engine continued to idle.

Five hours, or more, on one engine in a swell would be no fun. Carolyn was already unable to hold our original course.

Down below there were no pipes adrift or other visible problems.

"Let's try the obvious first," I said. But Jeremy was already kneeling beside the obvious - the fuel filters. We put our heads together as I looked for the guidelines which showed in which direction to turn the cocks to switch filters. I was still tracing them out laboriously when Jeremy had turned them.

I followed him back to the wheelhouse. He eased the port throttle forward. We waited with bated breath but there was no response. We were now steering south, instead of south-east.

"Can you hold this course O.K.?" I asked Carolyn, and she nodded, concentrating on the wheel.

"Let's get the trouble-shooting manual out," I said, and for want of anything else to do shoved the port throttle forward again.

There was a lovely roaring noise and we were all systems go again. Clearly dirty fuel had been our problem. Jeremy's flick of the filters had done the trick. But it had taken a few moments for the new flow to work through the system.

"What did you do?" Jeremy asked in some legitimate amazement.

I shrugged nonchalantly, "It wasn't difficult," I said with great modesty and total honesty.

Basking in the limelight as technical trouble-shooter didn't last beyond the time that the outline of land began to show up on the horizon. There seemed to be a lot of it.

I had a look at the chart. Gozo, the island to the north of the mainland was scarcely eight miles long. Malta was only twice as large. I had been expecting our view on the horizon to be little dots.

We closed the land and turned south to follow it. It ended suddenly giving way to a tiny island before the next landfall. This tiny island was unmistakably Comino, lying between Gozo and Malta. Relief – we were where we should have been.

I relaxed. So did Carolyn who always picked up my vibes and had been watching me. A dot on the map can be a remarkably large sprawl across the horizon I'd now learned.

We were making for the capital, Valetta. Carolyn was now in her standard cruising position. She lay tummy down at the sharp end, nose over blue waters, dolphin and flying-fish spotting with the end of the journey in view she had moved to the vertical, and it was her cry of, "There it is," which alerted us.

We saw the town of Valetta rising proudly above us on a peninsula. To the south lay Grand Harbour, home for many years before to the British battle fleet. We were heading for the yacht harbour creeks of Marsamxett, lying on the north side.

We were a thousand miles through summer - and light years from our last winter, spent in the familiar comfort of our town home. This would be our first winter aboard Jernica. We weren't quite sure what lay ahead. But we knew it would be in port, because despite the popular lay idea that the Med is always a sweet flat blue, in winter it can be as rough and unpleasant as any stretch of sea water; and the air bitterly cold.

Apart from the simple question of how we'd find winter life aboard ship, was Malta the right place? We'd asked just about anybody we knew who'd been there for their impressions of the island. It had been like asking about mothers-in-law. It was marvelous. Or lousy. Nobody was indifferent. And nobody could quite explain their reasons.

Now we would find out. Jeremy was coaxed out of the engine-room for a first glimpse of his winter home.

"Looks great," he said feelingly, and to prove it didn't rush below again: so we thought Malta had struck the first blow.

It did indeed look impressive. High on our port bow fort St. Elmo merged into the massive ramparts standing guard over Valetta. The sandstone glowed warm gold in the late afternoon. It looked noble, solid, inscrutable, a fitting repository of a history of centuries of violent assault and heroic defence.

Nicholas elbowed me off the wheel.

We passed Sliema Creek, most exposed of the inlets, and nosed into the yacht marina in Lazarreto Creek.

Carolyn, gazing through the binoculars emitted a loud, delighted cry.

I grabbed the binoculars. "Where is it?"

"Where's what?"

"Didn't you just see an empty berth?"

"No!" She snatched the binoculars back impatiently. "Look! There's a Wimpy Bar!"

The two boys heard the message and came forward to stare through the glasses in wonder at Nirvana after so many months in the wilderness of mere Continental cuisine.

But the berths here were full. We turned back to continue into Msida Creek, the next one along. We found a berth. We were among mostly local boats here. The quay was wide and backed by pleasant villas. It seemed quieter than along Lazaretto.

As we eased in, a roly-poly figure with eyes twinkling behind his glasses gave us guidance from the shore. We discovered his name was Joe, although the same was true for most of the male population of this intensely Catholic island.

"Call me Joe on the Boat," he suggested, after we'd berthed. Our Q flag was raised. Coming from Italy it was flying rather as a triumph of hope over experience. But a cheerful uniformed figure soon hailed us from the quay.

"Manuel Island customs are closed now," he called.

"You should have let us know you were coming. But some officers will be here from Valetta in about half an hour. Sorry to keep you." He waved and walked off.

We shouted our thanks for the courtesy which wasn't so much unusual as unique. When the customs officer appeared, middle-aged and quietly spoken, his first words were, "Sorry to keep you waiting."

He didn't so much clear us as provide a friendly information service about Malta and the harbour. His briefing included essential literature detailing charges for berthing, fuel, water, electricity and times of weather forecasts.

As he was leaving he said, "You will stay for the winter? You'll like it here." After that welcome, we told him, we were sure we would.

Joe-on-the-Boat was still there as we stepped ashore. He'd been waiting in case we needed to know anything.

"Where can we eat?" I asked prompted by my muttering adolescents.

Rosemarie murmured in my ear. "How? We've got no Maltese money, and the banks will be shut."

Joe solved both problems. We piled into his car and fell out of it at the "Astoria". This back street hotel in Sliema then run by a huge Englishman, Phil, and his Maltese wife Vera, regularly provided us thereafter with our best value food on the island - home cooking. Phil also provided some of the friendliest company and the cosiest bar.

We had no problem paying because Joe had stuffed some money into my hand.

"Pay me back when you've been to the bank," he said.

In the next few weeks Joe-on-the-Boat's car became our family taxi, running us to engineers for Jeremy, riding stables for Carolyn, and shops for Rosemarie.

We were embarrassed by the volume of his hospitality not least because there was virtually nothing we could do to repay him. He would scarcely accept a cup of tea, a bottle of whisky wasn't possible.

We found a similar disposition everywhere. Shop assistants took pains to direct us to other shops selling wares they lacked. Strangers walked out of their way to accompany us when we needed directions. We were several times told, as perfect strangers in shops, to bring money next time when no change was available.

We met Charlie. He was a large character inside a small man. He was the watchman on the quay. He was seventy-four years old, an ex-fisherman and as he used to tell us with a chuckle, twenty years in the Royal Navy. These years at sea had turned his face and hands to the texture and toughness of grained leather. Small but still muscular, he could clamber over a gunwale and into a dinghy as nimbly as a boy.

Among other jobs he looked after the ground chains used for mooring. He was another who could not be inveigled into a tea, or beer.

At Xmas we thought we'd got through to him. "Come on Charlie," I said. "You can surely have a whisky today."

His leathery face cracked into a grin, showing two teeth. "Alright little bit whisky." We poured him a snifter. He downed it at a gulp, Maltese style. I went to pour another but he held up his hand, chuckled a "No thank you," and was gone.

With his sturdy independence went a still nimble brain at guarding his domain.

The boys were learning sub-aqua diving and I had been press-ganged into an instructional course for their club on the navigation/seamanship aspect of a diver's life.

One day we took a dozen assorted divers out as part of the course. Coming back into our berth after any day out, our practice was to sound the horn and

Charlie would come rowing out within moments to hand us the line for the ground chain. This day there was a good breeze blowing which meant we needed the line sharpish if we weren't to drift.

We arrived. I tooted. No sign of Charlie. We started to drift and at the wheel I had to play with the engines, tooting as I did so. I had been looking forward to demonstrating my boating skills to the watching students – although often I let Nick handle the berthing. As my engine joggling became slightly more frenetic, the meaning of "pride comes before the fall" began to percolate through to me. Nicholas with binoculars fixed on the shore said, "Blimey. There he is."

I took the binoculars and said "Blimey" too, plus one or two other words not in the instructional manual. Charlie was ambling along, very slowly descending into his rowing boat, pretending he was an old man.

He began very laboriously to scull towards us, while I tried to keep the bow alongside the buoy to which the groundline was secured. I was also hoping to keep out of the way of passing round-the-harbour cruises.

I stepped outside the wheelhouse and shouted, "Come on Charlie."

Instead of his usual beam, he shrugged and continued his funereal progress. Arrived at last at the bow Nicholas leaned down to take the line, and nearly fell overboard through the fumbling inability of Charlie, old sea-dog, to hand it up.

At last Nicholas signaled it was up, and wrapped around the drum of the winch. As we eased our stern backwards I suddenly realised the bow wasn't following in the approved manner, I leaned out of the wheelhouse.

"Come on Nicholas. Control the line," I called kindly - for the simple reason that we had agreed to maintain family-crew decorum for the day, no matter what emergency, with our diving student guests appraising every move.

He called back kindly "I am. But it keeps getting stuck."

His job was to let out the line as we turned, tightening it progressively as we backed, but not so much as to impede progress. It required a reasonably light touch.

"What's up?" Rosemarie enquired kindly.

"Nicholas says the rope's getting stuck," I said almost kindly, with sufficient hint of sarcasm I trusted to make my disbelief clear. He was obviously not doing it properly.

Then, as we waggled jerkily backwards our stern began heading for the adjacent boat. We reckoned by now to be able to do this sort of maneuver as a crew faultlessly.

I went forward. "What's happening with that bloody line," I hissed kindly to Nicholas. "You're snagging us all over the place."

My students (most of them teachers) were clearly beginning to look down their noses at this demonstration.

Nicholas snapped, "I told you! It's not me! The bloody rope has got knots in it." We examined it together. It became clear that our line, normally expertly coiled, now contained a succession of knots, loops, whirls and heebie-jeebies such as no sailor had ever witnessed before.

We staggered into our berth with our sniggering students shoving our sides off the adjacent boat by force-majeure. As we tied up I bellowed at Charlie, sitting calmly in his boat watching the commotion, "What the hell did you do with our mooring line?"

Fiercely he shouted back, "Why did you give the line to this other boat instead of leaving it where I tell you? They mucked it up."

What Charlie had thought I'd done, I hadn't; I never got to the bottom of it, but he was under the impression I'd asked somebody else to do his job of bringing the line out. Hence transpired the mysterious transformation of our impeccable groundline into a tangled web.

He was a very fierce guardian of his independence.

But next day normal relations were restored. Rosemarie mentioned the potatoes we were buying were seedy. In the afternoon Charlie's brother appeared with new potatoes from his garden. He refused to take money or anything else for them. Charlie was always - apart from that one time! - a cheerful friend with a good, if singular, sense of humour.

We took Jernica out for local cruising through the winter. On one occasion we took along an English friend and his wife. He had extensive experience, and was dying to handle Jernica back into her berth. I agreed. Maybe because the controls were strange, he was making a mess of it.

Charlie had handed up the mooring line, and was sitting watching from his rowboat. As our friend roared the engines back and forth and got into a tangle Charlie's frown etched deeper.

191

Finally he could control himself no longer and as we gave another lurch he stood up and shouted in genuine concern to the kids assembled on deck, "What daddy doing? What daddy doing?"

"It's not daddy," they called back. "It's a friend," and they pointed to the wheelhouse.

He stood on tiptoe in his boat the better to peer at the wheelhouse, where he saw the unfamiliar figure struggling away. At which he virtually collapsed guffawing into his boat, and his cackle followed us until Jernica came to rest.

It slowly dawned on us why Malta was liked very much, or not at all. To visit Malta is in many ways to take a trip back to Victorian England. We found a sturdiness and helpfulness, the bedrock of old England, alive and well in Malta.

Long rows of terraced houses in pastel washes of yellows and pinks could be back-street Brighton at the turn of the century. The houses had small enclosed balconies where Granny can watch her world go by. Steps are scrubbed, wood and chrome competitively polished, down the meanest street.

We found bars called "Friends to All" and a chemist called "The Economical British Pharmacy".

The comparison stops with the town of Valetta, the capital. One enters through walls which, massive and golden in colour are more reminiscent of Jerusalem than Brighton. Within, the streets are narrow, crowded with shops and shoppers, a neat Kasbah. On all sides the streets lead down to the harbour, and to massive forts dominating the harbour which like the walls were built by the warrior Christians, the Knights of St. John.

Yet it might be disappointing for anybody seeking the life glamorous. There is an absence even of simple things which create atmosphere in other Mediterranean countries - such as street cafes, outside restaurants, and alive-o discos. The streets lack the vivacity which is the lure of so many warm climate countries.

As in Victorian times, some might feel an absence of sparkle in the lifestyle.

We liked it for the warm, unselfish friendliness of the people. And modest food was at least served at appropriately modest prices. And whatever the whims of some of the governments there is undoubtedly a warm feeling for Britain in the hearts of many Maltese. They demonstrate this by kindness to perfectly strange visitors.

Berthing wasn't expensive and we had water, but no electricity on our quay. So Jernica, and even more Jeremy, were at the mercy of jenny's whims for the whole of the winter. Water proved expensive on the basis of metering which seemed to reflect the island's budget needs rather than our consumption. The cost hurt more because the water tasted so salty it was difficult to enjoy a cup of tea.

We settled down cheerfully enough having overcome the delirium of Wimpy Bars, and milk from "real" milk bottles - instead of the plastic containers of France and Italy. We developed a winter routine.

The kids were spending hours a day at their correspondence courses without nagging from us. In these pre-internet days we had informed the correspondence college of Malta as our port to pick up the kids' latest results. They were always waiting expectantly for their latest results, and they duly arrived.

Torn, a local English resident and ex-teacher with numerous degrees was impressed with Nicholas's work, having agreed to give some coaching.

Jeremy received back his latest Physics test and growled away. We asked him how bad it was." Eighty three per cent," he said.

"That's terrific," I complimented him.

"I was hoping I'd get more like a hundred," he grunted. For the next hour he seemed to do nothing except frown over his paper. Then suddenly he appeared waving the paper, and wearing a more cheerful expression. They'd forgotten to add one of his marks to the total. He'd got ninety per cent.

Carolyn too was getting 60's and 70's. At school she was always one to avoid homework.

The boys joined the local British sub-aqua club although Jeremy was a year under-age. Carolyn found riding stables. The kids began to make the friends they had missed during the summer.

Diving regularly each week over the whole of the winter, the boys became skilled and disciplined at the sport.

Their fast-growing maturity was demonstrated in tragic manner. When they were away diving, there were typical parent-type niggles of anxiety in the back of our minds, although two of the strongest divers in the club, a Maltese friend Joe, and our Astoria friend Phil, were always high in praise of the boys' abilities.

One evening the four set off on a night dive together with Robin, a young Canadian pro diver, and Geoff, a middle-aged, lively, warm-hearted giant of a man who had been a Canadian navy officer, chopper and fixed-wing pilot, and professional diver.

At one in the morning a distraught Robin appeared on the boat, with Nicholas, still dressed in their wet suits. And no Jeremy. We were, for a second, terrified.

The news was terrible enough. Geoff had died in the water - (of natural causes as it turned out). After a tremendous struggle Joe had brought him ashore. Then for hours the boys had joined in trying to revive him and seeking assistance.

The sudden death of this friendly, lively, man was a shock. But in such a tragic test, we learned from the praise of the others on the scene that the boys had behaved with the calm and discipline of mature men.

There were tests of a happier nature. Carolyn couldn't sleep the day before she was due to ride in a ladies-only horse race at the Marsa race-track. Her horse was given no chance. I put a pound on her to win, and with the large crowd roaring she came home second out of a field of fourteen.

After the race we met her, elated and beaming. I gave her the grave news she'd cost the family the fortune I'd have won if she'd come in first.

"Well in a way I did, really," she said. The winner was a ringer, put in at the last second when the original horse fell ill. But they didn't want the disappointed girl jockey to be without a mount; and the Maltese racing community is very tolerant.

"It doesn't matter," she said her face all aglow. We gave our sixteen-year old jockey a big kiss.

We made many friends. On one of our days out with Jernica we took along Jacques, a Canadian helicopter pilot, his wife Lillian, who was one of Canada's leading artists, and their children, Philip and little Sophie. The boys had met Jacques through the diving club.

We berthed in Mgarr, the quiet colourful harbour of Gozo. The colour was provided by numerous Luzzus – traditional wooden fishing boats, all at rest, and gathered together to paint a canvas in bright reds and blues.

We all trooped off Jernica to make the short trek to the grandly-named church of Our Lady of Lourdes dominating the harbour from a high hillock. At the entrance to the church stood a portly priest. It became clear that progress would be greatly facilitated by an appropriate donation to good causes. Apart from a marble altar, the interior was simple, unlike its name. The church was built in honour of a local lady who, apparently, performed miracles. It acquired its title at the end of the nineteenth century when a visitor noticed that rocks on the hillock resembled a Lourdes Grotto. That was reason enough in this very Catholic island.

There was nothing else to see. We returned cheerfully to Jernica to begin a circumnavigation of the virtually uninhabited and featureless island. Our last anchorage was worth the whole journey. On the west of the island, the bay behind Fungus Rock is almost circular and land-locked.

Jernica and her passengers were alone there. We all plunged in and swam and dived and snorkelled in our own lagoon in total peace. The young and older kids were having a great time together. Apart from our shouts and calls and laughter there was no sound to suggest there was a world elsewhere.

But I was keeping an eye on the clock. There was another world. We had to get Jacques and his family back to Mgarr in time for the ferry back to Malta. We were staying on for another day.

Jacques' snorkel slowly surfaced. I beckoned. "We'd better get going," I yelled.

Jacques splashed around lazily and more or less yawned at me. His kids were swimming and having a great time. "It's nice here," said Jacques in his lispy French Canadian accent. "What's the hurry?"

"The ferry," I shouted. "No problem, no problem," said Jacques, which was his inevitable answer to just about any question, and disappeared back under the water.

When we nosed into Mgarr later the ferry was coming out and this had the strange effect of causing everybody to start howling with laughter. Unsurprisingly, the decision was made for both families to spend the night aboard.

After a terrible meal at a local nightclub we returned late at night to Jernica. We ate Rosemarie's apple pie, no better on earth, and drank and talked under the standard canopy of stars, surrounded by a fleet of Luzzus, the colourful local fishing boats, with lights twinkling down at us from the few buildings on the surrounding hills, and the silhouette on the ridge above of the church.

Then we carted out the camp beds and sorted out which corners we'd all be sleeping in. Sophie and Philip were excited at sleeping on a boat.

It was a totally messed-up day enjoying the company of friends to the full in a way we knew was only possible with our Jernica.

In return of course Jernica had to be given her full quota of winter care. Jeremy busied himself exorcising devilish things he'd not been able to deal with in the summer.

He closeted himself with small diagrams discovered in a do-it-yourself electronics magazine. One day we were terrified to hear a great wailing sound on the boat. We raced into the wheelhouse to see nothing more frightening than a great smile spreading over Jeremy's face.

"It works," he announced. We were now equipped with an electronic bilge alarm he had made. He pressed his test button again and we all shouted, "Yes, yes, we know," above the siren's din.

Later I heard the sound of violent squabbling on the quay. It was most unusual. I went out swiftly to break it up.

"It's my turn to clean the dinghy," Carolyn was shouting.

"No it isn't. You did it last time," Jeremy said angrily.

I coughed and returned on board.

Rosemarie had been kept busy varnishing, with Nicholas as assistant helping to rub down.

She must have felt she needed a change for she descended below to help Jeremy clean out the engine-room bilges. Emerging, she said with eyes uplifted, "I think that must be about the most basic job on the boat."

"No it isn't," said Nicholas holding up a piece of somebody's toilet system. He was establishing himself, albeit under protest, as the ship's bog specialist. He had made the serious mistake of repairing his own, at which point he was the expert and source of salvation when either of the other two went wrong - as they did, becoming bunged up with salt which set like iron, and – when even hydrochloric acid had little effect - needed iron muscles chiseling and hammering to restore.

What was becoming the routine of daily life was interrupted in a pleasant and very unusual way one day under our blue skies. From a short distance away we witnessed a gracefully- lined sailing boat approaching under full sail. Nothing much different about that. What was most unusual – and for our teenage boys – a matter for slightly open mouths and wide- eyes – was that the crew consisted of five ladies, four of them teenagers. Equally unusual, was that the girls had made no concession to sailing mores, but were busy about their tasks on deck in what looked like normal town dresses. There was a man at the helm. The Stars and Stripes fluttered aft, not often seen in the Med.

The space next to us was vacant, and with what looked like super efficiency the boat – tellingly named "Liberty" - wheeled, the sails were lowered, and shortly after we had taken their lines, they were snugly berthed stern-to

After they had settled down, we introduced ourselves. The pretty blonde teenagers, Libby, Joesy, Katie, and Margaret, were the daughters of Tom and his wife Jo. And we soon understood why their seamanship had looked so skilled and effortless. They had spent weeks crossing the Atlantic in their fifty foot 'Morgan' sailing yacht. And I learned much later that Tom after purchasing his yacht had learned to handle it by sailing miles down the rivers and through the challenging weather of the eastern seabord of the USA; and at one stage, when being overtaken by a hurricane while well off the coast had taken the decision that it would be safer to ride it out at sea, than to make for the nearest port. He had done so safely. As they say in the music-halls, "Follow that!"

Tom was a highly successful engineer and banker, a very young fifty. I was to find he had one of the liveliest and enquiring minds I had come across, and he was full of natural good humour.

He had left success at home to spend more time with his family. Jo, we found, shared the same easy humour.

"It's rather unusual to find a crew of four teenage girls," I commented, shortly after we'd met, "and come to that I suppose not often people have four daughters."

They weren't the most original remarks in the world, and I got my come-uppance. "It's not all that unusual," Tom replied with a very broad smile, "and we have five more daughters back in the States."

I assume I must have opened my mouth for a few seconds, because Tom added with a grin, "and there's no way we can be teased about it that we haven't heard before."

The boys and Carolyn had made their own friends in Malta and soon the Liberty girls were joining them. They had found what Nick described as a place selling 'the most amazing Pizzas' and this haven was early introduced to the girls. Carolyn and the boys enjoyed their company on our diving expeditions and also on visits to the cinema. Rosemarie was able to enjoy the nearby company of a fellow Mum. One of the great pleasures of cruising is to find new friends and we soon felt very close to this family.

Tom and I found we were both interested in political ideas. Over the weeks we sometimes took a break from shipboard duties to take ourselves off to a nearby cafe to discuss ideas which interested us both. We found much in common and in a relatively short time became good friends. He struck me as having the personality and knowledge to make waves in the US political scene as he had evidently done in his business life. But forseeing the future remains a gift of the Gods, rather than of man.

As Spring approached we were immensely sad one day to see them take off. They were heading for Greece. We would also be heading there before long. We had discussed where we both might head to, and had promised to keep an eye – and radio ear – open for each other. So as they hoisted sails and headed away, and Tom waved his goodbyes to us from "Liberty's" deck we could at least look forward to our next meeting.

We nearly secured our first charter. With the boat carrying a home for five and a school, chartering to improve our finances was a reasonable consideration; but we'd need more time than most boats to get organised.

One evening after dark we were hailed from the quay. I beheld a large young man, his dark glasses a trifle incongruous as there was little light on the quayside and no moon.

"Is your boat for charter?" he asked.

"Not just now," I told him.

"Well, I would like to charter it," he insisted.

"We're not available I'm afraid," I repeated, but it seemed with not quite enough conviction, for he persisted.

"You'd just have to go to Italy and back."

I said, "I don't know really."

"We would give you £4000 a week," said dark glasses.

That was something like four times the market rate. I didn't actually say "welcome aboard" but I did say, "When do you want to leave."

"Tomorrow."

I could hear now a whole cacophony of alarm bells, sirens and other warning sounds. It wasn't Jeremy's work this time, just noises in the back of my head. I explained that it wasn't possible. We'd need time to refuel, and provision, quite apart from making space available.

"Alright then, Sunday," he said, which would give us two days.

"No," I said. "No, Sorry," and withdrew.

The family was furious with my peremptory dismissal of a financial savior for such unsubstantial reasons as noises in the head. Rosemarie was already working out all the evenings she could have got away without cooking, by dining out.

"Look," I said, "I'll lay odds in the morning you'll hear that Public Enemy No.1 round here has broken out of jail. Or you'll hear a couple of million quid's worth of hashish has been hijacked; or something like that."

"But you didn't even ask!"

That was what irked them most. But I really didn't want to know. Customs have a nasty habit, with boats found in suspicious circumstances, of nailing them solidly to the quay, and that would be no way to treat a lady like Jernica; let alone its crew.

Our curiosity was soon satisfied. Dark glasses approached another boat along the quay whose skipper was adventurous enough to enquire into the details. He was required to carry four hundred cases of whisky; and not to Italy but to Islamic points east, where the health-giving fluid is banned to all, and therefore much in demand at skyrocket prices by higher-class residents.

"You see," I said. "We couldn't have done it."

"You're right," somebody replied "We've only got room for three hundred cases."

With such moments to enliven our routine, Xmas seemed to be suddenly upon us, with parties galore.

And then it was New Year's Eve. We decided we wanted to see in the New Year only aboard Jernica. As midnight approached we gathered on deck. The sky was clear and the moon reflected like a bright lantern in the softly moving waters of the creek. The air was mild.

As midnight chimed, a ship's horn blared over the roofs of Valetta in Grand Harbour. Our horn noisily joined the New Year's chorus rising all around from all the yachting harbours.

We toasted the New Year, and each other, and Jernica, and the toast, "Happy New Year" was alive with meaning.

It's Some Dirty Bottom!

The turn of the year allowed us to look forward to spring, and leaving. So it was back to scraping, rubbing down, painting, and varnishing. We all learned to bend bones in directions the Lord would have been surprised to know he provided for, and to regard anybody with fingernails intact as a sissy.

We took a break to celebrate our first anniversary aboard. We invited three dozen friends and four dozen turned up. Our Maltese friends, the kids' friends, and families and crews from other yachts helped us make the night one to remember.

Rosemarie had prepared a feast and with the booze flowing we waited for somebody to fall overboard.

Nobody did. But memories decreed that at least one crew member should be laid low in bed - this time Carolyn with tonsillitis. She had the benefit however, of a get-well kiss from comedian Norman Wisdom, who we'd met on a friend's boat. This seemed much better black magic then my five hundred Francs worth of drugs a year before, as Carolyn was up and about within a couple of days.

When the last guest had departed and the kids bedded down we sat among the débris in the wheelhouse. A bright moon caught the brass on the wheel and the varnished wood gleamed. Alongside, the moon traced the ghostly spars of our neighbour "Andando", a large square-rigged sailing boat. Seaward, a light flared on the water from a fishing-boat.

All was silent.

"I'm not dreaming am I," said Rosemarie. "Tell me I'm not dreaming."

It was back to reality next day as Jenny again came to a halt, with a dramatic rattling sound. Earlier in Jenny's life Jeremy had watched carefully as Joe electrician, friendly and efficient, dismantled the alternator. Now he tackled it himself.

He disconnected fuel, water, and electrical connections and the exhaust system. Then he groveled in the oily black drip tray feeling for bolts it was impossible to see.

We borrowed a mule and hoisted the sick lady off her bed onto some stretchers we'd laid ready. Jeremy could now sit in the bilges to get at the electrics.

More electrical disconnection and he was at the field coils. As thick as a man's torso, these bundles of copper windings and magnets, producing twelve thousand watts, could scarcely be lifted off the ground.

Jeremy, sitting, had to slide this bulk along studs which were eighteen inches long. The studs were bendable - so he had to support the whole weight.

Nobody could join him, to help, in his cramped, dirty position in the bilge. That done, he had to remove the armature from the flywheel. It was nearly as heavy as the fields.

Again he had to take the full weight, and between every move trying to uncramp legs and back and trying to keep the sweat out of eyes; trying to manoeuvre spanners around corners and under cracks where the tips of the fingers have to do the work of a hand; and then finding a nut a different size from the rest; or the one with the rounded head, or stripped thread.

And all the while he is smothered in oil which stings hands and arms increasingly covered in cuts and grazes. Doing this non-stop for three days.

It will be done only for good wages; or for love. Even for love, at fourteen, it sometimes becomes too much. At last Jeremy found the cause of the trouble; four bolts sheared on the plate holding the armature to the flywheel.

Removing the plate he found a tiny speck of metal between the surfaces which had, over time, thrown the whole massive bulk out of balance. When it was repaired Jeremy had to repeat the whole process in reverse, for reassembly.

His pride, and the applause he received, when finally the old girl wheezed into life again, was as well earned as anything he is ever likely to do in his lifetime.

There was more boat-work to be done outside. Especially in today's polluted waters, a hull quickly builds up barnacles and other sea organisms which substantially reduce performance. The last hurdle before we could put out to sea again for summer was slipping the boat to clean and anti-foul her bottom.

We chose a slip at the head of Grand Harbour. We watched nervously from aboard as Jernica made her first passage ashore, hauled by steel cables.

The moment we were settled and chocked on dry land, we were living in the middle of a work-yard. We donned boiler suits. We knew we must scrape off the barnacles and weed immediately after hosing them, or they would set like rocks.

Nicholas was first down the steep ladder, like an infantryman leading the assault over the top. On the ground he took one look at the hull and shouted up, "Boy! Is that some dirty bottom!"

He grabbed a scraper and was soon chipping away enthusiastically. We joined him with equal fervour. We were crouched underneath, working on the hull over our heads.

As pieces of barnacle and flakes of old anti-fouling fell into our eyes and nostrils our enthusiasm became a trifle dimmer. We carried on scrape, scrape, chip, chip.

Next day, barnacles gone, we had to sand the old anti-fouling smooth and clouds of the poisonous dust choked us.

Then we began applying the anti-fouling paint. With arms uplifted the paint dripped down all over us until we all looked like victims of some deadly plague. In all it was some of the hardest and dirtiest work we'd ever done.

We kept at it for three more days. By then we'd finished all the scraping and applied one coat of barrier paint and one of anti-fouling.

We were exhausted. I suggested we might let the yard finish the job, only to be met by threats of violent revolution from the kids who were determined we should finish the work ourselves.

Both Rosemarie and Jeremy celebrated their birthdays in this setting. The celebrations were not elaborate. For Rosemarie, a quick round of "Happy Birthday" followed by a speedy return to the scraping and painting. It wasn't we didn't love her any more, but we all wanted nothing more on earth than to be finished. At least she escaped cooking in the evening.

We were invited for dinner to a boat being looked after by our diving friend Robin. His girl-friend made a sauce, but as we sat there exhausted and starving, she couldn't find the spaghetti in the ship's stores. While waiting we had entertainment of a sort from diverse cockroaches parading up and down the wooden bulwarks of his characterful old boat, once a Dutch barge.

Fortunately Robin kept us plied with wine and his girl-friend finally found some star-shaped pasta used for sprinkling in soup.

When she put it all together it tasted good, and for Rosemarie it had that extra succulence of a meal prepared by someone else.

Jeremy was a little luckier. He got "Happy Birthday" and a present. He'd yearned for a diving watch. But knowing all our available funds were being gobbled up by the tins of paint, now forming small mountains around us, he was sure he wouldn't get one. Indeed, the kids hadn't had much in the way of pocket money since we'd left London.

We decided however that if we couldn't return a little of the devotion he'd shown to our boat-home, we didn't deserve to have one. We gave him a parcel the size of a hat box. He peeled off one wrapper; and then another, he kept going and finally unearthed the watch. He had tears of joy. We went back to our scraping.

Being on the slip, the bow was up at an angle. It made walking difficult; and also put our bed up steeply at the foot. But Rosemarie wasn't one to be hassled into change, and she simply piled up her pillows to try and maintain an even keel.

One night I was woken by a startled cry. "Arrgggh!"

I sat up in bed, alert. It couldn't be the anchor chain; we were ashore. "What is it, what's wrong?" I'd also had the impression of violent movement.

There was a silence. Then a puzzled, "Where are you?"

"Where do you think," I replied, "Here! In bed!"

"Oh."

I'd got fed up with the feet-up position and gone to sleep at the wrong, but higher end of the bed. In the middle of nightmares about scraping the hull (which we all had) Rosemarie had been woken by a ghastly, scaly creature poking at her face. She started fighting it.

It turned out to be my foot. I was lucky she didn't beat it to death.

One of the jobs we did while on the slip was to fit a speed-and-distance log. I blessed the marvels of modern technology for relieving me henceforth of the problem of translating revs into knots while my brain was being scrambled in a swell.

After five days non-stop, the blessed moment arrived when we left the slip, and could rest.

We fuelled and watered and went the round of friends as we waited for the settled spring weather which would enable us to make the next leg of our voyage - Greece.

We'd decided on a direct route from Malta to Zante (also known as Zakynthos), southernmost of the Ionian Islands. We'd agreed not to follow the usual motor-yacht route to Greece, hugging the foot of Italy, round to Corfu. Five pounds a day still rankled in our minds.

And so did Godfather; especially as the one we'd met seemed to be a beginner, from tales we'd heard from others about Italy's deep south. It is common practice in at least one of the ports on this route for a shore man to demand a substantial fee for taking a mooring rope and placing it over a bollard.

Ronnie, of neighbouring "Andando" told us his story. A Scot, he had made his dream come true the hard way. He had built his ninety foot square-rigged sailing boat himself over a period of years, on a stretch of the Thames.

An Italian importuning a do-it-yourself seafaring Scotsman on behalf of 'services' not rendered is of course liable to be disappointed. So it was in a southerly Italian port where Ronnie had berthed. The reaction to his refusal was such however that Ronnie genuinely feared for his stern lines after dark.

He attached the thinnest sewing twine to a line, pulled it through a porthole and attached it to a bell on the edge of his bed. Any interference with his lines, and the bell would fall off the bed. The twine was otherwise, he was sure, invisible.

He was roused in the early hours by the bell. Dashing up on deck he found a child tugging at the string, looking to see what might be coming up, and watched by adoring Mama.

Ronnie restored the alarm and took more trouble to hide the twine. At dawn, the bell shattered his sleep again. He raced aloft to see a small deputation - the harbour master and one or two other officials. They were busy playing with the twine.

They beamed at him. "Bon giorno! Is this how we wake you up in the morning?"

The seagoing advantage of the route by the foot of Italy is you're never far from a port. The disadvantages, apart from the shore-based human ones, are that the route leads through a succession of windy bottlenecks - the entrance to the Straits of Messina, the aptly named Squillace (Squalls) Gulf, and then the funnel-like entrance to the Adriatic.

So we saw good reasons for staying out to sea, following the direct west-east course. It would provide our longest voyage yet, 330 miles and two days and a night at sea.

We listened to the string of unfavourable weather forecasts which seemed to form part of our routine on such pre-take-off occasions. With mutinous mutterings among the impatient crew, I telephoned the local Met office somehow hoping I might encourage them to give me a good forecast. The best the Metman could offer was winds of force seven - near gale - with little prospect of improvement.

I awoke at six next morning. The ship was motionless. I looked out. The sea was glass. I remembered gale forecasts at Cagliari, while seas stayed smooth.

I woke Rosemarie and the kids. Carolyn gave me the usual grunt, scowl, and elbow, but when I said, "Upsy - daisy. We're going to Greece," she was up, all alive-o.

In no time Jeremy was busy in the engine room and Carolyn was securing the dinghy with that very careful attention to detail which comes only of hard experience.

The motors roared. We threw off the lines aft. We handed Charlie the ground-line for the last time with great sadness. His waving figure and toothless beam disappeared from sight, but fond memories will remain always.

At 0700 our first winter aboard Jernica ended as we cleared the outer harbour and headed for the open sea. We gave a few toots for good friends still lazing in bed on this fine morning, hoping they would hear, and remember us.

There was only a slight swell. I went aft to double-check the dinghy.

"You'll find it's perfectly alright," said Carolyn from behind, "and I've already had a go at the gear on the coach roof."

I mumbled something like, "Aye, aye Miss," and returned to the wheelhouse.

Nicholas passed through in a hurry. "Where are you off to?" I asked.

"Lazarette. Check the steering greasing. Can't remember seeing anyone else do it," he said and disappeared.

Jeremy's face poked above the engine room floor.

"Watch the charging on the port engine will you? And don't do your usual trick of opening up the engines straight away. Keep them at 1500 until I tell you."

I watched these self-reliant young people bustling around. Rosemarie passed at that moment. I said, "Where are you going?"

"Where d'you think?" she said. "The galley. There's two day's food to prepare in case it roughs up. And first, I'm nailing everything down."

Carolyn appeared. "What do you think?" she asked, "does it look like reasonable weather?"

"I think so," I said, "but I'm not worried. You lot are quite able to look after me and mum." That much was clear.

"I hope if we see dolphins again they stay with us."

"Just don't look them in the face," said Nicholas in brotherly fashion as he emerged from the lazarette.

Land faded. No other vessel was in sight, nor any dot visible on the radar screen. We were alone, but we felt only a tremendous sense of exhilaration as we headed once more towards the open sea and a new season of life and school aboard Jernica.

It was sad for all of us leaving friends. But we looked forward to meeting new ones.

Toilet-Roll Tourists

We were steering north-easterly on course for the Ionian Islands the fruitful cruising grounds tracing along the south-west coast of Greece.

We saw only three other boats on our horizons the first day at sea, and the feeling of isolation reinforced my usual niggling fear that the compass might have, at some time, conducted a misalliance with a passing piece of metal, and so would try to lead us astray.

Indeed, fixes I'd taken leaving Malta and comparisons with hand-bearing compasses suggested we might have an error of five degrees. We hadn't had the compass swung in Malta. It came home to me that this could be a mistake if we ended up cruising down the main street of some Greek coastal village.

I made adjustments and as insurance crossed my fingers. We were headed for Zante. Privately, I was ready to settle for any of the Ionian islands. As they extend 100 miles from Corfu in the north to Zante in the south, I thought the chances were fair.

As light slowly faded the sea lumped once or twice. We all became wary, little lumps can be messengers for bigger ones, but this time we were lucky. We agreed watches for the crew, and the night passed uneventfully. Next day saw us cruising steadily east on calm waters, looking forward to our first sight of Greece.

The conversation was somehow familiar early afternoon.

Nicholas (peering at the radar screen); "Land's shading in sixteen miles".

Me: "Can't be. It's too early!"

Nicholas: "I'll kick the radar. It's got no respect for your chart work."

In bright sunshine we gradually closed the coast.

"Where are we exactly?" Rosemarie asked as we all stood on deck gazing at our first Greek coastline.

"It's probably somewhere in Greece," said Nicholas.

"Greece you think? That's good. At last the family are beginning to show some confidence." Skippers have to keep their end up.

The coast was steep-to and rocky. But for once a feature marked as 'conspicuous' on the chart was actually visible. A large white cross showed up stark and beautifully prominent on one of the headlands. My aiming point.

I said casually, "We're abreast of Zante - almost exactly halfway along the west coast." There was a remarkable absence of gasps of admiration.

"Oh good, that's where we were heading for, wasn't it?" said Rosemarie as she headed for the galley.

We cruised southwards, hugging the coast, admiring a number of spectacular caverns of red rock, as large as cathedrals. We rounded the south coast promising ourselves a more leisurely inspection later of the large, attractive bay there. The west coast leading up to Zante harbour was green and wooded, and we all gratefully absorbed the rich colour after the barren hills of Malta.

We headed into harbour to one ribald cry of, "Why does the sign say "Welcome to Venice?"

The harbour was wind free, the water placid, despite the afternoon north-westerly blowing fresh and kicking up the sea outside. It was spacious, almost circular. The buildings by the water's edge were low and graceful; a copy of those destroyed in the 1953 earthquake but no less appealing for that. The town huddled close behind, rising up into an arc of high green hills.

Berthing was trouble-free, the quay sparsely occupied this early in the season. Our reception reinforced our first agreeable impression. A middle-aged customs officer came beaming up the gangway and made us feel like long-lost friends as we completed the transit log.

His work completed, he shook hands all around and asked, "Would you like to see round the island?"

"We'd love to," we said, delighted but puzzled.

"Then I will bring someone tomorrow," he said. "He likes talking English." We thanked him.

Next morning we heard a tooting from the quay. We saw an old gentleman waving from his car.

And so we met Georgios; and his miniature toilet roll. On it were recorded literally hundreds of English phrases. He had taken them from teach-yourself books and Linguaphone records of the 30's.

We commenced a unique guided tour of the island. We drove along roads pink-tinged with oleanders. There were sweeping views over green rolling hills and glimpses of distant bays. We began to understand why the inhabitants remained there in force, despite the island's history of earthquakes.

Georgios began conversing. "From the bottom, bottom?" - he turned to us for approval of his words. As we nodded, he continued, "From the bottom - bottom?" More nods, "of my heart - heart?" Turn.

Nods and "Heart - very good," encouragingly, from us.

"From the bottom, bottom of my heart - heart - I welcome you - welcome," - pointing at us, eyebrows raised questioningly.

We smile, "Welcome, yes, welcome good!"

"From the bottom - bottom of my heart, heart I welcome you - you to Zante!"

The rest of the family squashed into the back of the car, made approving, congratulatory noises.

It is my turn to respond.

"We thank you in return ... "

But Georgios was busy unraveling more toilet roll. We are driving along what could have been an English country lane. Pretty. And twisting and narrow.

As he reads he is also driving. He is driving on both sides of the road. I remind myself it is impolite for the passenger to grab the wheel. Nobody else seems to be on this road, luckily.

"Lee-Cester - Leester - Leicester Squeer!"

"Square, Leicester Square, yes, good," we say "Square."

I said, "You're speaking very good .... "

"I - I - I ... " He interrupted, pointing to himself eyebrows raised.

"I - yes, very good," we all shout, nodding like those toy dogs people place in the rear window of their cars.

"I - I am very pleased, pleased to meet, to meet you." He glanced up from his toilet roll in time to swerve away from a tree.

As he wrestles with the wheel, brakes and accelerator, it is my opportunity again. "And we are very pleased ... "

Toilet roll unravels. "England - England is bigger - is - bigger?"

"Bigger, bigger, yes bigger", we all shout and nod.

"England is bigger than - is bigger ..... "

"Bigger! Yes!" we scream.

"Is bigger than Way - Way -- Is?"

"Wales, very good," we all chorused encouragingly, the while looking with increasing apprehension at the road winding ahead to which he seemed quite oblivious."Good. Well done!"

We pass a large white, building smothered in hibiscus with gracious porticos, of some importance, maybe historical.

I point, I speak very slowly. "What is that lovely building please?"

He looks at it and nods. "From the bottom - bottom?"

"Bottom! Excellent! Well done!" we bawl.

"Bottom of my heart I - I," he points at himself, looking at the roll. This time I take the wheel to avoid a truck bearing down on us. The driver gesticulates angrily. He seems to think we shouldn't be on his side of the road. Strange.

Georgios looks up, then down again. "I welcome - welcome?"

"Welcome, welcome, welcome! Yes, welcome, good!"

We were never in any real danger though. He never took the car out of second gear. He came next day too. The kids found their studies pressing. But we felt indebted by his genuine wish to be friends.

Rosemarie and I went touring again. It was better this time though. Georgios' wife was front-seat passenger, so she was able to take the wheel from him.

Through Georgios, while nodding and agreeing and leaning away from the oncoming cars, we saw Zante.

One of our valued pilot books didn't think Zante deserved its tile of "Flower of Levant." Everybody carries their own image of beauty. For us, Zante remained the most attractive island we saw in the Ionians. Thickly wooded hills, green lawns down to snug coves, small villages suddenly appearing around corners in the hills.

The shops in the port were plentiful; the shopkeepers extremely friendly and helpful. We found prices high after low-priced Malta; but a good meal with wine in the tavernas was cheap by any other Mediterranean standards.

There were no supermarkets. Because of the heat meat was not put on display in the small shops. I accompanied Rosemarie on our first shopping expedition.

We asked hopefully in English for chicken. The shopkeeper grinned and nodded vigorously.

"He understands," I translated.

"No England," he said.

Rosemarie adopted the time-honoured method for dealing with foreigners who do not understand English. She assumed he was deaf.

"Chicken," she bellowed at the top of her voice to the bemused shopkeeper. "Have you got chicken?"

He retreated a little, still smiling, raising his eyes up and down.

"He doesn't understand," I translated again.

Rosemarie was having none of this, with starving children. A crowd was now gathering in the shop, curious and giggling.

"Chicken!" Rosemarie shouted in an even louder voice. Then she began wagging her elbows up and down in tune with a bowing of the head and neck, the while prancing knees-up all over the shop screeching "Cluck, cluck, cluck, cluck, cluck!"

The crowd in the shop now laughed out loud, and began jabbering excitedly at the shopkeeper.

A beam of understanding spread over his face and he disappeared down behind his counter. He reappeared, came round the counter and began prancing all over the shop as Rosemarie had done shouting "cluck, cluck, cluck." Then with a flourish he opened both hands to reveal eggs.

There was wild applause all round, and we left the shop with the eggs.

In the next shop Rosemarie kept it simple. Breathing in through her mouth and snorting unmistakably pig-like, we emerged triumphantly with pork.

We were heading next for Corfu, where we were due to pick up a school-friend of Carolyn's. We decided to leave in good time and enjoy the leisurely cruising we felt the Mistral had hassled us out of the previous summer. We would return to explore Zante's coasts later.

The blue of sky and waters merged as we headed northwards. On the east coast of Cephalonia, the next island, we found some small deserted coves and white beaches where we stopped to swim.

For an overnight anchorage we headed for the adjacent island to the east - Ithaca, ancient kingdom of Ulysses.

S. Andrea, a cove in the southwest was mentioned in lyrical terms by one of our favourite authors on places in the Mediterranean. As we headed on, I read aloud from his book. "The bay winds inland for nearly a mile between cliffs scented with thyme and there are oleanders in bright splashes along the slopes."

Rosemarie said, "There has to be one place the Lord designed for us. That sounds like it."

I checked the radar picture as Ithaca loomed closer. I adjusted course and said. "We'll shortly be going straight up the spout of Andrea."

Nobody was there to applaud. My crew were lying about in indolent postures all over the deck with scarcely a stitch between them.

The sun was so hot we had been heaving buckets of water over the teak deck so that it wouldn't burn the feet.

The bay drew closer. The entrance was bang on our bows. I waited to be blinded by flashing oleanders set in carpets of thyme. A winding mile of it.

Obviously, I wasn't looking quite right. All I could see was a dark shallow bay at the head of which straggled a tiny stretch of scruffy shingle. We closed right in. No colourful anchorage revealed itself. There could be only one explanation. Our objective must be a few yards off, hidden now by the headlands closing around us.

The family had mustered the strength to rise to their knees to view the night's haven. "Doesn't look much, we'll see what's round the corner," I said.

"That doesn't look like the bay described in the book," said Rosemarie, demonstrating once more her facility for total awareness at times when she might reasonably be expected to be immersed in the galley attending to the family's welfare.

"It must be just round the next headland," I declared strongly.

We turned west. There was a tolerant silence. We rounded the aforesaid headland. No deep colourful bay. But there was yet another headland before us.

"We'll just poke our nose round the next one," I said fairly cheerfully. The tolerant silence seemed to have become a little more intense. Our bay wasn't round the next point either.

We searched the short south coast for a good forty minutes, in which time the skipper's reputation as a navigator was looking rather dodgy.

The whole crew had soon taken over my business of running the dividers over the chart or matching the coastline with the chart.

"This just has to be it, no question," I said savagely, as we again arrived at the selfsame dark gloomy bay we had first approached and declined to enter.

"What are we doing back here?" Rosemarie enquired on behalf of the jury.

"This bloody place," I said, "is unquestionably, indubitably and bloody undoubtedly the missing garden of Eden."

As we nosed slowly in, the bay insidiously changed its dimensions. It became longer. The cliffs around, very high and steep, had created from outside the illusion of shallowness. Even so the eastern arm was barely half a mile long; it was no winding creek and there were no flowers! Rather, the steep-to sides made it dark and gloomy.

We were sad at losing a beautiful mile-long winding bay choked with oleanders, but we dropped anchor. The night was calm, the stars very bright; the sea and Jernica were so still we could have been floating on air.

As we sat on deck, the calm seeping through our souls, Rosemarie said, "Look! A new moon! We must bow three times and wish!"

I bowed and wished. Then I said, "That'll make sure there'll be no more foul-ups."

"You shouldn't reveal your wish," Rosemarie chided "It won't work now."

She was right, again. The gremlins were back next morning. In the engine room.

We had planned a leisurely start. Down below, Jeremy pressed the starter button. We heard a "bang". Smoke and an acrid smell came wafting up. I rushed below.

Jeremy was looking at the battery box, more indignant than fearful.

"What's happened?" I asked anxiously.

"A battery's blown up," he said bitterly, as one betrayed by next of kin. He hauled out his voltmeter and started poking about. Finally he concluded there might be a short circuit in the port engine starting-motor, though he wasn't certain.

"But if that's the case," he pointed out, "we can't use the other bank of batteries to start the engine. We'll blow them too."

We studied the chart. The nearest port of any size was Sami, five miles west of us on the island of Cephalonia. It was described encouragingly in one of our guide books as the new commercial centre of the island.

"Commercial centre. Engineering shops galore then," I forecast to cheer Jeremy up. Ferries called there regularly.

We started our one engine and weighed anchor. The Ithaca channel tends to be rough, even in good weather. This time it was benevolent, so we had no trouble steering.

Halfway across I saw Rosemarie leaning over a book and muttering.

"I'm looking up genders," she explained, frowning in concentration.

"Genders?"

"Is motor feminine or masculine?" Rosemarie mumbled at the book. Then "Ah! Mia Mihoni!" She was learning how to explain, "We have only one engine," in comprehensible Greek. I should have known it would be something practical.

Our first sight of the port wasn't encouraging. It looked like the archetypal Hollywood one-horse town. Along the sea-front were the kind of single-storey clapboard buildings which pass for gambling saloons in Western films.

There didn't seem to be that kind of excitement though, or indeed, anything much at all behind this facade. The few buildings soon gave way to firs, bush and scrub in a wide plain cut off in the far distance by a sharply-rising range of mountains.

Sami didn't look as though it would be teeming with electrical engineers.

There was the prospect of our first berthing on one engine; it's difficult enough going astern when one engine is fitted - as we'd noted with many motor-sailers, where this is the common specification.

Twin-engine boats working on one can be more troublesome as the screws are obviously not fitted down the centre of the keel.

The quays were fairly empty and it didn't look as though we would have any problems. Nevertheless Rosemarie perched herself forward, and shouted "Mia Mihoni!" at the port policeman watching us.

He scratched himself.

We reversed for the quay. The wind was gusting. But Nicholas dropped anchor and Jernica behaved like a well-bred lady, going astern under the influence of one engine with not too many a wobble.

Rosemarie and Carolyn stood by the stern lines. A boy on the quay watching held his arms out. Carolyn threw her line. He caught it. As he was looping the line over the bollard, the policeman stepped forward.

He muttered something at the boy. The boy looked up in surprise, let go of the line and shrugged at us. To our amazement the policeman heaved the line back at us and gestured for us to leave.

Rosemarie bawled "Mia Mahoni," and heaved her line ashore. The policeman picked it up and threw it off.

We were still a dozen meters short of the quay. But we'd slowed more or less to a stop. Nicholas on the anchor didn't know whether to let out chain or stop. The yacht began to drift off line.

I went aft and bawled at the unmoving figure, "One engine! Take the lines. We've got to berth."

Carolyn heaved her line again and made looping motions with her hand. The boy took it and stooped but the policeman flung it off again.

Rosemarie forgot all her convent-school decorum. "You silly bugger," she cried to the uniformed figure. "Let the boy take the lines!"

Jeremy was on deck watching, ready to burst.

I said to him, "I'm taking her right in. Jump so you can take our lines."

I returned to the controls. As I got there I heard Rosemarie shout in alarm, "What are you doing?"

I looked out. In disbelief I saw Jeremy flying through the air in a mighty arch and then into the surging sea.

Rosemarie raced into the wheelhouse. "What's he doing?" she cried.

I slammed the engines into neutral.

"I told him I would take Jernica right into the quay. I wanted him to jump ashore, not bloody swim for it!" I said aghast.

We peered over the side, our mouths open. But with strong strokes he was gaining the quay. He hauled himself ashore at the feet of the astounded policeman. Shaking water over the officer he took up station crouched over a bollard.

Nicholas said," He looks like a guard-dog - a very fierce one!"

Clearly the port policeman had the same idea. He stood paralysed.

I took Jernica in again. Carolyn and Rosemarie threw their lines. Jeremy's willing hands grabbed them and in a few moments Jernica was secured.

I went ashore. I shook the policeman's hand by way of assurance that he was safe from the still-glowering guard-dog. He spoke to me in Greek, I spoke in English. We both shook and nodded our heads.

I then said, "One engine kaput. We go see the harbour-master." I set off to where I could see the only offices in the port.

The harbour-master turned out to be a friendly chap who as soon as I said we were an English crew began to talk about football and Bobby Charlton, I nodded and told him about my team Arsenal, and got on to Charlie George's screamer to win the Cup a few years' earlier. Whether he knew Charlie as well as world-cup hero Bobby I didn't know but we were friends.

He then came round to the problem. We couldn't berth stern-to because our anchor chain might trouble the ferry traffic. But we could berth alongside the very same quay.

A small gesture from the port policeman would of course have made that clear. But in these climes it seems that no well-trained port policeman will ever tell a boat to move away before the crew has dropped anchor. They are highly trained in the art of appearing totally unconcerned, or finding places to hide, until the last possible second. This provides them with much needed entertainment in an otherwise routine day.

Our policeman was not the most popular man when I returned to the boat and gave the news. We would have to first motor out and pick up our anchor – and that meant an extra duty for someone in the dreaded chain locker.

There were many dirty and difficult jobs on the boat. This remained the only one the kids argued over, and tried to skive-off from.

Berthed alongside finally, we set out looking for engineers. We explained our needs to a friendly taxi driver.

He smiled happily. "I can find you electrical engineers," he said, "No trouble." As we sighed in relief he added, "In Argostoli."

I recognised the rumbling and grating noises by my side as restrained frustration from Jeremy.

Argostoli was ten miles away across a steep spine of hills and our chances of finding the right man - and finding him free to return with us - would be slim indeed. We returned despondently to the boat.

Jeremy metered around the engine room again, but without any findings which might solve the problem. Then a large inter-island ferry made its way into harbour - the "'Ionion'".

I muttered, "There must be engineers on a boat that size." It must have been a loud mutter, for everybody assured me immediately that a daily walk around the harbour was essential for good health. Jeremy and I set off.

Supervising the crowd and cars thronging off the ferry was our friendly harbour-master. He was now resplendent in all-white uniform and peaked cap. He smiled at our approach. We were after all brothers in football.

We told him we were there in case we might find an engineer on 'Ionion' ready to give us a hand.

"Sure. Don't worry, wait here," he said and boarded the ferry.

A little later he reappeared and beckoned to us. We boarded the ferry where he introduced us to a man who looked like Anthony Quayle playing the part of a Greek engineer on a Greek boat called 'Ionion'.

John, the ship's chief engineer, had a warm, friendly manner. Jeremy explained what had happened.

John listened, put an arm around my shoulders as though we were lifelong friends and said, "I'll come. Just let me clear up a few things here first."

Our gratitude was heartfelt, not just because we'd found assistance. I realised how much we were asking. He looked tired. Greek ferries stop in summer only as long as it takes to shoot one mass of cars and passengers ashore and shoo aboard the next. Long hours, seven days a week. No holidays. It's the common Mediterranean problem of just a few tourist months to make a year's money. Time off for these crews is precious.

We were lucky, as the ferry was berthed for the night. When John appeared again he had two other smiling shipmates in tow.

We returned to our wondering crew leading a fine deputation. The harbour-master was introduced, followed by John, Alex his electrician, and John's number two. The nearest we could get to pronouncing his name was 'Three Hundred', which we christened him.

This secret cabal descended into their temple, known to ordinary mortals as engine-room. Jeremy looked like a priest who'd just been told it was all a mistake, and he'd be going to Heaven after all.

I followed at a respectful distance. Alex poked about for twenty minutes, checking with Jeremy and John.

"The battery split under the load," Alex declared finally. "It was too old. That was all. There isn't any short-circuit in the motor."

Jeremy's face lit up and he said, "Great!"

As bad news goes this was indeed marvelous. It meant we could, after all, use the remaining bank of batteries. We were back in business with two engines.

I set out celebratory glasses and a bottle or two, but we began to learn more about Greece. John would have none of our hospitality. He insisted we join him instead at one of the tavernas on the quayside for ouzos.

"You are in our country so you are our guests," he explained laughing over our protests. As in Malta, we were up against the embarrassing problem of not being able to return a kindness; or rather, we could only return it by agreeing to accept more!

We sat at a table on the nearly-empty quayside. Passers-by were mostly locals. The ouzos flowed. With each refill another of John's passing friends would drag a chair up to join us.

Soon we had a dozen or more at our table. Each was contributing to the ouzo flow. Every attempt we made to contribute was laughingly refused.

Jeremy whispered, "Anyone would think we'd fixed John's engines!"

Several of the men started singing a Greek song, and in a moment Rosemarie and I, inspired by ouzo, and Carolyn, shy but inspired by the atmosphere, were hopping and leaping and knee-bending and circling and clapping on the quay with the dancing crowd.

Our highly inexpert performance was greeted with cheers and back-slaps and roars of laughter.

As we finally swayed back to our seats I said to Rosemarie, "What a fabulous crowd."

She said to me, "Wonderful! Do you think there might be any shops around with fresh milk?" Rosemarie, champion Mum.

John had heard. "Milk? Come!"

In a trice we were saying goodbye to our new friends, and following John to a shop across the road. An old lady appeared. He spoke to her and she disappeared through a back door.

We waited. And waited a little more. We imagined her rummaging around a large storeroom.

At last Carolyn could contain herself no longer, "Where has she gone all of this time?" We shushed her to be quiet and patient.

John thought it a perfectly reasonable question. "To get the milk," he replied.

"Ah," Carolyn, yet a little later. "But why is she so long?"

John chuckled. "She has to find the cow."

We laughed. Great sense of humour. Typically English too.

John saw our amused expressions. He laughed in his turn. "It's quite true! You get your own milk here! No bottles!"

Carolyn looked aghast. "You mean it comes straight out of the cow?"

Rosemarie said, "Modern cows all give pasteurised milk. Don't worry!"

Carolyn seemed not to put the trust in her parents' words which is expected of a dutiful daughter. The Greek lady reappeared carrying a large jug of thick warm creamy liquid.

We beamed too, but town-bred Carolyn peered into the jug with a frown of suspicion and wrinkled nose which had John roaring with laughter again.

When we left Sami next morning we felt as despondent as though we'd been saying goodbye to very old friends. We didn't know we'd be seeing them again sooner than we thought.

We cruised north, luxuriating in the fine weather, a leisurely pace and two engines working. For our night's anchorage we'd decided on Sivota bay, on the south coast of Levkas.

Radar seemed to confirm we were heading straight into the mouth of the bay. I refrained from making any public announcement.

We were passing through an uncomfortable steep swell. I sensed the crew might become abusive if our entry into Sivota's calmer waters was anything other than highly competent and swift.

Following our recent experience, I'd checked the chart doubly carefully. The bay was another nearly a mile long. And it seemed to wind inland.

As it hove into view I raised the binoculars. "Not another shallow, non-winding bay!" I groaned.

Before mutiny could break out however I said to Jeremy on the wheel, "Keep going in." Slowly the bay began to open up. As we moved around a sharp bend to port it was clear I wasn't going to have to hang anybody from the yardarm today for impertinence.

The family were all making noises of approval at the lovely waters opening before us. After the dog-leg, we had arrived in a totally enclosed lagoon. The gentle slopes on either side were studded with palm trees. Old fishermen's cottages and tavernas with gaily-coloured awnings fringed the shore.

It was one of the most picturesque settings we had encountered. We had it all to ourselves. We dropped anchor in glorious solitude.

With sighs of contentment we abandoned ourselves to our various versions of care-free relaxation in the midst of quiet beauty.

Carolyn got busy with sun-cream. Nicholas propped Dostoevsky in front of his nose, doubling as a shade to the hot sun; Rosemarie put her feet up to read a cookbook; Jeremy started examining yet again the outboard engine to the dinghy.

Suddenly the tranquility was shattered. There was a cry from Nicholas. "Gawd blimey! Rubber ducks! Scores of 'em!"

We were soon surrounded by a 'rubber duck' fleet. This is a group of small sailing boats on hire. The crews are novices and hoist and lower sails and perform their other manoeuvres on signals from their professional leader who they follow like ducks behind their Swan.

The title - which we'd picked up from other boats - is patronising. But all the crews we ever saw were enjoying themselves tremendously. And it seemed a fun way of learning to sail.

We watched their leader rowing furiously from boat to boat, taking each anchor which he then rowed out to the dropping point, leaving his charges with the job only of winching in.

We swam and lazed and I decided to try some writing. If inspiration was to come anywhere, then it had to be in such lyrical surroundings. I sat down at my typewriter.

As background noise I noted Jeremy saying he was going for a run in the dinghy, to try the outboard. I muttered at him not to go out of the bay because of the rough conditions.

He grunted and mumbled at this order, and departed.

Working, my sense of time became dulled. But it was much more than an hour later when I said to Carolyn, sprawling on deck, "Have you heard from Jeremy?" The walkie-talkie was by her side. Jeremy had the other.

"Not a word," Carolyn replied.

"Has he appeared at all while I've been working?"

"No," Rosemarie said, "He'll be alright. He's probably found some interesting place to potter about."

We called him on the walkie-talkie. There was no answer.

I said, "He may not have switched on."

"Even if he has, it probably wouldn't get through the hills around us," Nicholas pointed out.

"He'll be alright," somebody said again, but with less conviction.

We kept about our business. But now we all had one eye to the entrance to the bay - or at least as far as we could see. The bend cut off any view of the sea.

Long minutes ticked away without sign or sound of Jeremy and our anxieties grew. We were also much more conscious of the increasing weight of wind over our heads, pushing the branches on shore into a lively dance.

Another fleet of rubber ducks was coming in. As each boat passed I shouted to ask if they'd seen our dinghy. None had.

I asked Carolyn, "Did he have flares?" It was our rule not to take the dinghy to sea without flares. She said anxiously, "No. He didn't think they were neces-sary with the walkie-talkie."

It wasn't unreasonable. You only notice obstacles like hills when you need them not to be there.

I said, "I'm going to borrow a dinghy and go and have a look."

At that moment another 'duck' came in - "Merlin".

I shouted, "Have you seen a white dinghy and outboard anywhere? Probably drifting with a boy aboard?"

He replied immediately, "No. But would you like me to go out and look for him?" Our thanks were heartfelt and I scrambled over the side of the sailing craft with binoculars slung round my neck.

I chafed as David - the professional skipper of the fleet - continued into the bay to put off his crew, Sue, so that she could look after their ducklings. Re-passing Jernica we arranged to call in on the radio.

Leaving the shelter of the bay a stiff breeze and a pronounced swell hit us to increase my misgivings.

"Where to?" asked David. I really didn't know. But I was now certain the outboard had failed. I pointed southeast - down wind.

The swell had a lumpy, strange motion for me on this small and unfamiliar vessel. I stood on the coach roof, holding the glasses with one hand and clinging to the mast with the other. The rest of the family could only sit by the radio. At least I could do something.

I began to scan with the glasses as well as I could. I couldn't see clearly because of the unsteadiness. White shapes appeared off the crests of the shifting waves. Strange blobs; whitecaps; or a small dinghy?

I spotted a small boat. "Over there!" I called to David. But after a few minutes more we could make out the outline of a local fishing boat. I felt the disappointment as a physical blow. Through the glasses I could see the surf thudding hard into Arkudi, a small island downwind.

We turned to cover the southeast track again. Crossing the entrance to the adjacent bay I turned the glasses inshore. Still nothing.

"We'd better head further out," I said to David. For ten minutes I strained my eyes at whitecaps and blobs of various kinds as the wind frothed the wave-tops. I was anxious.

I followed yet another white blob through the wobbling binoculars. I looked again. The shape stayed the same. More solid than white horses.

As we approached I could make out a low white hull; and a single figure. Another fisherman? They were liable to sit out in all sorts of strange weather. I put all my effort into holding the glasses steady. Now I could make out the shape of an outboard. And the single figure was rowing hard, back upright.

"That's him!" I shouted to David.

He followed my pointing finger and grinned. "Soon have him in tow," he said.

I tried to stand higher and wave. Slowly we drew closer. I said, "He's having a tough job in this sea."

"I'm more worried about the chap behind," said David. I turned. A Greek fishing boat with outboard engine was following directly along our wake; and gradually overhauling us.

"He's only after one thing," said David, He meant money.

Small boats in trouble on the sea have to consider if they can afford to be saved. The laws allow scope for extravagant claims. If the caique arrived first and Jeremy took his line, the skipper would claim salvage.

But we arrived first. Jeremy was rowing desperately to stay his drift. We were very close to the rocky Arkudi shore and the sound of thudding waves. He gave me a strained but relieved grin.

David threw him a line and Jeremy secured it to the dinghy, only then did the caique veer away.

"Hello," I called to him. "You alright?"

"Yes, thanks," I didn't open my mouth again. I wanted to blast him for leaving the bay; but I felt only sheer relief.

He drew slowly astern on the tow rope and stopped rowing.

David said "Want to try the VHF?" I thanked him. In my sense of relief I'd quite forgotten the others. In the cabin I picked up the microphone and pressed "transmit".

"Jernica Jernica, this is Merlin. Over."

Nicholas' voice came back, excited, relieved. "You've found him!" I could only look at the mike wondering if it had transmitted anything without my knowledge.

When our procession returned, Rosemarie explained Nicholas knew Jeremy was safe from the tone of my voice.

Rosemarie asked Jeremy. "Were you worried?"

"Not really."

"Why not?"

He said, "I knew Dad would come."

I had a sneaking feeling that that simply meant he knew I was a fusspot but that didn't stop me downing a large whisky while he told us what had happened.

"I was testing the outboard. I was just outside the bay. It stopped. I had a look, a wire had come off the ignition system. I tried to hold it on. But the chord which you pull to start the engine also broke. I had to wrap it round the flywheel."

Even when it wasn't broken, it required two hands and a good pull on the cord to start the engine. Jeremy only had one hand available, the other holding the wire.

"The trouble was," he said, allowing himself a grin, "when I did manage to start it, I got an electric shock from the wire and had to let go of it! I couldn't win that one."

By now Rosemarie and I hated the outboard and vowed never to buy a second-hand one again. Without a working dinghy, one is trapped on a boat at anchor.

But the reviled object was still one of Jeremy's babies. By late evening he had it repaired again so that we could take our hero David and his shipmate Sue ashore for a night at one of the tavernas. The ouzos, food and company were a great way to end the day.

It was days before I could bring myself to ask him why he took the suspect engine out to sea.

"What was I supposed to do?" he grumbled. "Go round and round Jernica?"

Rescued By The Demon Drink

I was still working out an appropriate riposte next day. But jenny, our star-turn, once more claimed our full attention by the time-honoured method - she stopped working.

"It's the water-cooler this time," moaned Jeremy.

Heaping curses on the world's most deficient second-hand engine didn't have any effect on it. We couldn't see anywhere on the chart that might have an engineering shop. So we upped and made the short run for Port Ithaki. We knew our only salvation - "'Ionion'" and our friends - called there.

Arriving, we found a berth alongside the quay. It lay in the unprotected channel leading in. It had a reputation for being windy. But it wasn't long before we saw 'Ionion' entering - and we were delighted to spot

Alex and Three Hundred waving at us from on deck. John wasn't on this trip.

When we met this time, there was no time even for ouzo. They were going straight out again. We felt mean greeting them with our problem. But they left with the usual smiles and our ailing water-cooler, promising to deliver it back on their next trip to Sami –(in fact it was only a couple of days later and we were all ship-shape in the engine room again).

After they'd left I checked at the harbour office for any messages for us. There were none.

Back on board I said to Rosemarie, "We have a problem."

She said, "Couldn't they do the water cooler?"

"Yes. But it's money. There's no message from the bank."

Having given up carrier-pigeons which could carry information in a few days, the banks transfer money by the latest marvels of electronic technology, which was taking a minimum of three weeks.

Of course the day you order it, the money is taken out of your account. What happens to it in the long mystery period before it arrives? The longer he can sit on it, unmoving, the more millions the happy and grateful transferring agent can earn as he gets interest at day rates on the sums trapped within his web of immobility.

That was the picture we saw. But gnashing our teeth wouldn't buy us fresh-food, water (more expensive than wine in some ports) fuel, or all the emergency buys always cropping up to keep the boat running and in good order.

We were certain the money would have arrived by now. We were down to the drachmas equivalent of £7.50.

We'd come across other crews in similar situations and we'd muttered words of sympathy. As usual, the consequences looked much more horrific when they were staring into our own faces.

It wasn't even as though we could rely on financial succour arriving in a day or two. It could be weeks.

"What are we going to do?" Rosemarie enquired. I'm the one supposed to answer that kind of problem.

I could only shrug and raise my eyebrows in approved local style.

She pointed dramatically at our feet.

Where the engine room stopped the storeroom began. Lying there, ready for our evening pleasures, were some cases of duty-free whisky.

Foreign flag yachts are allowed in all countries to purchase goods duty-free. They are strictly for consumption on board.

We had not infrequently been asked at various ports whether we had any duty-free for sale. We had no desire to abuse our privileges. Nor were we ready to risk finding the goods - and even the yacht - impounded; and by no means last on the list of "no no's" we had no wish to land in some dark damp Mediterranean house of correction. We liked the sun.

So in response to Rosemarie's pointed finger, I said, "Look. This is serious. We could go in the nick."

But she was a mother faced with the prospect of starving children. And I was a provider who couldn't provide.

Our salvation came from fate, circumstances, sheer luck, call it what you will. In a previous harbour, where we had declined a proposition to sell booze, we had been told that the proposer's brother would be interested if we ever got to his port, and we felt so inclined. He lived, glory-be, on the island of Ithaki - where we were berthed.

"What was his name?" I asked.

"Surely you remember?" replied Rosemarie.

We both frowned in concentration and went through possibilities. We ended up both looking blank.

"Look, we really can't risk it," I said. "Anyway, what will we do in the evenings?"

"Think positive. It's only demon drink we're getting rid of," said Rosemarie.

That day Carolyn made friends with the skipper of a rubber-duck fleet. He came to drag her and Jeremy off to a disco which was round the other side of the jetty. The opportunities for them to enjoy the company of friends were few. So we saw them off for their evening-out with ninety per cent of the family fortune clutched in their hands.

As they left, we were for the first time ever busy doubling up the lines securing us to the quayside. It was not merely the force of the gale. It was blowing straight up the channel in which we were lying, heaping seas against us. It was impossible to sleep in our aft cabin. The seas pounding on the stern sounded like giants hammering at our heads, trying to break their way in.

We spent a miserable night. As the kids rolled up bright and cheerful from their merry-making at three in the morning, they found their parents in a very bad temper, prowling about checking lines.

The next morning a bleary-eyed Rosemarie said, "We haven't got a bean. And this isn't the place to sit around waiting for funds." She gave me what I had no trouble in recognising as a meaningful look.

I said, "I can't remember his name. But I can remember his business - and there's only one here."

In a trice we were on shore and very shortly in a young Greek's office. We established first that he was indeed the brother. It didn't take long to fix a price.

Back on Jernica I said, "That was the easy bit." I pointed at the Customs house looming above us. I had never seen such a tall one, with so many overlooking windows, so near to our berth.

Rosemarie had time only to ask, "How else do we eat or pay for water?" She was otherwise busily engaged stuffing whisky galore into our very large shopping basket on wheels, originally designed for the innocent task of trundling goods back from supermarkets. We were lucky it was designed with a very large flap on top which could be clipped down.

We wheeled the bulging vehicle on deck. It was hot as usual. I was glad of it, as a cover for the sweat.

We decided to move in the afternoon. Siesta can be a religion, rather than a habit, with Mediterranean Man. We were counting on it.

We manhandled the thing gingerly over the bulwarks and onto the quayside. The fact that nobody else was moving only seemed to make our moves more conspicuous.

"Look natural," I hissed.

"I'm perfectly natural," Rosemarie declared with a big smile for onlookers. "But why don't you stop whispering in broad daylight?"

We set off along the quay. In a few steps we were outside the Customs house.

I laboriously pushed the dead-weight trolley. The bag bulged fit to split.

"They're going to see this bag is stuffed full with something when we're coming off the boat to go out shopping!" I hissed on.

Before Rosemarie could answer we went over a rough piece of the quay. We were directly outside the door to the Customs. The wheels and springing hadn't been designed to deal quietly with contraband. The bottles started merrily clanking and ringing together.

"Aaargh!" I exclaimed. I put a hand on the heaving bag to calm it, but the tolling only rang out louder as I lost control. With another "AArrghh!" and a desperate gaze at the door only feet away I made to resume two-handed control.

Rosemarie was quicker. "Here let me push it!" she said, grabbed the handles, and trundled on with a gorgeous smile at the world.

I fixed a stiff grin on my face and held my eyes on the distant horizon rather than the windows of the adjacent building.

However I couldn't resist a cackle. "I wonder what some of the Sisters would say if they could see you now?"

Rosemarie had been head girl at her convent school.

She laughed, "Sister Catherine for one would say, 'Oh! How exciting!'"

Arriving after what seemed to me like the Long March - in reality only a few minutes - at the buyer's offices Rosemarie marched straight in with the hot cargo.

I saw an elderly man hanging around outside the door. I thought that this wasn't a good idea. Tongues might wag.

I hailed him in the usual smattering of phrase-book Greek and pigeon-English used to address natives.

He smiled. "I been in England. What you want?"

I looked around and began asking him about the history of the port, where the ferries went to, and anything else that came into my head. Meanwhile I led him away from the door.

We ended with the usual smiles and nods as Rosemarie emerged. I felt I'd made a reasonable contribution.

She gave me a slight nod and I breathed easily again for the first time for a day.

As we walked back with guilt on our shoulders but a load off our minds I said, "How did it go?"

She said, "Very straightforward. Only problem was, he was dead worried there was nobody watching the door."

"How do you mean? Couldn't he find anybody?"

"No. He put that old chap there. But then you came up and led him off, gabbling away."

We left to pick up our repaired motor in Sami and for once we were allowed to entertain John and his friends on board.

We set off north from Ithaca towards Levkas a large island just off the Greek mainland to our east. Before arriving there, we found ourselves entering one of the most enchanted of all cruising areas.

Along the south-east of Levkas lies the island of Meganisi. There is a two-mile channel between Meganisi and the small island of Kalomo. We passed through the very short Meganisi channel into a scene of fjord-like beauty - with Greek-like sun.

It was a large, seemingly inland sea. All around us the softly blurred contours of hills and islands hovered in a shimmering haze above a glassy lake.

Bordering this 'lake' to the west is the coast of Levkas. The mainland of Greece eight miles to the east, sweeping round to create a northern shore separated from the island of Levkas only by a narrow canal.

We glided in this wonderland.

There was no wind. It was hot. The faces of the crew reminded me of that famous old Bisto advertisement where two kids rapturously inhale the gravy aroma. "Ah! Bisto!" Now it was, "Ah!Meganisi Sea!"

Many small coves indent the northern coast of Meganisi. We discovered the loveliest. We anchored close by the soft sandy shore where trees ranged along neat terraces of white broken stone. We could swim to our home from the beach. We were alone in a wonderland.

We walked, swam, and lunched, and would have been happy to spend the rest of our days there; but we spent just two days, swimming, snorkeling, barbecuing, sunbathing, reading, sleeping. We were at last living the lifestyle our home-based friends assumed we had enjoyed since the day we bought Jernica.

The only fault we could find with this hot haven was the wasps. But even they were lazy and indolent in this setting and presumably because it was too much of an effort, never stung anybody.

We left reluctantly. We travelled on, past the island of Skorpios, which was the Onassis family's island. There was the unusual sight on a Greek island of splendid man-made gardens. It's also one Greek island where tourists were not welcome.

We sailed on. For the night, we anchored in a small cove opposite the village of Nidri, on Levkas. Several friends had recommended this anchorage. It was pretty. But we didn't like it. We couldn't say why. Our feelings assumed a strange and tragic significance next day.

We passed through the Levkas canal separating the Greek mainland into open sea. Then we steered east to close the Greek mainland. We were heading for Parga. The seaside village held happy memories for us. It was the only place we had ever visited in Greece when the kids were very small.

First we put into Preveza, our first time on the Greek mainland for fuel and water. We had no sooner berthed alongside than a young and enthusiastic port officer rapped on our handrail.

I raised an alarmed eyebrow at Rosemarie which meant, "Whisky?"

But the demand was only for papers.

We dutifully handed him the ship's papers, passports and everything else we could think of. He looked at them with a frown.

"Papers, papers!" he said.

We pointed at the documents in his hand and smiled encouragingly.

He shook his head. "Papers, papers," he repeated and jabbed a finger at me. "You, captain. You papers."

In France and elsewhere local yachtsmen must have some licence of competence. Foreign boats are not restricted in this way. For example, it is not mandatory in the U.K. This was the first time we'd been asked - as it appeared - for my driving licence.

I made sure it was Carolyn who fetched my Yachtmaster's certificate and handed it to him. He returned her beam.

He opened it full out and his eyes lit up with delight. The certificate is a very handsome document - in navy blue hard-cover, with elegant script; and a good, sound, rubber stamp.

I saw he was reading it upside down.

But he was full of admiration. "Good, good, good," nodding with heartfelt approval.

He handed it back beaming at Carolyn and we were free to fuel up, take on water, and depart.

We set off to go northerly up the west coast, seemingly with the broad seas to ourselves. Then a dot appeared at sixteen miles on radar. We watched it casually as it began to close us. I guessed it must be making for Paxos, the small island south of Corfu as there wasn't much else in that direction.

Soon we could see sails. Meeting another boat on empty seas always rouses spirits - and curiosity. We stared through binoculars. I saw the Stars and Stripes. There was something familiar about the whole outline.

I said, "I bet that's Liberty!"

"Can't possibly be!" everyone exclaimed, before fighting for the binoculars in case it was. The family on 'Liberty' had been among the best of the friends we'd made since leaving London. We had met in Malta where they were also wintering, after crossing the Atlantic in their fifty foot sailing yacht.

As we continued to close the other boat Nicholas said, "I think you're right!"

I thought of asking for that epoch-making statement in writing. Nicholas was grinning, and so was Jeremy. Needless to say they were also looking forward to meeting Liberty - or more specifically her younger crew members.

Finally we had no doubt. I grabbed the VHF mike. "Liberty, Liberty, this is Jernica, Jernica. Over." We waited for a wisecracking reply. There was silence. I repeated the message. Then Jo's voice came on the line and confirmed it was 'Liberty' .

We tried to work out the odds against such a mid-sea meeting. I joked over the radio something about a British boat always being able to intercept any Yankee on the high seas, and asked to speak to Tom.

It was then that Jo told us haltingly that he'd died a few mornings before of a heart attack.

The terrible words didn't seem to make sense. After a few moments I could only reply that I didn't know what to say. We learned later that Tom had died in the bay opposite Nidri which we had, almost uniquely, disliked. Earlier, he'd been calling us every day on the radio to find where we were, but we hadn't picked it up.

That news increased our own deep sense of loss. Personally, after knowing him for only a few weeks in Malta, I had come to regard him as a great friend. We felt shattered; we knew that would be nothing compared with the family's own sense of grief.

We changed course to meet up with Jo and the girls in the island of Paxos and went on ahead, making for Gaois, its principal port. As we met Jo off Liberty in Gaois she still managed a smile.

As both families talked and dined that evening Jo and her family showed tremendous spirit. They were continuing their cruising itinerary. And then sailing back across the Atlantic. That's what Tom would have wanted them to do and they were doing it.

A few days later, indeed, on their way to Gouvia, where we had arranged to meet again, a French-crewed 'Swan' racing yacht approached them, challenging them to race. 'Liberty' was only a cruising boat.

But the challenger had chosen the wrong bunch. The girls quickly whipped up the sails and the male crew on the racing vessel were left chasing their wake. Their faces were still red when they appeared later on shore to offer a bottle of champagne to the victors.

We waved au-revoir and our hearts went with them as "Liberty" left Gaois. Then it was business as usual on Jernica. Nicholas on the quayside scraping caked salt out of the toilet system; Jeremy changing oil in the generator, and Carolyn working nobly, as she pointed out, at her school books.

Gaois is one of the most picturesque harbours in the Ionians. We approached through a very narrow channel, which creates a river-like setting. This led us to the main anchorage which is just about in the middle of the village square.

On the other side of the inlet was a small green island. It was crammed with livestock. That evening we watched a boatman row across with their feed. By the time he arrived, rams, lambs, cockerels and chickens were all jostling, waiting at the water's edge.

One wily old sea bird flew in, perched on a rock amid the mêlée and didn't leave before it had been flung a fish. It was obviously a regular.

The square was filled with gaily coloured cafe umbrellas. Centre piece in the square was a white church topped by a belfry and red-tiled roof.

In the narrow streets behind the square we found food shops and tavernas. We experienced again that child-like delight in helping strangers which we found was a hallmark of Greece.

I asked at the local grocers for the 'OTE' - the telephone office. An old man with a weather-gnarled face, bright eyes and a bushy moustache was being served. He rapped out a stream of instructions in Greek, to which I could only shake my head, shrug and smile.

He laughed, and then suddenly took my hand. Still holding my hand, he led me out of the shop and along the streets before finally depositing me at the OTE. He cackled with delight when I said "Thank you very much," in my phrase-book Greek.

We departed reluctantly for Corfu next day, and Carolyn's school-friend. The main harbour in Corfu town is not beloved of yachtsmen. Possibly the fact that it is noisy - a few yards from a main road, wired in like a P.O.W. camp and untenable in northerly blows has something to do with this lack of affection.

We decided to give it a miss. We made for Gouvia, a few miles to the north. A new marina was in course of building in the broad bay, fringed with green hills. We tied up at one of the half-deserted quays. All around was churned earth, ready for new building.

Our lines were taken by a middle-age couple - John and his wife Maude. We learned they had journeyed from Britain in a smart 45ft. motor yacht designed primarily for speeding around flat inshore waters, rather than offshore seas. They too had horrendous memories of the journey to Calvi in Corsica, albeit for different reasons from our own.

Later, John told us what happened. "We were some miles short of Calvi, when I saw we didn't have enough fuel to make the coast. The swell was really rolling us about. But I had no alternative but to run on one engine. And if that wasn't enough," he added, "I'd decided we'd have to drift into the coast."

Needless to say John and Maude were both terrified. But they made it, as terrified crews do so often.

In a gap in the conversation Maude commented, "John nearly put his foot in it. He thought Rosemarie was the au pair!"

"Why," I asked, extremely curious.

Maude told us. Immediately after we'd arrived Jeremy and Carolyn had set off in the dinghy, water skiing. Nicholas was reading. I was nowhere to be seen (I was making vitally important post-passage notes as I carefully explained). "Then," said Maude, "we saw Rosemarie appear with pail and scrubbing brush working furiously on the coach-roof and handrails."

I pointed out that, like most other crews, we always washed Jernica clean of her salt coat on arrival, and that Rosemarie was simply more conspicuous because she easily became bored if she wasn't busy and merely lazed in the sun like others. This was in fact a reasonably accurate analysis. But it earned me a face full of wet leather as I said it lounging by Rosemarie when she was washing down the handrail.

Nicholas, in fact, was able to justify his own time out of sight. He beckoned us into the kids' loo aft. "Look," he said. He pumped the evacuation handle. It worked easily, smoothly. Previously, it could be worked only by an Olympic weight-lifter, of which we were in short supply. We all crowded round the handle in turn gazing in genuine admiration at its smooth efficiency. Nicholas had again been dismantling and chipping away for days at the usual solid build-up of salt.

He was now congratulated by the admiring throng. Such are the triumphs that light up a day on a boat.

And then, of course, the jenny's starting-motor packed up, to end Jeremy's leisure activities. I hefted the motor to a firm in Corfu. Jeremy came too of course, not letting his badly-behaved charge out of his sight.

In the engineer's office, I was given an estimate for the cost of the repair. Although we were accustomed to Mediterranean boat-work prices, I must have looked just a little bemused.

The agent set out to explain. "I'm afraid we'll have to make the parts, he explained, "There aren't any spares around."

"But you could get the parts flown out," I suggested, from our experience.

He wrinkled his neat moustache, frowning. "No, no. They wouldn't do that. Anyway, why bother when we can make it?" He smiled at us and held his arms aloft at the simplicity of it all.

The motor was, in fact, standard, and widely used. A spare part would be inexpensive. And we couldn't afford the price he'd quoted for making it.

I sat there a couple of hours talking, drinking coffee, laughing. Jeremy could no doubt have completed a dozen jobs back on Jernica in the time, as he kept darkly hinting. But our engineer friend didn't seem busy; and we didn't actually have any appointments. And in the Mediterranean, sitting around talking and drinking is sometimes the fast way to get things done. Even when it isn't, it can be interesting.

After we had become acquainted I said I had an idea. "I know the manufacturers. I'll send them a telex and tell them the very difficult problems you're having with their standard spare parts. They know me. I'm sure they'll send some."

He thanked me for my help. Then a few moments later said," You are my friend. I will perhaps find something for you."

He made a few 'phone calls. After a few minutes he embraced me and said he'd found spares. The bill was reduced to one-quarter of the original.

As we headed for a bus, Jeremy said, "I didn't know you knew the manufacturers."

"I don't," I said. "There's more to being a good engineer in the Mediterranean than groveling about in drip-trays."

"Hm'm."

Three days later I picked up the repaired starting-motor. Jeremy and Carolyn greeted me on the gangplank. To my surprise it was Carolyn who took the motor, cradling it in her arms. She looked rather pleased with herself.

"He's strained his back," she explained, jerking a thumb at her younger brother. "I'm going to install it." She swelled up like a pouter pigeon. Jeremy looked dubious.

In her 'working' bikini (i.e. the one with the most paint on it) she descended below with Jeremy. While he directed, she groveled and spannered. When later the generator started up once more, Carolyn was standing with oil-grimed hands and body looking as proud as if she'd just finished building the Eiffel Tower.

We picked up Julia, Carolyn's friend, and welcomed her aboard. But she was unlucky. Near-gales kept us locked by the quay, the dinghy rolling and pitching by our side. But we woke one morning to windless blue skies.

Julia's eyes lit up as we took in the aft ropes and commenced winching up the anchor. "At last," she said with a happy smile, "cruising in blue waters."

There was a snappish shout from forward "Give us a hand!" The anchor chain was coming up thick with foul-looking mud and slime.

"Could I be of any..?" Julia started to offer. She hadn't finished her sentence before some pitiless crew member thrust a scrubbing brush in her hands.

For half an hour our team winched, stopped, scrubbed like mad, winched the next filthy portion of chain, stopped, and scrubbed. Great clouds of black mud sprayed out from the brushes. Julia's body took on a reptilian appearance. Native white poked through great splodges of thick goo.

"See," said Carolyn cheerfully, "it's not all lazing about!"

But Julia had the last laugh. In a day's fishing the score was Julia six, crew one. We never found out how she managed it. She didn't know either.

A couple of days later we rounded the north coast and berthed in Kassiopi. There was just enough room for us on the jetty.

Caiques jammed with tourists pour into this pretty harbour during the day. But they leave in the evening and we found enough space to fall noisily over one another and other diners at one of the quayside restaurants in our version of Greek dancing.

Next morning on deck I saw some figures waving at me from the end of the gangplank. I looked hard and then again.

"Di and Eric!" I called in delight.

They were our best friends in London. We ushered them aboard and soon had ouzos in their hands. The meeting was incredible. We'd arranged to meet them in a week's time, at Gouvia, after Julia had left. But they'd come to Corfu early, and didn't know where to stay. Some stranger had suggested Kassiopi, and here we all were!

Once more we were able to enjoy a totally unexpected reunion with good friends, which is one of the great pleasures of the boating life.

It was overcast and windy next morning. We old timers looked out and pulled the sheets over our heads, but Di and Eric thought it was lovely weather for sea.

I pointed out the hazards, including the anchor warp of a small sailing boat alongside, trailing at a sharp angle across our bow. Our guests were merciless, however, and we started off.

Sure enough, the cross-wind pushed at us, and to Eric's chuckles we snagged the sailing boat's warp. Jeremy beat Nicholas in the race overboard with snorkel and flippers. The first recorded embarrassing moment in leaving harbour, (recently anyway), ended without further ado. Catch 33 of International Regulations at Sea is that embarrassing moments shall only occur with guests aboard.

We anchored finally on the east coast, in Kolura bay. It was pretty and quiet; reposeful. No wind. We ate, sat and drank a glass or two on the aft deck in serene contentment.

Eric sighed, which for a doctor is a major achievement. He said, "This is the life."

"Certainly is," Di replied.

I should have warned him about letting the Marine gods hear such complacent satisfaction. Our champion fisher-girl had departed, with hugs, and we headed south for Paxos again, new ground for Di and Eric who otherwise as tourists had visited more Greek islands than most Greek sailors.

We anchored in the delightful northernmost bay, Lacqua. A simple village sat drowsily at the head of the bay. A screen of painted fishing boats bobbed at a small jetty. Sandy beaches lined by trees fringed the shore.

As we anchored into the north-west wind it began to freshen. Yachts streamed into the anchorage. By late afternoon a full gale was blowing outside. Jernica's bows, held into the wind, were at right angles to the bay's entrance, facing north-east.

A vicious swell soon began surging in, walloping the boats on their exposed beams. It was uncomfortable.

We got busy securing movables, in between trying to keep on our own feet. The fact that everybody else was similarly suffering didn't improve our tempers.

What we really needed was to be anchored not into the wind but into the entrance to the bay. I didn't fancy hauling up the anchor however in this heaving crowd of close tethered boats.

In the white flecked, churning waters of the bay, the dinghy was lurching up and down like a demented roller-coaster. There was very little room for manoeuvre. The shelter had filled with yachts of all shapes and sizes driven by the gathering blasts of wind.

I decided to move our bow to face the opening into the bay, and then secure a line from the aft deck to one of the trees on shore to hold us steady.

"The outboard is u/s of course," Jeremy said, following up the thinking. "Bloody bolt's sheared." We decided the epithet was permissible. Rowing was out of the question.

"Here's where the intrepid frogmen take over," said Nicholas. Equipped with flippers, masks and snorkels, our two divers plunged into the seas. Between them they were dragging one hundred meters of rope.

Laboriously they finned their dead-weight of rope to the shore. A competent bowline, a loop around the rock, and the boys waved us the O.K.

Carolyn and I aboard began heaving up the slack line, securing it aft. As it tightened, Jernica began turning her bows towards the entrance to the bay.

As we turned into the rollers, our movement became negligible. I stood for some time watching the anchor chain. It seemed solid.

Frogmen back on board, we all congratulated ourselves. The other boats were still rolling and heaving and we gleefully imagined the envy with which they would be observing us; and thinking, what a bright fellow, the skipper.

Eric muttered something about Pythagoras. We were all seated drinking tea and talking in the wheelhouse an hour and a half later.

Carolyn gazed aft and said, frowning, "Dad aren't we a little close to the shore?"

I looked out, equally casually. Then I bellowed, "Jeremy! Start the engines! NicholasRosemarie! Get a knife! Cut the aft lines! Quick!" Nicholas was already racing forward to haul in the anchor.

We were yards only from rocks on the water's edge. The whippy line, well inshore, was still pulling us back and I knew the last few feet to the beach shallowed quickly.

The engines roared, I shoved the throttles forward, waiting fearfully for churning noises. But we leaped ahead. Nicholas dived at the ropes. Under the strain of the engines, they began to unravel. He had only to touch them with the knife to slice them through.

A few seconds more and we were out to a safe distance. I throttled back. Everybody started breathing again. The general conversation was of the order of "Phew". Some kind member of the brotherhood of mariners witnessed it all and coiled the rope on shore for us to collect later.

Against the angled tug of the rope aft, the anchor had pulled out of the ground, as any competent ancient Greek mathematician could have told us, and Eric had.

Now it was my turn to envy the other boats, fast at anchor, albeit rolling. By this time, late evening, no reasonably sheltered space was available. We chose a spot and settled down humbly to an uncomfortable night rolling with the best of them.

The wind continued to howl. I took the first anchor watch. Nicholas took over, and I told him to wake me again at 0300 when I'd take another turn.

I woke at five to find him still sitting, watching, the BBC overseas service for company.

"Didn't want to disturb you," he said.

The wind was quieter; but we knew it was only crouching in some corner, recharging its energies ready to spring again on a signal from the sun now climbing in the sky. I decided not to wait.

By seven o'clock we were on our way down the coast. The swell, behind us, was untroublesome. Within the hour we were snugly berthed in Gaois again alongside a jetty. The silence and calm there had that special polished quality after a storm.

A gale quickly blew up again. We learned much later that the other craft in the bay had remained trapped several more days, so we were lucky.

The time came when we had to wave a sad goodbye to Di and Eric. We were to retrace our steps south before turning east for Athens. We decided to stop by Sami in Cephalonia again to meet "Ionion" and John and crew.

"Ionion" berthed soon after we were inside the harbour. We all stood on deck and someone spotted Three Hundred waving at us. We were sorry to learn John wasn't aboard. But that evening we entertained Three Hundred, Alex, their wives and nieces on board.

The wheelhouse was filled with laughter and fractured Anglo-Greek conversation, totally comprehensible to anyone able to smile or nod. As usual, it was difficult to know who was entertaining who. They brought enough ice-cream and cakes with them to feed a fleet. We were discovering again that it is very difficult to out-hospitality the Greeks.

My dreams that night were interspersed with loud squeaking noises. I dreamed the "Ionion" boys came by and said, "Don't worry about the noises - you can't do anything about it."

I woke up in a sweat. Rosemarie mumbled, "What?"

I said, "The jenny. It's even squeaked into my dreams." She condescended to open an eye - normally regarded as my night-time job.

"There is a squeak," she announced.

I leapt out of bed, ready to finish the jenny once and for all. I tracked the noise down swiftly - even a red setter couldn't have competed with my determination to find the target.

I was somewhat disappointed. It wasn't the jenny. I manhandled away a big rubber tyre alongside us on the jetty. Supposed to act as a fender, it had been squeaking and scraping along our hull with the rise and fall of the swell. I returned to bed.

Rosemarie cocked the other eye open. "Well?"

I said, "It wasn't the jenny. It must be learning to keep out of my way." I went to sleep happy.

SAILING IT IS
WONDERFUL IS IT NOT?

A few days later we were back on the east coast of Zante. We anchored for the night in a cove by Cape Katastarion. The water looked like a still crystal stream and there was a wide beach.

"Looks like a little piece of England," said Carolyn.

"Just the right place for a shore visit then," said Rosemarie. She dumped some bags on the deck. We peered inside and poked. Meat and potatoes were wrapped enticingly in foil.

"All we need," she said, "is a fire. Then we can have a barbecue. So get cracking somebody."

Nicholas and I got cracking. We dinghy'd in to the beach. I looked around.

Jernica sat still as though she were riding on air. The beach was of clean white pebbles. A steep cliff rose from a few meters back of the beach, topped by green fields and hedgerows. We could see cows and sheep grazing around a large farmhouse.

"It's idyllic," I said to Nicholas though I'd promised myself not to overdo the word on our travels.

We began gathering large stones for our hearth, and collected driftwood.

"Obviously animals think it's idyllic too," said Nicholas. He was threading his feet carefully between the droppings of sheep, cows, goats and horses. Alerted, I began to do the same.

Then we noticed a shepherd boy had appeared, and was watching us, grinning. We bid him "Yasoo." He carried on grinning.

We lit the fire and built it up. As the embers began to glow, we placed the foil wraps in them. In the brushed light of the waning sun, the rest of the family dinghy'd ashore. They brought wine, bread, salt and mustard; and Rosemarie had made garlic bread.

The ravenous horde fell upon the food. The meat was only a little burned on the outside.

"Not a bad restaurant," said Jeremy.

"That's what the animals think too," said Nicholas,

I was about to tell him not to repeat his wisecracks when I saw all eyes staring behind me. I turned. A veritable Noah's Ark procession was straggling towards us. Cows, sheep, goats, and horses.

"My God!" Rosemarie said, "I didn't make enough for them!"

Fortunately, they were more interested in water. They stopped some yards away. We saw they were at a well. We were surrounded by a cacophonous moo-ing,

bah-ah-ing and neighing and enough quadruped fart-
ing up and down the scale for us to get bored with saying, "It's the ship's biscuits."

There was no jostling. The animals waited their
turn, like a crowd of well-bred diners passing through
busy swing doors at the Ritz. Each would drink its fill,
and move on. Finally they straggled away and disappeared back up the hill. We made gestures inviting the
shepherd, who had remained, to join us. He smiled but
seemed too bashful.

With the departure of the animals and their gas-
eous chorus we ate in tranquility. Jernica was sitting
quietly on the water as though watching over us. The
embers of our fire glowed more deeply seen through
wine glasses.

I raised my glass to Rosemarie and we held hands. I
was about to say something again about it being idyllic
when a large rock crashed on the ground about a foot
away from us. It was followed by a liberal sprinkling of
stones.

We all sprang up. On the slopes above us we spotted the farmer's family. Half-a-dozen kids and their
mother. As we watched, one of the older boys picked
up a stone, grinned at us and heaved it. We ducked.
Clearly it wasn't only an attractive beach. It was a farm.
I could see their point of view. But dented heads were
now at issue.

"Parrakolo-Mi!" I shouted. I trusted this translated
as "Please don't." I'd learned the phrase to discourage
swimmers who used our dinghy as a diving platform
when we were anchored.

The woman smiled at us and we exchanged friendly waves. My sigh of relief was stillborn when another rock came hurtling by our heads. The woman turned to the boy and said "Mi" but as she was grinning fondly at him all he did was to wait a few seconds before his next broadside.

Since appeals to reason weren't working I thought we might try lunacy. "Let's have a singsong," I suggested. Carolyn and Rosemarie loved music but both were both tone deaf. "At least then they'll have a reason to fling rocks at us."

We started off into "Ten green bottles."

Jeremy said, "Now we're for it", and we all looked above apprehensively.

Possibly our stone-throwing companions were music lovers and couldn't stand the cacophony. Or maybe they thought we were calling up reinforcements. One or two more stones accompanied by one or two more half-hearted "Mi's" from mother followed. Then they disappeared.

We stayed on into the warm velvet night, lazily re-kindling the fire, and as we lay back keeping our usual watch for the fiery traces of shooting stars which was never unrewarded with a fine display.

Next day we were back in Zante harbour. But we decided we must take avoiding action against our most hospitable but difficult friend Georgios.

Another day out under the aural assault of his toilet-roll was saved by the appearance of "Ventotene". This "Gin-Fizz" sailing vessel was crewed by Jean-Yves, his wife and family - two teenage girls, and a boyfriend.

We took their lines as they came in to berth, got talking and Jean-Yves, plump and smiling, was desolé to learn that we'd had practically no sailing experience - which wasn't for lack of trying, as we told him.

In our pre-Jernica days we'd chartered a sailing boat for a day on the Solent to see if maybe that's what we should opt for. It was October. We hoped there wouldn't be too big a storm. We arrived, that winter's day in England, to bright blue skies and not a breath of wind. The charterer smiled and assured us the weather wouldn't last. We motored out to the middle of the Solent. There the owner goose-winged his sails to catch any wisp of wind.

We sat and waited expectantly for the moment to arrive when we would at last experience - sailing! We sat and waited. We waited. We ate lunch looking enviously at the motor craft moving freely around us.

We waited, sitting still in the middle of the Solent. Late afternoon the monotony was broken. I'd instructed the kids to line up two objects on the shore for any signs of movement.

"We're moving," Carolyn shouted triumphantly.

"Great!" we all shouted. I looked again.

"Yeah, great. But we're going backwards!"

The ebb tide was taking us down the west Solent, out to sea, while our bows were pointing to harbour, goose-winged and all. With an embarrassed grin our host started the engines and our day's sailing adventure was over.

Now we happily agreed to try again with our new friend and his clearly experienced and pleasant crew, especially with a breeze guaranteed to catch their sails.

As we sailed out of Zante on "Ventotene" we knew this would be different. White horses were galloping outside the harbour, chased by a good breeze. Jean-Yves was at the helm in the cockpit, his girls coping with the sails.

"It's good weather for a sail," he said brightly. "We'll go round the south coast."

The boat's motion inevitably was different from Jernica's. We were riding along as part of the wave movement rather than over it; the novel motion did not immediately meet with our total approval as the odd pale face among us revealed.

Jean-Yves tacked to take us south. We bobbed along with Veronique and Marie-Helena their two attractive daughters busy handling the sails.

"We'll try the Spinnaker," Jean-Yves announced suddenly. "That will be great fun for you!"

He called to his daughters. "Put up the spinnaker!" There was some scuffling forward. A sail flapped ineffectually. More scuffling.

Veronique came aft and began a quiet discussion with her father. He finally gave a shrug and explained to us with a grin, "The spinnaker is new. We've only used it twice ourselves." Fifteen minutes later, amid much giggling the girls had worked out how to do it. The spinnaker rose majestically, 'Ventotene' surged forward.

"It is wonderful," Jean-Yves said gesturing at the magnificent spread of canvas forward. "Is it not?" We agreed it was. There was a sudden loud crack. I saw in one moment the spinnaker filled to straining and the boat beginning to heel steeply.

Close around us, as though suddenly attacked by some monster mixer, the sea was churning up into a white froth. The wind was making a whistling noise through the rigging. The spinnaker as we lurched was trying to scoop itself under the water.

"Take the spinnaker down! Quickly!" Jean-Yves shouted.

Veronique and Marie-Helen rushed forward. Jean-Yves battled furiously with the wheel against what was obviously the spinnaker's attempt to take control. As he did so he hollered instructions. The girls scrambled about but the sail stayed high, dominant; still trying to scoop water up and the boat under.

Veronique came back aft. With a strained grin at her father she said, "We don't know how to get it down."

In one movement Jean-Yves handed her the helm and darted forwards and Nicholas and I went forward with him. We threw ourselves onto the twisting and squirming canvas monster as it tried to drag itself overboard, with the boat possibly following.

When it was under control, we returned aft where Veronique was steering, heading back for port. We all breathed a lot easier.

Then she said to her father, "What's that funny squeaking sound when I turn the wheel?" Jean-Yves thrust his head over the stem, and then up to the heavens.

"The line from the spinnaker is caught in the rudder!"

If my kid's faces looked a trifle bleak it wasn't only the rough sea. They had last winter dived on a wreck just outside Valetta harbour. It was a sailing boat which had gone down only two days earlier. Entering port in rough weather its engine had failed and it had been swept onto the rocks.

The boys during their dive were the first to discover what had gone wrong. A line from the lowered sails was wrapped around the propeller. So while they didn't know anything about sailing, they knew all about lines trailing aft.

This sea however was only uncomfortable, not stormy. And while the spinnaker was clearly novel, our hosts were obviously highly competent sailors. Jean-Yves took over the helm. The handling was obviously not easy for him.

"Not far to go." I pointed reassuringly at the harbour entrance a few hundred meters away.

Our helmsman, coaxing the wheel, steered away from it.

"Oh blimey, of course we're tacking," someone said. It was a novel experience for all of us. We watched the entrance pass us first on one side and then the other, getting closer tantalisingly slowly.

Jean-Ives tack was skilful, and despite his difficulties his final leg took us plumb through the middle of the harbour entrance. Safely berthed, he said, "You know, it was quite dangerous, with the spinnaker." We told him we'd had every confidence in his crew, which was true.

It was equally true that we all agreed with Carolyn when we stepped back aboard and she said from the heart, "Good old Jemica!"

Meanwhile, John and Pat with their kids Eilean and Patrick arrived in Zante on their sailing boat, "Shadow of Lome". We knew them from Malta. Eilean was pretty and Jeremy's age and they seemed to get along. So he was wearing a big grin, engines for once having to compete for attention.

Tourists were now in numbers parading around the port. That also meant that tourist attractions were available for the children on shore. That evening they all went out on their hired vehicles. They were mounted on bicycles which two people could pedal seated side by side. They went careering past along the quay waving and shouting.

They returned some time later pushing. A wheel had fallen off.

"What shall we do?" they asked anxiously.

"Take it back. What else?" I replied.

The return of the wheeled ruin went as follows, we learned later.

Hirer: "You've broken my bicycle. That will cost you 400 Drachmas for repair."

Carolyn: "It wasn't our fault."

Hirer: "H'm. I'll settle for 200 drachs then. But you'd better pay up."

Carolyn: "The wheel was wobbly when we set off."

Hirer: "Well alright. Give me 100 drachs."

Jeremy: "We want our money back. We paid you for a ride and we haven't had one because your bicycle was faulty."

Anywhere else, the hirer might have turned nasty. But there is nothing a Greek so admires as one who knows how to bargain in a tight corner. He gave the broadest of smiles, patted Jeremy on the back, and said, "You're a good lad. That's alright then. You just forget it."

Rosemarie and I thought the teen-agers' education was making progress. But the time was close when more formal education would have to have a higher priority. With touring weather ending and winter in sight our next stop would be Athens. We were leaving Ionian seas for the Aegean,

The next morning we headed north-east for the Gulf of Patras and the Corinth canal. In the capital there was a British Council where the kids would be able to sit English school exams. They'd been working steadily at their correspondence courses.

When we turned into the landlocked waters of the long Gulf of Patras we were looking forward especially to our stop at Galaxidi on the north side of the gulf. We'd been told it was very attractive. And from there we could visit the famous ruins of ancient Delphi.

As we made into the port it lived up to the description we'd been given. Looking forward, thick pine woods spread across nearby slopes. They swept round behind a white, paved promenade fronted by terraced villas and small bushy trees. We could see a row of simple tavernas along the seafront road.

It was here we met Horst and Helga. The German couple were sailing through the summer on their yacht 'Sonderling V'. We also befriended Ted and Linda, young Canadians, who were getting away from everything aboard their sailing boat. The name of their yacht told their story - 'Alternative'.

They recounted how they'd been sailing near an old lone Greek fisherman one day. He'd suddenly changed course to approach them. When he was within hailing distance he stood up and shouted in English, "There is no alternative!" He then turned away, back to his fishing.

We saw Delphi on the wrong day and the wrong time. Sunday was free entry day to public museums and sites. We arrived with ten thousand others (roughly, we didn't count) just before the peak of the noon sun. Carolyn groaned. "We should have consulted the oracle. He would have told us this was a bad day for a visit."

"She," corrected classics-student Nicholas. "The oracle was a she."

"I know that," scowled our liberated female.

We hustled and jostled and sweated. The two famous pinnacles, backcloth to the whole scene, didn't look any more magnificent than two steep hills might be expected to look to perspiring tourists forced to climb their slopes. There was a remarkable absence of site notices. We followed the guide books as best we could; or loitered with intent with flapping ears on the fringe of parties on guided tours.

We ascended to the plateau of Apollo's temple. It was here the priestess used to pass on the words of the oracle to kings, generals, statesmen - and anyone who could fork out the fee.

"It seemed to be a paying game," Rosemarie observed, noting all the Treasuries dotting the site.

Beyond the temple we reached the well-preserved theatre. We slumped gratefully into its stone seats.

Only Nicholas had the energy to ascend further, to the stadium. He was well rewarded. He returned filled with enthusiasm. The setting had struck a spark within him. History suddenly became alive. "The stadium looked as though it had never changed," he said, eyes aglow. "As I sat there I could imagine all the athletes performing before my eyes."

Otherwise we departed with memories primarily from the museum sculptures; the noble head of the youth Antinous, and the alert eyes and flowing drapes of the charioteer.

Next morning we were some 2500 years and a few miles on from Delphi, heading south-east as the gulf turned in a long neck towards the Corinth canal, gateway to Athens and the Aegean sea.

"The signal's green for the canal," said Nicholas, looking through the binoculars. So with light fading we headed towards the beginning of our journey through the Corinth canal.

As we entered, it looked as though some giant had sawn through the hills with a blunt bread knife. The cleft seemed hardly wide enough for the boat's beam. The rough hewn sides closed in on us, towering vertically for up to 200 feet. A thin seam of sky showed overhead.

We hoped nobody would fling anything down at us as we passed under the bridges which spanned the canal. Cars and people on them looked like toys; but some of the toys waved, and we waved back.

It isn't a long journey – only about four miles. The glamour was dulled a little as we emerged again into open sea. The coast port-side could be described only as messy - concrete buildings, big tankers and oil storage tanks. But it was the Aegean, of mystery and allure; it didn't look "wine-dark" but we knew Homer had been here before us.

We were charged a small fortune for the trip through the canal. I pointed out to the official that we weren't carrying cargo, such as gold bricks, but he was unmoved. Of course, if he had asked double or triple there was nothing we could have done.

We anchored for the night half way to Athens in the bay of Salamis island. We were just short of the village, where fishing boats by the score were stuffed along the quays. There was a bright full moon and there was no way of telling if the one in the sky or the water was the real one. The lights of land twinkled in a broad arc around us. It was memorable.

On the beach round the corner the Persian Emperor Xerxes had sat on his golden throne waiting to tick off the score as his fleet sunk the Greek ships. But the Greeks had been waiting to draw his numerically superior fleet into the narrows, and wiped them out. All in all it was a romantic place to sleep.

Next morning more mundane thoughts filled our heads. A winter berth; and 'O' and 'A' level exams for the kids, in Athens. We were soon threading Jernica through the traffic block outside Piraeus, the main port of Athens. The seas were thick with bulky, stained cargo boats at anchor waiting their turn to enter. Then, high above this modern mass of rusting metal we viewed with growing excitement the imperious, elegant temples of the Acropolis looming ever closer. The Parthenon no longer just a picture in their history books for the kids.

We were making for Zea marina, round the corner from Piraeus. We'd been advised to berth right inside the harbour - where Zea becomes Passa Limani.

We found both arms of the harbour extremely crowded. And the eye's view all round was disappointing, especially after our early glimpse of ancient beauty. Apartment blocks all clashing in shape and colour; no vestige of green; no hint of harmony or architectural style appropriate to a famed city of antiquity.

Nicholas was at the wheel. I went forward to try and spot an empty berth. The wind was very fresh. There was little enough room to spare. On either side anchor chains and warps reached out to snag us. But Nicholas kept us out of trouble, allowing my occasional note of warning to go respectfully in one ear before ignoring it out of the other.

We finally squeezed into a minuscule slot. We intended to remain in it only a few days anyway, while arranging a winter berth. Then we'd spend a few weeks final cruising before winter. Rosemarie produced tea, a comforting family routine signaling the end of a leg of the journey.

Days later, we still couldn't get a promise of a berth. Only an assurance that we'd have the highest priority because we were the only boat family there. We found that in itself disappointing. But we'd also been hoping there would be company around for the kids.

The two other - and more attractive ports - locally at Glyfada and Vouliagmeni were, we were told, even fuller. But after a week of car-filled roads, blasting motor cycles and enclosed by blocks of flats we'd had enough. We decided to make the most of the last few weeks of Greek summer. We set off for the east side of the Peloponnese and a view of the Aegean and Homer's seas and islands.

The Peloponnese peninsular lies on the opposite shores of the gulf dominated by Athens and we headed south for the island of Hydra via Poros. The trip was uneventful. The strip of water between the island of Poros and the mainland creates a green-encircled lagoon, broad in the north, narrowing to a sliver of a channel in the south. We came in from the north. On our port side were a number of anchorages.

As we passed the first, Carolyn said, "I'm sure that's 'Olympia'!" John and Velma's boat from Zante.

John was a Greek who had made it big in Australia. He returned every year to cruise his native waters where he kept a fast motor yacht. With the neck and shoulders of a bull and a quick temper he wasn't a man to cross.

We'd once been guests on his yacht for the day quietly at anchor outside Zante. A large open boat had motored past. It came very close and was going fast enough for its wash to send us lurching - and Velma flying over the deck to injure her leg. The man at the helm must have known this would happen and was perhaps having some kind of fun; or he was an unusually poor sailor.

John went red in the face and native Greek came spewing from his mouth. It required no translator to know it wasn't complimentary. In seconds our anchor was up and within minutes John had caught the other vessel. He returned the honours. He circled it at high speed to send it spinning and lurching and seas flying over its deck. The while, atop his flying bridge, he bawled in Greek to the man at the helm what he thought of him. We were also terrified as we thought the open boat would sink. It didn't only because John was a good enough seaman to stop at the limit.

Albeit he was our host, we disliked his behaviour. On this occasion there was at least a reason, But from our observations men at the helm of very fast motor yachts could be a danger. It had something to do with caring little for others, and with ignorance of the elementary rules of the sea and boat handling. These predatory yachts will invariably have professional crews. When the owner's aboard though, he's the driver. At last, he can go flat out without traffic lights or speed limits, totally unaware of the dangers of a different environment and the different skills needed to avoid his behaviour having unexpected consequences.

However we also remembered John and Velma for their hospitality. We'd discovered through them Greek restaurants. We'd also been introduced to their fridge cabin. Velma was Australian born. John and Velma shared their countrymen's love for beer. One cabin had been given its own refrigeration. It was stacked from floor to ceiling with beer. We were never thirsty when aboard "Olympia".

As we passed the second bay, Rosemarie called out, "Isn't that 'Sonderling' over there!" They were German friends from Galaxidi. Jernica had led us to another evening with friends unexpectedly encountered.

Next morning we set off for the famous island of Hydra sitting close to the base of the Peloponnese. The Hydra channel was only five miles away. Our course took us via a narrow gap between two small islets just off the mainland. The area is renowned for its swell, and as we approached, the sea heaved about.

Then Carolyn said, "Look at that great hulk following us!" We saw a large ferry some distance off our stem. She was a little to our port side. To starboard we were less than half a mile off the coast. The gap we were heading for wasn't much more than a mile ahead.

"He's overtaking. It's his job's to keep clear," I said.

"How can you be sure?" Carolyn asked anxiously.

"It says so in the International Steering Rules," I said.

"In Greek?" Jeremy queried, as the monstrous shape drew closer.

I could also recall the regulations about getting out of a big boat's way in a narrow channel with restricted manoeuvring. But I couldn't see how to get out of her way. The restricted manoeuvring bit was my problem, not the ferry's. I had moved over some, but I couldn't close the coast any more because of shallows and rocks. Turning to port would put us across his bows. I could only maintain our course.

He was approaching at more than twice our speed. He had plenty of room to seaward. His obvious move was to slow down and fall in behind us. If it took us six minutes for the mile remaining to the gap, he would lose only three. His bows came surging up behind us.

Rosemarie joined us in gazing up. A cliff of metal seemed to tower scores of feet above us. "My God! She's a bit close! Shouldn't we get over! It's bloody enormous!"

The ferry's bows began to overlap our stern. I judged it would pass scarcely a few score feet away. And having made its decision, it pressed on. Its massive bulk started to race past.

We all shouted various variations of "Oh no!" some more obscene than others. The menace of the white foaming bow wave thrusting out from the overtaking vessel was unmistakable. No doubt everyone was re-membering, as I was, what a wash from a yacht very much smaller than this ferry could do.

Rosemarie fell down the stairs in a race to shut the portholes below. I yelled at Nicholas now at the helm to try to put the wash on our stern. In no time, it seemed, the ferry was ahead. Then her wash began to hit us. It tumbled its way towards us over the top of the swell. We were soon in the grip of a very short, very steep and turbulent sea.

We pitched violently. Nicholas sweated and strug-gled with the wheel. At one point he shouted "I can't hold it!" and I went rushing back to the wheel. There came an anguished cry from Jeremy. He'd been lean-ing over the sides watching in amazement the sea climbing our gunwales. Suddenly he remembered his engine-room portholes were open. He fell down the ladder to the engine room.

We struggled for five minutes, which seemed like five hours; the sea churning around and over us. Then we turned into the dying wake, nosed our way into the gap and were finally out into the relative calm of the Hydra channel.

"The galley floor's a mess," said Rosemarie breathlessly.

Jeremy was in a fury. He'd been too late. The seas had washed through his engine room. The product of countless hours of painstaking labour, polished rocker covers, brass-bright pipes, painted engines were all now covered in layers of salt. He found a fish in the scuppers.

It took us some hours having arrived in port for our anger to soften.

Hydra is one of the busiest Greek ports in summer. It is small. But it has a famous history and a pretty village. It is popular with tourists. Hydrofoils as well as conventional ferries are jostling in and out ceaselessly. They race each other brazenly for a place on the small quay, rather than sit outside waiting.

One of the fastest and cockiest was called 'Mania' and anybody who's seen bathers and small-boat skippers alike leaping about to escape its racing wash won't ask why. We timed the average turn-round time of any ferry at not more than three minutes.

So we could console ourselves that if they had no respect for smaller yachts, they had none either for each other. When the harvest is ripe the farmer must work non-stop; their harvest was the tourists, a crop which withers to nothing in winter.

Jeremy was less forgiving. For days he was busy cleaning away all traces of the unprovoked assault on his territory. We tried to console him by compiling a new Steering Rule. Nicholas posted it in the wheel-house. 'Rule 272' he read. 'Keep the hell out of the way of local ferries, under any condition.' It was as well that we didn't know the day would come when we would need to tack on another amendment.

Hydra presented a magnificent vista. The port is set in a natural amphitheatre. In the foreground are castle ruins, a windmill and large old and elegant stone buildings. Behind, the small town climbs up the bowl of the hill, white terraced houses and villas dovetailing with each other. The old waterfront terraces are white with splashes of colour - yellows, reds and browns. The large ornately decorated shops reminded me of card-board toy facades I'd bought as a child.

The rectangular harbour was small enough to cre-ate a feeling of intimacy. It had witnessed noble affairs of State. It was Hydra which supplied the ships and men which led Greece's fight for independence some one hundred and fifty years before. This special place in Greek history and affections has helped local groups in their fight to maintain the architectural unity of the town, even as it developed as a world tourist centre.

Ashore, as we walked the cobbled streets, every new curve exposed fresh views of arches, courtyards, steps, all of perfect proportions. As we returned to Jernica we passed lines of donkeys. Paniers strapped to their backs, they waited patiently to transport cargo from the boats. There are no cars and motor bikes on the island. The dreaded scrambler's roar which otherwise fills Mediterranean roads is worlds away.

We were berthed on the sea wall. As we'd entered we'd had another of those odds-against port meetings. We shouted to a man in the bows of a German yacht asking the best place to berth. He'd indicated the sea wall. After watching us intently he called out, "Weren't you 'Crionna' at one time?" We shouted back that that was her name when she'd first come off the builder's slip, seventeen years before.

"I thought so," he called. "Couldn't mistake her, I was her skipper!"

We were excited at meeting Jernica's past. We were disappointed when our ex-skipper's bosses took to sea before we'd had a chance to talk.

But we made new friends, in one of the ways peculiar to cruising yachts. A young man with fair curly hair shouted to us as we began to berth, asking if we needed assistance. A large smile, which was somehow familiar, accompanied the question. We recognised him as a yachtsman we'd first seen in Gaios.

He'd had one of those days all skippers dread and invariably get sometime, particularly on single screw boats. He'd wanted to back in. His yacht wanted to go in a circle. The harder he tried the more she veered off. Eventually Jeremy and Nicholas dinghy'd out and took his lines ashore. He'd earned nothing but our applause for he never lost his good-humoured smile and easy manner during a long and trying performance.

"You'd have been shouting your head off at everybody," I remember Rosemarie saying. I thanked her for her noble support, but could only silently agree she was right.

Now, at second or third time of chance meeting we all felt we knew each other. Willy introduced us to his wife Loretta aboard their sailing yacht 'Ananahi'. They were both journalists and spent the summers sailing and writing with their two very young kids.

Next morning we were washing the boat down when Nicholas suddenly uttered a cry and dashed towards 'Ananahi' carrying some of our spare fenders. Willy and Loretta were somewhere on shore.

Nicholas was trying to save Ananahi from a not uncommon fate in Greece. We called it, "Yes we have no fenders."

It started the first time a local boat of fifteen ft. beam tried to squeeze into a berth three feet wide between Jernica and an adjacent yacht. We had watched its approach with horror. Her hull was streaked and dirty. There wasn't a fender in sight.

Me, calling: "Where are your fenders?"

Local skipper, (smiling, under any circumstances) "Don't worry."

Their stem was now level with our bows - across our bows. Me - a bit louder: "Haven't you got any fenders?"

They now began to scrape down our side. The family were working like demons, pushing off, and inserting our own fenders. The local crew made palms up and raised eyebrow signs to show they could not understand our fear.

Local crew: "But yes! We have fenders," still smiling - indulgently now at our panic. Their streaky hull was now creaking and groaning along our pristine paint, to the anguished cries of the family. Carolyn is puffed up, arms waving, face red, threatening to assault them if they take off any more of her paint.

They were very pleased she was paying them attention.

Me - bawling: "Well, where are they then - your fenders!"

As their hull shoved and skidded between us and the adjacent yacht one of the crew grabbed what looked like a greying sausage which had just been run over by a steamroller. He held it up, and called cheerfully, "Yes, we have fenders!"

They were nearly berthed now. In desperation I shouted, "Why don't you use them then!"

They regarded us with frowning lack of comprehension. "Well, we haven't berthed yet."

Sure enough after grating and cracking down our sides they came to a halt and then with great beams and a flourish inserted their thin pieces of chewed rubber as best they could between our hulls.

We all collapsed in exhaustion. We found it happened on other occasions, with the same replies. Clearly fenders were for putting down after the hulls have had a good scraping.

We stopped asking and always kept our own spares handy.

Nicholas reached Ananahi in time to preserve its paint-work from the assault.

Meanwhile the wind had been blowing up. The sea climbed over the wall and poured itself in buckets over our aft deck. It blew a storm.

The harbour had been crowded. Now boats came over from the main quay where the incoming swell was making conditions hazardous, to double berth on our side. They parked between the bows of the boats already there, the inside yachts being used as passageway to shore. More yachts swept in to escape the seas now raging outside, and squeezed in to whatever triple berths they could manage.

It's an ill storm that doesn't make a few friends in harbour. Late evening, as giant hands pushed us around, we sat over dinner with Willy and Loretta. I was trying to lure their younger daughter Vitaea who was just learning to speak to say, "Ay-yo Michael". She always addressed her father as "Ay-yo Willy".

The next stormbound day we met Andreas and Leah on their neighbouring motor yacht. He was a retired Greek admiral and, we learned much later, a genuine war hero. He had an encyclopedic knowledge of just about every Greek boat we saw. As a Greek-flag boat passed he would tell us who built it, when, in what material, its length, breadth, and modifications.

Leah was one of those people inclined to say whatever she was thinking the moment she thought it - usually in the middle of one of Andrea's sentences. It was fortunate they both had a sense of humour.

Through them we visited some of the impressive historic family houses of Hydra - one of which was built of old ships' timbers. We were amazed to see a clematis bush the size of a tree trunk growing inside it.

The kids weren't quite so lucky. Teenagers seemed in short supply. This lack of teenage companionship had been the one drawback of our life on the boat. It worried Rosemarie and me. We mentioned it.

Nicholas said, "I think you worry about it more than we do." Carolyn said, "Think of all the other people we meet." In Hydra we had been fortunate.

The storm passed. We said goodbye to our friends. I earned a shy, parting "Ay-yo Michael" from Vitaea, so our stay had been a success. We cruised leisurely in waters calmed after the storm to make the short distance westwards to the island of Spetsai.

Cigar Cigar To Win

Baltiza bay was the old harbour of Spetsai. It is reputed still to be the safest. We were lucky to find a free berth at the head of the bay. However it was rather like being in the middle of a huge workshop - interesting but unkempt; muddy and grimy.

We rode a horse and buggy to town and the new harbour where the boats rolled to the wash of the passing ferries. Late into the small hours at Baltiza two discos on the water's edge blasted so loudly we contemplated leaving there and then.

"It's such lousy music," Nicholas complained.

Next morning we departed for the northern end of Spetsai and one of the loveliest bays we'd found - the western-most cove of Zoyiori - 'oy-yoy' bay to the family. A couple of days spent tramping over green hills restored our respect for Spetsai. Hills in the Aegean are usually scorched brown.

We decided we should see some more of ancient Greece. With the seas some of the calmest we'd encountered, Jernica sauntered the twenty miles north to the head of the Argolokis Gulf, and the mainland port of Nauplion.

The entrance was picturesque. The islet of Bourdzi on the portside has a solid old castle atop it, now a hotel. Dominating the cliffs to starboard stands the old Venetian fortress of Palamedi. We tied up at a clean quay with ample space and a choice of smiling taxi drivers.

We were soon on our way to the ancient ruins of Mycaenae, home of Agamemnon, the king and commander of the Greeks in the Trojan wars. After Delphi we were prepared for disappointment. But this site gave us strong vibrations of doom and destiny.

Going through the massive Lion Gate, traversing the king's impressive Cyclopaean walls, and looking down at an eagle's view of hundreds of square miles one could imagine the sense of power seeping through the warrior king.

The construction of his Treasury of Atreus impressed even our twentieth-century plastic and Concorde kids. We stood in the centre of the circular floor. But we could see that the basic building block of this circular structure was rectangular slabs of stone. Perfectly preserved, the building was as big as a church; but it was built in the shape of a beehive with the dome sculpted to come to a point at the top.

We departed still shaking heads in wonderment. We left it to the kids to walk the 999 steps to the top of Palamedi fort for its panoramic view.

Returning down the gulf, we made some short stops but soon everybody opted to spend more time in Hydra. After a few hours we were berthing near our old position on the sea wall. Our good friends Leah and Andreas were gone. Instead we came in alongside a German sailing yacht.

There was plenty of room. Our fenders hung down as profuse as sausages in a pork butcher's shop. But a rather aged gentleman aboard the sailing yacht watched our approach with grim face.

"You must be careful!" he shouted. We smiled and nodded like Greeks. Only we had good fenders at the ready. We understood his concern. We drew closer. As our stern came alongside his bows the girls handed him our ropes, with a smile and a, "Please".

He ignored their offer. "NO!" he shouted, "I look after my own boat first!"

The quay was deserted. With some wind, the anchor dropped, making no way and with nobody to take our stern lines we began to swing.

He hollered, "Watch what you are doing! Look out!"

I heard Jeremy say to him, very quietly, "If you want to look after your boat, the best way is to take our lines."

We had to start shoving his boat off. I pointed out to him the wisdom of Jeremy's remark but he still refused to take our lines.

"Back us up to the quay," I said to Nicholas now at the wheel. Jeremy this time remembered not to swim. At the right moment he jumped, and we were soon secured; miles from our irritable neighbour.

Rosemarie said, as we growled about it over tea, "It's the first time in two years anything like that's happened."

It was true. The uniqueness of this encounter made us appreciate the more how warm and friendly people invariably are in boats.

It was clearly not meant to be our lucky visit to Hydra. We started to rock. The wind began to whistle. "Not again," everybody groaned.

The sudden storm was even stronger than on our previous visit. We decided we needed more scope on the anchor. Nicholas remained on shore to take our lines for when we came in again.

We started out, the winch running. But as we hauled up it became clear the anchor had snagged some other chain. I went forward where Carolyn and Jeremy were preparing a rope to free the chain - Nicholas was the ship's usual specialist at this job. I said, "We'll hoist it all above water and then ... "

"Yes, yes! We know," Carolyn said testily. "There're two of us here already."

I returned to my subordinate's position on the wheel. We manoeuvred about taking a little more time than we should have, but eventually the obstruction was freed. We made ourselves another fifteen meters of scope and dropped anchor again. We reversed, and were soon berthed again with plenty of holding in the anchor against any storm.

To our surprise the normally phlegmatic Nicholas came tearing aboard, shouting at the top of his voice.

"What was going on out there?" he yelled. "I've never seen such an incompetent job! Why didn't you loop up the anchor instead of putting the whole rope around it ... " he ranted on and on, in detail.

Jeremy and Carolyn argued back, fairly half-heartedly, because Nicholas was ticking off very precisely the things he'd noticed done wrong.

I grinned and said, "I was actually ordered back into the wheelhouse, Guv'nor. I thought they did alright."

He shouted, "I was ashamed of the whole performance!"

I said, "Calm down, stop shouting." Rosemarie was smiling broadly.

"What's so funny?" I asked.

"He sounds just like you," she said.

The wind increased in force. The skies turned black and the wind howled as it is supposed to do only in the Arctic, not in the Aegean in summer. The ferries stopped running. Seas hurled themselves over the wall once again, and on over our stern and even our bows.

Anybody educated on travel brochure pictures of the Med in summer would have been very surprised. By the second day the surge in the harbour was substantial. Suddenly, we found ourselves pulled forwards, lifted up and then shoved back. We heard a metallic crunching noise aft.

We ran out, hearts in mouth. It wasn't the worst we'd feared - the stern being crunched on shore - but our aluminium gangway was now V-shaped.

The middle was a jagged mess of metal. Jeremy and I squatted with the mangled remains on the aft deck. Driving spray, and frequent bucketfuls of sea slopped over the wall on us. It was cold.

We scratched around in the lazarette and found some old angle irons.

"What do you think?" I asked Jeremy.

"Get me some self-tapping screws," he said, "and I'll have a go."

I hastened to the local chandlers for the screws. For most of two days Jeremy worked on the gangway with hammer, electric drill and screwdriver, sitting on the cold aft deck under constant assault from waves coming over the wall.

Wetness was not the only problem. Water over his electric drill could have given him a shock ranging from nasty to fatal. He had the skill and foresight to plug into a 110 volt battery rather than our 220 volt generator power.

The evening he finally repaired the gangway the three kids used it to escape the howling wind, in favour of the howling local disco.

The clatter of the gangway warned us of their arrival back on board in the early morning. We were sitting in the wheelhouse talking over a glass as Carolyn and Jeremy burst in.

Jeremy shook himself like a dog and said "Phew! We nearly got soaked through."

"We ran like mad," puffed Carolyn.

They'd had to walk the last twenty yards to the boat on the narrow quay under the threat of waves breaking over the sea-wall.

"Where's Nicholas?" Rosemarie asked.

"Oh, you know Nicholas," said Carolyn. "He wasn't going to run."

"My God," Rosemarie gasped, looking astern. "What - what's that?"

In the dank, greenish light a large sodden bundle of clothes could be seen shuffling on the gangplank. We began to make out a head swamped under rats-tails of hair, and large staring whites of eyes. A sodden T- shirt was pulled half off the shoulders. The legs of the Being seemed to be wrinkled and misshapen - until we realised that they were saturated trousers wrapped tightly around the skin.

The Being began moving towards us, arms out like a Frankenstein mummy.

As it arrived on deck, Nicholas' voice emerged in a monotone. "I was walking along and I got hit by two bloody great waves. I'd have been drier if I'd gone for a swim."

We all stared transfixed.

Suddenly Nicholas chortled. Then he began to laugh. We all began to laugh. Soon we were all propped up on the deck roaring with laughter until a head popped up from an adjacent boat to complain we were making more bloody noise than the bloody storm.

The black storm continued for four days. When we finally left in calm seas it was like being released from some madhouse where the inmates had been constantly shrieking and wailing all around us.

It was the warning. Winter was approaching. We set course back to Zea Marina, a winter berth, and exams.

I'd phoned Constantine, a friend we'd found in the capital, asking if he would check on the berth available to us. We gave our time of arrival.

His partner, John, met us, waving, at the entrance.

"You can go over there," he shouted pointing to an inside corner of the outer harbour. We wanted to be much further inside, where Zea becomes Passa Limani. We knew a swell could blow through the outer harbour. But this would do while we sorted things out.

We waved and thanked him. But as we moved on, one of the marina boats came to meet us.

"No room, no room," the men aboard shouted. "Go there!" They pointed.

"But they're pointing back to the entrance!" Rosemarie exclaimed.

"Where to?" I asked our water-borne shepherds.

They pointed in the same direction. I shouted at them we'd been assured we'd been given a berth. I hung around in the middle while they reluctantly returned to consult John.

Then the marina launch returned with a note from Constantine to say we'd have to go where they directed. We ended up double-banked alongside the quay right by the entrance. Every passing boat sent a wash rolling into our sides.

Before we'd left previously we'd been told our request had the "highest priority" because of the kids aboard. We were the only family, as far as we knew, living aboard.

"Bloody fine priority," Rosemarie commented as we rolled yet again.

Encouraged by this and grunts and scowls from the rest of the family, I went grunting and scowling round to the port office. The chief wasn't there but I saw one of his assistants. We learned to call him The Mouth. He always shouted.

"No room!" He shouted.

"We were told by the port captain we'd be given a berth," I said.

"No room! You must leave!" he shouted. He didn't know anything about "highest priority". I pointed through the windows to a dozen desirable and empty berthing slots. The logic didn't have much effect. So I took to shouting at a higher level of decibels. This had a better effect.

He said we might - temporarily only - tie up later that day alongside the fuel quay which was tucked into a corner. A sailing boat there would be leaving.

I returned with the relatively good news. In the afternoon I approached the sailing boat to ask the skipper what time they were leaving.

He looked at me cautiously, "Why?"

"We're told we can come here when you've left."

"Ah." He gave me some news. As far as he was concerned, he said, he was sitting there until he'd found a berth inside.

I said that sounded familiar.

"Why don't you tie up alongside us," he suggested.

That afternoon we slipped out into the middle of the stream. The launch sped towards us. "What are you doing? Get back! Get back!" the gesticulating crew shouted.

"We're going over there," I pointed to the fuel quay.

"No room! No room! Wait there!" They sped for the shore.

"Don't be silly, there's plenty of room, said Alice," I heard Nicholas growl over the rails.

"Don't put The Mad Hatter's tea party in this class," I replied despairingly. "He was sane.

We watched the launch speeding back towards us.

"Watch out, the Mouth's aboard," said Jeremy.

"Why have you left your berth?" his great foghorn voice echoed out at us.

I foghorned back, "Because you told us to!"

He thought about that for a few moments. Then he shouted "Who told you?"

"You did."

Another, longer pause, then, "Ah. Alright. But it's only temporary!"

As we tied alongside the sailing boat he came alongside again to remind us we could not stay.

"The funny thing is," Rosemarie told him, "If there was anywhere else to go we would be delighted."

This was the start of the battle of Zea. It was played with intensity and didn't conclude for two months. It was played to Mediterranean rules.

We discovered there were empty berths available. But if officials make a citizen's life too easy, their own position, and earning capacity from diverse sources, might be remarkably diminished. For us, there was no-where else to go. We knew the other marinas along the coast were full; and we had to be in Athens for critical exams.

Andreas and Lea, our friends from Hydra, turned up for lunch. The admiral gave me some advice, basi-cally, the rules of the game.

"In Greece, everything is seegar, seegar, - slowly, slowly. You stay here. Don't move. If anybody asks for the skipper, he's not around. It will be alright, you see." And then he grinned at me. "And don't complain that everybody shouts. It is not England. It doesn't mean anything. You may shout back - only do it louder!"

We had learned Andreas's story earlier. He had smuggled himself aboard an old fishing boat to get out of German-occupied Greece during the war. He'd joined the allied forces. The following boat-load of of-ficers were discovered, and all shot.

He had been ostracised during the regime of the Colonels, because he wouldn't toe their line. Any ad-vice from Andreas was good.

So we began playing 'seegar'. The marina staff would come alongside in the dinghy banging on our rails at eight in the morning shouting, "No room, No room! You must go!" There would come further verbal assaults from the quay.

In the interests of "seegar" I took to creeping off the boat at 07:45 and sitting peering at our decks from a cafe balustrade thirty yards away. I could see the girl's arm-waving to the assault parties. 'The skipper is un-avoidably absent,' shrug, shrug.

I was returning to the boat some few days after our latest entry when I saw a local motor yacht racing an English sailing boat into a nearby space on the quay.

An official, standing by our own boat, was waving his arms, rooting for the motor yacht. We were cheering for the red ensign. He won. As this scene ended the official screamed "JER - NI - CA!"

I descended from the ship's bicycle behind him and said "Yes?"

He turned "You! OUT! OUT! No place! You go out!" He was bawling at the top of his voice which, since he was two feet away, was a trifle deafening.

As only that morning we had grudgingly been given permission to plug in to shore power, this latest advice was too much. All my lofty decisions to take things calmly and seegar, seegar were blown away by an internal gale-force storm.

I shouted at the top of my lungs. "The port captain's given us permission to berth here and take electricity! Come on you! We'll go and see him!" I mounted my bicycle and glared.

He looked at me rather puzzled, then said, "I am the port captain." There was a longish silence.

I said, "That's good. I've been meaning to see you to get our electrics connected up."

He was in fact acting port captain for the off duty period of the main staff. It required more long arguments but we finally got our electrics too. The shouting match was forgotten, as shouting matches are in this part of the world.

Early next morning however we again heard the dreaded, "JER - NI - CA!"

"You go," said Rosemarie, not unreasonably as I hadn't escaped yet to my hideout. I went.

"You're in my place! You must go!" A man was shouting from the quay. After about ten minutes of verbal brawling I said finally, "The port captain put us here, you'll have to go and see him." He strode off glowing red. The family emerged from their fall-out shelters below.

"Now what?" said Rosemarie wearily.

"Our apoplectic friend has gone to the Capitainerie," I said. "I think we need reinforcements. I must go find that agent."

A friend on a sailing-boat had recommended him to solve local problems.

I found him. He smiled as he listened to our story

"In Greece," he said, "Everything is seegar, seegar. Do what everybody else does. Just don't move."

I returned to the family. They told me the port captain had come storming along with Apoplexy demanding to see me. Told I wasn't there, he didn't believe it, which wasn't unreasonable, albeit true this time.

"When the captain comes back tell him to go to the port police," he had commanded.

I made tracks back to our agent and repeated the command we had been given.

"Don't go. Seegar," he said.

"Of course," I said, "Seegar seegar. But rather than sit around waiting to be arrested, can you speak to someone?"

He picked up the phone. A long shouting match got under way as soon as "Jernica" was mentioned. Twenty minutes later there was calm and laughter over the earpiece.

Shouting in Greece as in any part of the Mediterranean we'd visited is a question of style, not anger. He put the phone down. "You can stay where you are. It'll be sorted out tomorrow."

"Cigar, cigar," I said.

He chuckled. "This is Greece. Don't worry. Just keep out of the way."

I returned carefully to my balustrade eyrie. I was just in time. Apoplexy appeared again, shouting. I could see Rosemarie on deck engaged in evasive manoeuvres. The performance required much arm-waving - and was repeated several times over the next hour or so as I sat skulking.

I crept back later, feeling the more like a criminal as I kept my eyes skinned for signs of Authority.

A visitor was on board, a middle-aged lady who'd got chatting as she'd passed by. Rosemarie had invited her on board. She was living on another boat in the harbour with her English husband. We told her our story.

"Oh yes," the lady said. "They come banging on our rails every morning shouting we must leave."

"What do you do?"

"I just tell my husband to stay in the loo, and I tell them he's not on board." She laughed. "They don't believe me of course."

Nicholas said wonderingly, "A whole marina filled with skippers loitering in the loos!"

"What they want," said our lady guest, "Is for you to say 'Eff it. No more of this. I'm going,' then they've won."

"Cigar, cigar," I said.

"That's it, exactly," she said with a big smile. "Cigar, cigar, to win!"

I was off the boat at eight next morning. Only just in time. The launch arrived just as I seated myself at my observation post. I could hear only odd cries and shouts but could see much waving of arms.

Rosemarie pieced it all together for me later. First," she told me, "Jeremy shouted, 'the warders are coming'". We agreed this was either a justifiable Freudian slip or a moment of inspirational invention. They banged on the handrail and did the "JER-NI-CA!" bit, and bawled. "You must move! You must move!"

Rosemarie continued, "I told them you weren't here. They shouted some more and then left." She went on, "Then the Mouth appeared. Carolyn was on deck." The scene then went like this:

Mouth: "You've got to move. Immediately!"

Carolyn: "My father's not here." She added firmly, "Nor is Nicholas." (He'd been recognised by now as Male No. 2 on board, and therefore the Responsible who could move the boat in the absence of The Captain. He'd been sent to view bookshops in Athens.)

The Mouth took a step forward. "Then I'll come on board and move you!"

Carolyn put up a hand. "Don't put a single foot aboard! If you want anything go and see our agents."

She told us, "My hands were shaking while I was talking to him."

I thought it was time this stopped, seegar or no seegars. I went to see the agent. I said, "I know the rules by now. If we do move from the corner, we'll never find another space. We'll be out. But we want a berth. Time to settle this once and for all."

He laughed as ever, picked up the phone and had another long shouted conversation. He obtained a promise for us. If we moved out of the corner, we wouldn't be chased on and out.

With this promise we all got busy with the lines and hauled forward. Apoplexy slipped his yacht behind us at which his face acquired a natural complexion and he beamed at us. It was the day the hassling stopped. We weren't yet accepted as permanent residents, but they knew we wouldn't leave.

The Mouth and his heavies now began to emerge as human beings. We learned how boats arriving after us had managed to find snug berths inside. Some three hundred and fifty unauthorised boats had entered.

Of course, they were the winners. It was all Mediterraneanly simple. No application. No request for priority. No rules. Above all no getting on somebody's list as, 'Requiring Permission'. Anonymity is the game. Obeying the rules is another peculiarity of those who go out in the mid-day sun.

The carefree ones slipped in after dark, when the staff weren't on duty. Friends waiting on the quay took their lines. And there the vessels stayed, the crews or owners departing immediately for Paris, St. Moritz or wherever for the winter. Fait-accompli. Nobody to listen to thumps on the hull, or shouts.

We'd done it all wrong: a) officially, b) with advanced notification, c) by the light of day. We had gone and upset the whole system.

The day came when we were allotted a berth. It was on the outer wall alongside one of the hydrofoils. Heavy south winds would bring the seas and flotsam over the wall, high though it was. They also created an uncomfortable swell.

The hydrofoils coming and going about their business set up their own seas. We looked longingly at the masses of empty boats packed inside the still, safe harbour of Passa Limani. But we had a berth.

One morning at seven o'clock we were all awoken by a resounding crash on the hull. Five of us appeared simultaneously on deck in pyjamas and dressing gowns like pantomime devils shot up through the trap door. We wore the same kind of expressions.

One of the hydrofoils stood off us. Its crew were looking back. The foil had wrecked a small work-raft which we had tied onto our pulpit. The pulpit was distorted.

I climbed over our sides. There was no other damage. I sounded our horn. I wasn't exactly surprised the skipper didn't stop since he had passengers on board. But I expected he would call on his return. There wasn't too much damage.

He didn't come. I finally found him on the quay. I reminded him what had happened and asked why he hadn't come to see me. He looked at me as though I had said something very strange.

"It was all your fault," he said.

I said, "Eh? We were all asleep."

"If you were at sea, and there was a collision you would still be responsible - didn't you know that?" he demanded.

"Well, yes," I said looking round for the Mad Hatter and the Queen of Hearts again, "but we were not exactly at sea; we were berthed, in port. We go to sleep at night in port and don't keep a watch. We make something of a habit of going to sleep at night."

"It was your fault."

The conversation was repeated on both sides for some time before I bade him good-day.

Nicholas amended our Rule 272 to read "Keep out of the way of local ferries, under any conditions especially when you are berthed, sleeping, in port ... ."

Later that day Carolyn was working on the patched-up raft, filling in and painting spots on the hull. The same 'foil came into its adjacent berth at high speed. She was terrified. She thought it would hit her. He missed by a yard but if she hadn't leaped back on board she would have been flung into the water by the turbulence.

I was of the conviction that a further conversation with this particular 'foil's skipper might be entertaining but would be unlikely to be constructive.

I went to the Port Authority. I informed them of our problems and that I would be moving inside, hopefully with their blessing, but moving inside.

The next morning we moved off into the inner harbour of Passa Limani. We found an empty berth and moved in.

When we were secure and engines off Rosemarie sighed. "At last, we can relax." She gathered up her shopping bags and bicycled off cheerfully towards the local shops.

Shortly after she'd gone Nicholas shouted, "Look out!" The port guardians were hailing us from their launch. We scrambled to guard our lines. But their tone was friendly.

"You can stay - but we show you the berth," they called.

After some hesitation we decided they meant it. We let out our lines started engines, and they guided us to a berth on a different quay.

They waved and grinned like old friends as they departed. We waved back. The shouting war was over.

As we settled down again with the weight off our backs Carolyn said, "Hey! What about Mum!"

"Oh my God," I replied, already halfway down the gangplank. I made all speed round the port.

From a distance by our vacated berth I could see a forlorn figure slumped cross-legged on the ground. It was surrounded by a litter of shopping bags. A bicycle lay dumped across some of the bags.

As I approached, Rosemarie, for it was she, was gazing listlessly into the empty space where she had last seen her home.

I came up behind and touched her shoulder. As she saw me her face lit up with relief, and enquiry.

I explained what had happened.

Rosemarie slowly picked herself up. "When I left I thought everything was O.K. I just couldn't register, when the boat wasn't there. I couldn't imagine what could have happened. It was all a bit much."

She received a large hug and kiss there and then, and two very large whiskies on our return to Jernica restored our sanity and new relaxed mood.

Our great relief at being settled, the first day in the new berth, was substantially diminished by somebody who stole our collapsible bicycle.

It's been a smashing week," said Nicholas, remembering adventures with gangplanks as well as bicycles.

But we knew there was a totally different Greece outside Zea. We'd seen it in the old man leading me by the hand in Gaios, our friends on 'Ionion', and countless small kindnesses in shops and when needing any kind of assistance. A smile is good currency in Greece and will always be returned.

One experience we had in Kithnos was quite typical. We'd made a dash for this island, south-east of Athens to see one of the Cyclades before wintering. We found ourselves held up in St. Stefanou, a bay on the east coast by a heavy 'Melteme'- the summer gale that whistles through the Aegean and heaps up one of the world's most dangerous short seas.

We anchored alone in a wide bay with a sandy beach surrounded by steep slopes of loose rock.

We thought it would be nice to find some fresh local food. Carolyn and I decided we'd visit the head village of Kithnos. It was only five kilometres away as the crow flies, but we soon discovered we weren't crows.

The old fishermen on the shore from whom we'd asked the way looked at us as though we were crazy. He indicated we didn't want to go to Kithnos and tried to send us to a different village. After a short discussion leaving him shrugging, we set off for Kithnos.

There were no roads. Only uneven tracks. The path we started along was evidently a dried-up river bed. We laboured over loose stones and rock in the late morning heat. Then the path began to climb steeply. We scrambled upwards cautiously.

By the time we realised what we were in for it was too late to turn back. It wasn't Everest, but every time we thought we were at the top, we rounded a bend to find another steep slope ahead.

"The ancient Greeks knew how to discourage marauding Turks," I wheezed breathlessly.

"All we want is bread and tomatoes," Carolyn panted.

We followed the trail up two mountains and crossed a few hills until finally and gratefully we arrived exhausted at the village.

The few narrow whitewashed streets, and the houses, were beautifully clean, like every village we saw in Greece. The few people about looked at us curiously, but ready to return our smile and greeting. We found a shop selling bread, but none with tomatoes.

Carolyn was starving. I bought some chocolate from a shop. Carolyn took one bite, cried "Ugghh!" spat out, then handed the bar to me. "Try!"

I could hardly get my teeth into the dry, chewy plastic. It seemed suppliers didn't come up this mountain top very frequently.

We considered our return. We couldn't face another mountain scramble. But there would be only one kind of taxi - a donkey. We began to search the village. We cornered a postman.

His English and our Greek were at the same level of incomprehension.

But Carolyn wasn't her mother's daughter for nothing. She made big ears with her hands and began galloping around the street crying, "Hee-Haw, Hee-Haw!"

The postman looked on in amazement, and then suddenly began galloping around the street nodding his head, uttering "Hee-Haws" and beckoning us to follow.

To our surprise he led us to the local priest. We weren't completely sure it was the priest, at first. True, he was in flowing cassock. And he was outside his church. But he was busy working on the half-finished hull of a thirty-foot fishing boat.

We'd seen caiques built in all kinds of places. In Zante we'd seen an old man building a sixty-footer in a walled yard half a mile from the shore. He'd been delighted to show us his skills, and we were fascinated to watch. He knew no English except "Rolls-Royce. Goodie goodie," which he kept repeating.

Finally by sign language we asked how he would get the boat out. In the same manner he demonstrated that he would simply knock the adjacent building down.

How this Kithnos priest would get his caique down the mountainside to the shore far below strained our imaginations. But he was a man of faith. We had a more immediate concern - how to get ourselves back down.

The postman explained our needs with much pointing at Carolyn and flapping hands to ears and "Hee-Haws".

There was a muttered conversation between the priest and another man helping him. This assistant then followed the by-now approved routine. He smiled at Carolyn, put hands to ears, "Hee-Hawed" and pointed to himself.

We talked drachmas, an international language when assisted by ten fingers.

When we agreed a price Carolyn exclaimed, "Wow! That's more than a London taxi!"

"A London cabbie," I pointed out, "doesn't have to negotiate dried-up river beds up one-in-two mountains."

We all then set off at a remarkably fast trot which we recognised later as donkey's pace. We knew when we had arrived at our donkey friend's home as we could see our steed tethered nearby. But the family was about to have lunch.

We were ushered into chairs placed outside the door of their small house by his smiling wife. Some shy dark-haired children peeped out at the strangers from the doorway, but were shooed back inside.

We settled down to wait for them to finish their meal.

To our surprise his wife reappeared and offered us some delicious home-made chocolate cake. We'd no sooner finished that than she returned with a plate of beans in a tomato-oil sauce.

We tried to make it clear that we didn't want to muscle-in on their lunch arrangements. But as I pointed at my mouth and stomach and started to shake my head Carolyn commented, "They might think you're saying you don't like what they're offering!"

That was a fair point. Worse, it became clear they weren't prepared to eat until we two total strangers had been served. We were embarrassed eating their meal. But as Carolyn scraped up her plateful she muttered, "This is better than we've had in any taverna!" and we smiled and nodded our heads at our hosts in genuine appreciation.

Then it was the husband's turn. He thrust a full glass of wine in my hand over my protests - I didn't want to fall off the donkey's back. But his wife wasn't finished yet. She returned with clean plates containing fried eggs and meat. It too was delicious.

Carolyn groaned. It was ruining her slimming regime. But we were clearly not expected to refuse.

Only when they were satisfied we'd had enough, and we'd mimed enough to make it clear we'd enjoyed it, did they and their children settle down to eat in their turn.

Our mumbled thanks seemed of poor quality in comparison to their generosity.

We finally bade the family farewell, and set off on the donkey. There was only one saddle, as usual on a donkey, so we had to take turns. I magnanimously let Carolyn go first.

Immediately I discovered my mistake. A donkey's pace is very deceptive. From afar, it seems to amble. I found I had to run to keep up. After not many minutes, puffing, and all thoughts of chivalry gone, I summoned the younger generation down to ground level, and climbed aboard the beast.

By now I'd developed good sea-legs, but sitting in the saddle as it swayed precipitately from side to side with the donkey's gait, had me hanging on for dear life.

Carolyn saved a moment's breath to giggle as she saw me clutching at saddle and donkey hair, having just got off the same conveyance. "Yes! We thought a rolling sea was bad!"

We left the streets of the village and began first to ascend the surrounding hills. Carolyn had to run to keep up. With a grin the driver, trotting alongside with practiced stride, handed her the donkey's tail. The certainty of an available hand-grab support is one advantage donkeys have over Tube travel.

I could now console myself Carolyn was now hitching a ride, of a kind. But conscience kicked in, and on the easy slopes I let Carolyn take over the seat for a spell.

We arrived at the highest point in the route. Now we had to go down. From above, the slopes we'd climbed earlier looked an endless vista of shingle and crumbling stone steps; and quite vertical.

Hurriedly, as she swayed and lurched forward above this daunting vista, Carolyn offered me the hot seat. As we started down, I hoped the donkey knew what it was doing. I tried not to look, and not to will it where to put its feet, but failed.

The view of the distant sea was magnificent, but from my perch, terrifying. The situation was not helped by the minder shouting "Sh-sh-sh-oooohh - aahhh!" in a loud shriek, and whacking the donkey on the legs with his stick to make it descend faster, when I wanted desperately to slow it down.

We were descending in a zigzag. At each turn there was a low wall with a sheer drop below. Once the animal didn't turn soon enough. It scrambled to a juddering halt, forelegs stiff, over a sheer precipice. Slowly, very slowly, so that I could appreciate every long moment, I toppled forward over its neck and began to hang further into the abyss.

Just as I thought of doing a bit of shrieking myself, there came an "Oooohh - aaahhh!" shriek, a thwack and a tug from our guide. The donkey swayed slowly sideways, like a badly-designed boat rolling and then I found myself back in the saddle, safe; until the next turn.

We arrived back at the boat exhausted, with a totally new respect for the ability of donkeys, an expensive loaf of bread and a vivid memory of Greek hospitality.

We remembered these kindnesses as well as our more recent experiences as we settled down the first evening in our new berth in Zea. The kids set to their schoolbooks. But there was more than book education to come.

Jeremy took on a new identity - "the Mikro" - the little one. The Mikro first made himself known around the port when the port electrician plugged our electrics into the shoreline.

Our fifteen-year old stood watching, returned to his engine room, and then back to the electrician on shore.

"You haven't got the polarity right," said Jeremy.

The electrician looked up, noticed the young lad for the first time shrugged, and went to close his manhole. "Makes no difference," he smiled, "is good."

"It's not right."

"Is good."

"Come please." Jeremy beckoned and with a smile and a shrug the electrician marched off with us to board Jernica and descend into Jeremy's engine room.

He checked a dial of some electrical kind or other and showed it to the electrical wizard.

Jeremy got the polarity changed, even at the expense of the electrician's smile disappearing.

The same friendly and understandably condescending smile and pat on the head greeted our announcement to Kostas, the permanent engineer on the neighbouring boat, that little Jeremy was our engineer.

However Jeremy had been unknowingly advertising some of his skills. When he wasn't in the engine-room he was on the quay or aft-deck working on items which were a mystery to me - but not, it turned out, to observant neighbours. He would sometimes have friendly eyes standing over him, watching with interest.

One day Kostas stood at the end of the gangplank and hailed us. It was the first time I'd noticed that people when embarrassed actually do shuffle from one foot to the other.

"Is the Mikro on board?" he enquired diffidently.

The little one appeared and after a short few words disappeared with Kostas to fix an engine-room problem on his boat.

Later, quite unknown Greeks would appear in regulation uniform of dirty vest and shorts asking for the Mikro. Jeremy would disappear round the quay with them. He usually reappeared covered in black, and grinning in delight at having discovered more engine-room mysteries. We felt it was some repayment for the work that Ionion John and his friends had performed for us.

As winter drew in, we looked forward to the occasional Greek lunch ashore. We enjoyed the traditional lamb, stewed, kebab'd and garlanded in various ways.

In Piraeus we discovered that many restaurants cooked only for lunch. Evening dishes were the midday ones warmed up. We learned to enjoy it.

On our first arrival, we couldn't comprehend why everyone seemed to be saying "Taxi". The polite Greeks were saying thank you, "Endaksi".

We spent little time in the capital. The traffic jams were endless and noisy. On our first arriving in the port we had found we were out of practice in crossing these teeming roads, and closely resembled myopic ninety-year olds when we had to do so. Although we weren't myopic we nearly ended up deafened, as Athenians drive on the brake, accelerator and horn, in reverse order.

Half-built concrete buildings seemed to abound. We discovered it was because the top half could then be built without tax penalties, if the family grew.

Of course, visiting the Acropolis was top of our list. The approach was through disappointingly seedy roads. At the ancient site itself we were impressed most by the streets which had been excavated at the foot of the famous hill.

The work had been done by Americans. We weren't surprised. There was no evidence of local care for the cradle of democracy. Every day a thin layer of white dust settled on Jernica and its neighbours. They came from cement factories.

Our Greek friends told us there had long been a battle to stop this pollution. It had failed.

The boats could be washed daily. The Acropolis was falling to pieces. One solution offered was to replace the stone with plastic copies.

Shopping around the port, I learned the fingers-to-forehead sign language. I had decided to treat myself to a packet of some small cigars I'd discovered. I went to a nearby kiosk to ask for them.

The vendor, beaming, put his knuckles to his forehead, fingers spread like wings on either side, and flapped them up and down meanwhile raising head and eyes to the sky several times and nodding vigorously.

I smiled, held out my money.

The flapping and nodding got more vigorous. I nodded vigorously and smiled just as much in return and held my money our straighter.

Finally he bawled, "Occhi!"

I wasn't convinced yet. I walked to the next kiosk - I must have asked a little more insistently. The fingers, in the same gesture, wagged more decisively; the head and eyes wagged up and down more violently.

I had after all, lived a long time in England, where a nod is a nod is a "Yes".

I stretched out my arm with the money.

The smile became agitated, the hands waving enough for take-off.

I really wanted those cigars. I walked from kiosk to kiosk from Zea marina to the commercial port of Piraeus. I returned without cigars but with a clear understanding that when a Greek nods vigorously and waggles his knuckles against his forehead, walk away.

We adults learned other things. We were invited onto a neighbouring boat by the skipper. Carolyn had drawn our attention to him earlier.

"Come and look," she had hissed in scandalised tones one mid-winter's day. He was in the middle of maintenance. We went to the side of the wheelhouse and peered.

"Look!" The skipper was calmly slapping white paint over huge patches of rust on his mast. "Not a scraper or sander in sight!" said our expert, who had a few muscles to prove she knew what should come before paint.

But the skipper was a cheery, smiling chap. One day he invited Rosemarie and me on board for drinks. We were flattered. Hospitality offered in the Mediterranean, we had found, was generous and given with an open-heart. But the easiness with which Anglo-Saxons will invite acquaintances into their home - or aboard their yacht - is not shared.

"You like it here in Greece?" He was wreathed in smiles.

"We like very much," we said, dropping automatically into talking-to-natives argot.

We were sitting, at his invitation, three alongside on the cover of a rope box on his forward deck. We were heading towards spring with a bright, warm day - a release from the biting winds of winter which arrived from Siberia.

We were all in shorts.

Several bottles of Ouzo were set out on the deck. From past experience as we'd come aboard I'd said to Rosemarie, "You'd better be ready to run."

She replied, with good reason, "If I do, I won't need your advice."

Sure enough his hands started flying about as we drank, talked, and laughed together. His hands flew down on my thigh and then off again.

We all drank a lot more, and found lots more to laugh about. His hands came down again on my thigh, and stayed there. I gently shoved at them. They stayed locked firm. I pushed much harder. Instead of moving off, they tried to move closer into my crotch.

I couldn't quite believe it. But his grip was firm. Short of giving him a violent and un-neighbourly shove I could scarcely move. I sat paralysed. It's not my thing.

Rosemarie suddenly jumped up, looked at her watch, and exclaimed, "The time! My goodness - the, er, the children! We must go!" We had hardly just arrived.

She heaved me up, and shouting our "Efferistos - thank you," we made our escape.

So much for Rosemarie needing my advice.

My white knight said, "Didn't want to lose you. I thought you were going to choke to death on that drink!"

We recounted the episode to our Greek friend Constantine when he came to dinner that evening.

He looked quite serious.

"Tell me did he, er .." he floundered about for a moment for words, then, "did he touch your, your Mister importants?"

"Oh no, thanks to Rosemarie's experience of making quick exits," I smiled.

At that he started laughing. "That's alright then!" Constantine raised his wine glass. "Then all is well that ends well!"

In the winter, the kids went off to the British Council's premises in Athens for their English exams. A little later we heard they'd all passed. We were delighted for them all. We thought Carolyn had done especially well.

One day she had visited the Council for some pre-exam papers. She found the correspondence school had been teaching her the wrong syllabus for

Geography. There were only a few weeks before the exams. The school couldn't provide the needed papers.

Carolyn spent weeks in the Council library finding and reading the new books she needed. She passed.

"Two years," said Rosemarie, after they'd taken their exams. "The kids have grown up so much."

I nodded. "Do you remember coming back from Nauplion? When we had to take off from Oy-yoy-bay? That's when it came home to me."

It was our second visit to our favourite anchorage in Spetsai. In calm water, we'd dropped anchor plumb in the middle. This was much to the relief of the family who pointed out that I wouldn't need to disturb them creeping about in the early hours looking for things that go bump. Over in one corner of the bay some rubber ducks were at anchor.

"Nothing is going to happen here, with us smack in the middle," said Carolyn planting a kiss on her skipper's cheek, his occasional perk when he did the right thing.

We gave Rosemarie a night off and dined at the taverna on the beach. The moon was showing; but it began to flicker on and off like a lamp with a loose connection as low clouds thickened. At our taverna table we could see Jernica's anchor light beginning a little dance.

Some rubber duck crews arrived and began a heavy session of celebrations at a nearby table.

At about eleven o'clock we bid them farewell and dinghy'd back under a dark sky and stiff breeze to Jernica. As though waiting for this moment, a violent gust of wind roared over our heads. Within minutes it was a regular gale. The sky became a black whirlpool.

'Jernica' and the small sailing boats began heaving and pivoting to the swirling shafts of wind. A swell was beginning to surge in.

We trained a spotlight aft. We were no longer centre bay. Our anchor chain was stretched to its full scope. We gazed aghast at rocks now no more than a few yards from our stern.

"The kedge anchor," I shouted. We'd never used it before. Jeremy and I leaped into the lurching dinghy with the wind shrieking about our ears, man-handling the big fisherman's anchor we used as a kedge. We motored away and heaved it over while Nicholas tightened the warp on the winch.

Carolyn had meanwhile focused on one of the small sailing boats. "Quick," she shouted as we arrived back on board. "Shine our searchlight over there!"

We switched on the powerful beam and swiveled it round. One of the small rubber-ducks was practically on the beach. Others were performing a mad dance, skidding over the boiling waters.

We could see, with horror, the crews still carousing in the taverna. We sounded our horn and shone our light in their direction. We saw figures waving back at us and leaping up and down like monkeys.

"Oh God, pissed," said Rosemarie aghast. Not that it was unreasonable. Just untimely.

We persisted. We transferred the searchlight beam on to their scattered sailing boats, moved it about, and pounded the horn. Their antics slowed down, and suddenly changed to movements of a very sober variety.

We saw their dark shapes racing to the water's edge and splashing into their dinghies. They were just about in time to prevent total disaster. We continued using the light to help them fish for their worst placed yachts and dinghies and then studied our own position, the wind meanwhile moaning and shoving us around. We gathered on the prancing aft deck to watch the rocks.

"If we stay here," I said, "We'll need to keep a night watch."

"Even so," Nicholas pointed out, "If the anchor does drag we'll have no time to start the engines."

"But the anchor looks pretty solid, we're not budging," Rosemarie pointed out.

"That's fine while it lasts," I said.

"The wind came up suddenly. Maybe it will stop the same way?" Jeremy ventured hopefully over the yowling outside.

We were all focused on our taut and twitching anchor cable.

I studied the chart again. The mainland harbour of Portoo

Cheli was several miles away. It looked as though it should be well sheltered from this gale. We discussed upping anchor and going there.

"Let's go!" said Carolyn "What's the point of sitting up all night and worrying? Let's get out and into a sheltered harbour."

We would have to cross the Spetsai channel which ran open to the north-west. It would be funneling the violence of the wind.

"There will be a very nasty sea out there, and it's pitch black," I said.

The kids shrugged.

"Let's go, and fast," someone said.

"OK, let's do it." I quickly studied the chart to look at the lights marking the entrance to the longish tide-way leading into Porto Cheli.

Everybody set to. Carolyn jumped into the dinghy leaping about on our stern. With the swell bullying her about she secured it to the davit wires and winched it out of the water. Then she got busy with the lines to ensure that the dinghy wouldn't swing, however heavy the lurching seas. After our early frights to Corsica she was our acknowledged expert at this job.

The motors started, Jeremy went forward to help Nicholas on the winch to weigh both anchors.

At the helm I needed to keep an eye on the leeward rocks; and also keep out of the way of the sailing boats skittering about and re-dropping anchors. None were showing lights.

The anchors were stowed, we all braced, and I went ahead and steered out into the channel. The wind caught us square and in moments was hurling heavy seas onto our port beam, hissing up the hull and over the decks. We rolled sharply and did our flying fish bit. The windscreen wipers barely coped with the thick spray. (Rosemarie, I learned later, was at this moment laying spread-eagled over our stores in the hold).

If I headed directly for Porto Cheli on this course the beam seas would continue mauling us around. Old story. New ending - I pulled Jernica round to port to put the seas on our shoulder.

Jeremy took the wheel as I went to the chart table.

"Just keep her coming round until we're comfortable," I said.

"I know," he replied.

Nicholas had beaten me to the chart table. As I started running my finger over it he said, "It's O.K. I've sorted out the entrance to Cheli." As Jernica's movement through the water became easier, he called out to Jeremy, "What's our course now?"

Jeremy told him and our speed.

We both spent a moment with the chart and glanced at the ship's chronometer. Nick jabbed his finger at the chart, marking Cheli's entrance.

I said, "Hold this course, till I say." Nick nodded.

Some time later I gave Jeremy the new course. We turned with a following sea, our progress remaining comfortable. The black night and wild seas were lit by sliver flashes of moonlight through scudding clouds. Carolyn was peering ahead with the binoculars. She shouted, "There!" and pointed. A red light marking the entrance to the channel became visible ahead.

As we approached, the clouds parted to illuminate tumbling silver seas breaking over little islets and rocks on either side of the entrance.

I sped out on deck the better to see. The red light passed us close on the portside. I returned to the wheelhouse and lifted my arm, pointing left. "To port," I commanded from my memory of the chart. I did so with a little trepidation. It seemed to me some of the tumbling silver seas were in that direction, suggesting shallows or even rocks.

We didn't go to port but continued straight on. I must have looked confused but before I could speak again Nicholas bawled, "No! Straight on!" Then as I must have seemed even more confused, Jeremy and Nick both shouted together, "Look!" They were pointing at the radar screen. We were going plumb down the middle of the entrance channel. There, dead ahead, and certainly not to the nasty-looking left, was the clear outline of a harbour.

"Ah,yes," was my only comment, as I tried to find ways to make myself invisible. And so the kids saved the great skipper, and our beloved Jernica, from a frightful cock-up.

Inside the sheltered harbour there was again the feeling of unnatural silence and stillness after a passage through a storm. We approached deserted quays and Nicholas manoeuvred Jernica stern-to. Jeremy dropped the anchor and Carolyn nimbly dealt with the lines to secure us to the quay.

Rosemarie, freed from the hold, was making snacks and drinks.

I also made myself useful. I got out the whisky bottle.

The engines were soon silent and in the well protected harbour the violent wind was no more than a far-off whisper. The waters were still. We adults applied ourselves to the whisky. The kids were sitting around chatting and laughing.

Rosemarie looked at me and said, "We seem to be a bit superfluous."

I said, "Superfluous? Rubbish! Listen, I pour the best drinks on this boat."

We were in Greece. We were in a world of beautiful summer light and hospitable people.

We had more journeying to do. And one day we knew we must return to a more conventional life.

We wondered what further adventures and growing-up processes might lie in store for all of us.

But at that moment we knew we'd discovered more than new places and new friends since leaving everything for Jernica.

We'd begun to discover ourselves.

THE END

EPILOGUE – SOME YEARS LATER

Our adventure described in 'Family Aweigh' took place at a time when there was no GPS, no smartphones, no Internet, and satellite-accuracy weather forecasting was rare. We relied on Admiralty charts, dead-reckoning, and, for sea states, listening to local radio weather forecasts, never very trustworthy, aided maybe by a finger in the air to the wind. It was 1976.

The book also finished before the end of our voyage. And I know that there will be curious readers asking, 'What happened next?' in regard to the voyage; and also how did the crew – your kids - fare from the experience?

This is clear from those many readers who have taken the time and effort to praise the book on the 'Family Aweigh' Amazon page. Some have said it is among their favourite travel books. Two have chosen to turn their thumbs down at it, one describing how terrible it must have been for the children cooped up for a few years on a boat. The children, I can assure you, would disagree. But there could be legitimate questions about the outcome of their unconventional education.

And so now I supply some answers.

With apologies, the sea journey descriptions are not overlong as they are written from a failing memory, and a few remaining notes I retain rather than the meticulous logs and diaries I had kept, from which I was able to record 'Family Aweigh'.

The idyllic, boat-free tree-lined bays I described in the Mediterranean are today often filled with buildings and their once empty anchorages overfull with craft of every description. I know that because a couple of our favourite anchorages have been found by Jeremy on recent Med sailing holidays in the Ionians with his wife Jill. (He now loves sailing on the wind and recognised the bays because he now holds most of my logs and diaries; as well as a picture frame containing a photo of 'Jernica' complete with the boat's metal name-plate and date of launching by its Dutch builders). Even two shapely girls standing at the bow could not conjure up spaces today in most of the marinas.

The book ends with 'Jernica' moored in Piraeus. As spring arrived, we continued our cruising midst the many islands in the Aegean, where seas could be calm, and then round the other side of the island, blowing a gale. We travelled down to Rhodes where we found the son et lumiere of the castle standing directly behind the marina exceptionally and movingly well-performed.

From there we travelled down to southern Turkey, to discover and linger in even more empty heavily-wooded pastoral bays. We also enjoyed enormous lobsters exchanged over the boats' sides with fishing boats for cigarettes (which otherwise, Rosemarie alone smoked).

I explained how we dealt with the kids' education on the boat. Carolyn and Jeremy passed their 'O' level exams, and Nick his 'O' and 'A' level exams, to all our delight, sitting for them at the British Council in Piraeus. With exams passed, it was becoming time for the cruising to end so the kids might go off to higher education. We planned our journey back to the Côte d'Azur, where our adventure had begun.

But first we began the inevitable, and for us sad, experience of beginning to lose our crew, now developing into adulthood. Nicholas left to stay with friends we had made in Malta so that he could study for his next two 'A' levels. After he had departed the boat didn't feel quite the same, but the crew soon learned to cope with one hand fewer.exam

From the Turkish coast we decided to head back to Corfu, where we would make for Italy, then up the Italian west coast back to our start point, the Côte d'Azur. The most direct Italian port from Corfu was Crotone, just east of the southern Italian heel. The journey would be some 170 nautical miles so on a calm sea at our ten knots cruising it would take us about seventeen hours.

I waited until the local radio weather forecast was good enough, promising reasonable seas. We seldom found the local weather forecasts reliable. But it was all we had.

It all started serenely. But we were travelling west south-westerly. Albania sits immediately north of Corfu and we were travelling across the gap a little further to the north where that country sits close to the east coast of Italy. A likely wind-valley.

Night had fallen, and after a time 'Jernica' began to prove restless. And then I was recording, 'A Force 8-plus something, whipping up high, steep vicious seas.' The worst we had ever experienced. We were soon riding like a rodeo horse trying to hold our course. No way we could ride it by changing course. For a time the kids took turns at the wheel – it is easier to avoid seasickness by looking out towards the horizon, and concentrating on something. At those times I lay prone on the wheelhouse settee with my watch taking over as my navigation instrument. I have the note I wrote after our journey ended. "Lying horizontal I had sudden downward views of huge white foam-frothed valleys. They would tilt out of sight as we mounted, before reappearing in a raging fury of white-whipped waters."

Then, Carolyn, sturdy at the wheel, called out breathlessly, "Look!" A massive vertical wall of water was ahead, rearing ever higher. We held our breath, powerless, as we put Jernica's shoulder towards the rising mountain fast approaching. We rose and rose, and I believe we were all somewhat fearful. I know I was. Then suddenly we found we were on the other side, descending the slope. That was our 'Jernica', the most wonderful sea-boat.

It was much calmer seas and bright moonlight though which saved us as we finally came towards the entrance to Crotone. Our first sight of it from afar was of flames bursting skywards. We didn't know as we approached that it was an oil port, the fires coming from an oil refinery.

I took up the binoculars to look ahead to the entrance. Through them, suddenly, dead-ahead I saw a broad low menacing black shape lying above the sparkling moonlit water. Nothing had shown up on our radar, and no rocks or obstacles were marked on the chart. I shouted 'slow engines' as I raced forward out of the wheelhouse. Then I ran back and pulled at the wheel to turn 'Jernica' off her course. We just managed to glide round a huge iron mooring platform, carrying no lights, which we learned later was for oil tankers waiting to enter the port. I still sometimes shake my head to think what might have happened but for the grace of bright moonlight and calm seas at that moment.

The port itself was large and virtually empty and we had no problem in finding a mooring alongside one of the long quays where we spent a peaceful night after the usual 'thank you' whiskies, and cups of tea, according to seniority of age.

We then headed south-westerly down the Italian heel, and although that took us across the bay of Squillace (notorious historically, for gales and shipwrecks) we had no further sea alarums. Then we turned north for the narrow Straits of Messina between Sicily and Italy. Only about three kilometers wide, creating strong tidal currents, it is also known to have a whirl-pool somewhere about. It was certainly feared in ancient times when ships were reputed to be easily lost in the area.

This gave rise to the Greek legends of two sea monsters, one named Scylla on one side of the Straits, and if you steered to miss it, hard luck, Charybdis was waiting to get you on the other. We kept an eye open, not so much for monsters, as for troubled waters, but passed serenely through to the Tyrrhenian Sea of Italy's lower west coast.

As we then travelled up the Italian coast my most vivid memory is of putting into Salerno, just south of Naples. I remembered that during WW2 (when I was a boy in London, glued to the news bulletins, listening both for news, and in the evenings for those moments when the radio would warn of the approach of German bombers by suddenly fading and crackling. The normal radio signal could have been used as guidance by the planes.) Salerno was the site of a bitterly contested sea invasion by the allied armies driving north up Italy. As we had our first view of the port my first thought was, "Blimey". Tall hills rose steeply behind the port and must have given the Germans a really good oversight of the incoming boats filled with troops and equipment. No wonder the invading soldiers and seamen experienced such a torrid time.

But we were entering the port under clear Mediterranean skies on untroubled seas. We looked forwards to relaxing for a while on land. Then, from literally out of the blue, we experienced our own big

Salerno battle, and one of the biggest surprises of our whole trip. As we entered further into the port area into what we expected to be flat calm, a fierce wind exploded around us as suddenly as though fired from artillery, and the seas were cutting up. The sudden gale was so strong that we had great difficulty keeping upright on deck as we searched out a berth. And 'Jernica' was staggering around like a drunk, being pushed about as we had to enter the confines of the port at slow speed without much speed. Maybe too the staggering was due to the absence of one expert helmsman, now studying in Malta. To add to our confusion the port was chock-full of large commercial vessels. Only one berth was in sight, and we thought ourselves wondrously gifted that it allowed more than enough space to enable us to secure alongside.

But then the next problem loomed. No person was visible on the quay. It meant I had to steer broadside to the mooring, and slow enough so that we could throw our lines and jump on shore to tie up. I thought I generally did OK at boat handling, but the elements were laughing at my puny efforts. As I tried to steer close alongside, I was unable to hold the boat still. The crew were as anxious as I was as they crouched with difficulty on deck, ready with our mooring lines. I shouted, "Right, next time I get close enough, throw the lines and Jeremy get ready to jump ashore to grab them. I'll yell when to do it." I started maneuvering again. We closed the gap. I waited. We weren't yet near enough.

Then I saw Jeremy, forward, flying through the air. It was when time stopped. As he was still airborne, I saw him as though suspended, fearing, with heart in mouth, that he might plunge into the wavering gap, too-wide surely, between our moving hull and the quay.

He landed safely, I breathed again, and with deft speed he gathered the forward line, secured it to a bollard and raced to do the same as the aft line was flung to him.

When we were fully secure we all breathed a huge sigh of relief, my first words to Jeremy being, "You silly bugger, I said jump when I told you." We went to the wheelhouse to sigh and relax and for refreshment. There then occurred, not entirely to our surprise, but to our great dismay, the great Med phenomenon – the hidden authority who watches you tie up before magically materialising to shout that you can't moor there. But my protests were aborted when he shouted we were at the local ferry mooring. What's more, he bawled with utmost pleasure, it was due any moment. "Where's an empty berth?" I shouted back above the whistling of the wind. There wasn't an inch of space to be seen anywhere, huge though the port was. It was overflowing with large commercial vessels. He just shrugged, and his job done, walked away.

We took off again and we desperately surveyed the area for any space. None, it seemed. Finally I spotted what seemed to be the only gap, which I thought might be just about big enough for us, on the other side of the bay, between two huge cargo ships. Shoved and pushed about still by the unrelenting squall, we somehow managed to squeeze in between them, without the dramatics this time of crew members endangering themselves.

It was only later after this berthing manoeuvre that Rosemarie, normally the epitome of calm, told me she'd feared we wouldn't do it. I felt quite pleased with myself. That was, until later I found that our foremast was bent backwards, caught by one of the huge hawsers used to moor the neighbouring vessels. The mast carried a navigation light, and sometimes, equally important when in port a clothesline.

What upset us most was that 'Jernica', hitherto an unblemished beauty had had part of her nose bent. We straightened it later. I can't remember how or when that was but we weren't entirely happy until she had been fully restored and we could once again rest content that all eyes would be beholding her with admiration.

It was only recently that I read on Wikipedia: "The strong wind that comes from the mountains toward the <u>Gulf of Salerno</u> makes the city very windy..." My Tyrrhenian sea-book bibles had made no mention of it. (And Wikipedia, and all that goes with it was only to be conceived as a tiny baby as our journey was coming to an end.)

Just to the west of Salerno sits the lovely isle of Capri. On it is the hilltop Villa San Michele, (which I referred to above) built in the early 20th century by <u>Swedish</u> doctor, <u>Axel Munthe</u>, on the ruins of Emperor <u>Tiberius</u>'s <u>villa</u>. Possibly better known to some older Brits, also on its heights, was the house occupied by the most renowned pre-war singer Gracie Fields with her Italian husband. Nationalism, and the fact that Italy joined Hitler's war effort, despoiled Gracie's reputation during the war. But war's end, her superb voice, the fact she had entertained millions of allied troops, and her never-doubted love of Britain soon had it fully restored. Rosemarie and I had visited the isle and its famous sites earlier on our holidays, and so, selfishly no doubt, we decided to push on.

The family wanted to visit Rome, and we put into Civitavecchia marina. This ancient Roman port was about 50 miles from Rome. We arrived early morning and the family prepared to entrain for the capital. The harbour was quite full with plenty of locals about. With the plentiful dubious stories I had heard (in those days) about untended yachts in that country – plus he fact that Rosemarie and I had also visited Rome in our early pre-family travels - I decided to stay aboard. Rome was a first for the kids, and they all had a great time seeing the famous sites.

Another memory is the diesel seller on the island of Elba. In those days, certainly, we were always at the mercy of local sellers of diesel and water, who could virtually name their own price for their essential products. But having charged us a good price, just as we were just about to leave this merchant suddenly appeared again and shouted that we hadn't paid him enough. Fortunately, we had just coiled our lines and it was a pleasure calling out, 'cheerio old chap' as we continued under way – and away.

We finally arrived in San Remo, in Italy, then continued to Menton, a marina close by just over the French border. We remained there for some time, visiting famous gardens built by an Englishman early in the twentieth century and making friends with a number of families who had decided to drop anchor more or less permanently in this lovely town with historic British connections. One of my memories is going out to collect some oranges fallen off trees planted in the street from which Rosemarie could make marmalade – and hoping I wouldn't feel a flic's hand on my shoulder with the equivalent of "hello, hello, hello!'

Nicholas had rejoined us here and with Jeremy was busy applying for their higher education back in England. The first one to leave was Nicholas having secured a place at Bangor University. He'd decided to study psychology, but chose Bangor on the basis that the scuba diving scene would be good. We found him an old banger and the first member of our crew to depart, with sinking heart from the rest of us, set off to drive back to England.

Here is Nick's story. I think it shows that some three years living in an environment when initiative, decision–making, and tackling physical work were a daily occurrence had left its mark.

Nick writes: *I set off with a degree of trepidation, leaving the nest for the first time. The car was a Peugeot 204, right hand drive, with the gear shift on the steering column. It was a tin can, although it subsequently worked well enough to drive around much of the UK and to and from France a couple of times.*

I was doing about seventy mph along the Promenade des Anglais, a dual-carriageway on the seafront in Nice, enjoying the view, when there was a crunch and it went dark. The bonnet had flown up, and wrapped itself around my windscreen. This was inconvenient. I managed to slow down and pull over without further mishap. I unwrapped the bonnet, and crawled to the nearest petrol station, where, in pre-mobile phone times, I found a payphone, and called my parents to explain what had happened. I said that I'd have to come back. To their credit they were having none of it, and told me to sort it out and get on with it.

I borrowed a hammer from the surly petrol station attendant, and bashed the bonnet back into some semblance of shape. I then bought some of those bungee elastic straps with hooks on the end. The hooks went under the wheel arches, the straps holding the bonnet down and I drove back to the UK like that. Later I got a garage to fit some rally pins to better secure the bonnet - cheaper than fixing it properly - and with that it was able to pass the MO. The creases in the bonnet remained to give the car a distinct design appearance.

His departure saga ended with three degrees. An honours degree in psychology from Bangor, an MSc in underwater psychology from Stirling University in Scotland, and after he'd started work, an MBA. He also ran the diving clubs in both Universities, winning a national award for the Bangor club.

After he was awarded his MSc, with his supervisor he applied to a number of grant awarding bodies with what he thought was an interesting and useful proposal to study the psychology of professional divers, but despite receiving positive feedback on the proposal, none of the bodies thought that it fell within their remit, and so Nicholas realised he had to apply for a real job.

Ultimately Nicholas applied for over thirty jobs, and despite what you may think would have looked like an interesting CV, he had very few interviews. The last job he applied for – merely because he didn't have anything else to do at the time – was as a programmer with British Airways, and this turned out to be the one he got. Interestingly, one of the recruiters told Nicholas some time later that they nearly hadn't given him the job because they weren't actually sure that he would take to programming, and they were quite right. Fortunately, the recruiters at the time were also looking for people who might branch out and be useful in other ways.

He was. In 1993-4 the Internet was encroaching on the public awareness, and I had started a business venture with Jeremy *(see further re Jeremy below)*. He had assisted Jeremy and myself. His interest sparked, he wrote a white paper which became widely circulated in BA, to persuade one of the world's biggest airlines that it should start up something called a website. Going in to work each day with a mini-tower pc under his arm, and a long length of telephone wire, he gave demonstrations to many departments on what the Internet actually was. One of these demonstrations was to the Executive Leadership Team, at the end of which they applauded – apparently a rare thing, indeed had previously only happened to Nicholas when the crew applauded his faultlessly flushing sea toilet.

Among other means of persuasion he talked about 'surfing' the web by introducing a clip of the Beach Boys' "Surfin USA" to which music he strutted his stuff to the somewhat bemused audience.

Nutty promotion ideas notwithstanding, the web idea was finally agreed. It became one of the world's first commercial sites, which he still helps manage, often with awards as one of the best.

Nicholas recalls one of the problems of starting this early website – a problem unimaginable today. It had been decided that a key requirement for going live was to have information with phone numbers and addresses around the world on the site. There was no e-commerce at the time. The only source of global contact information was in the back of the company's printed timetable. Nicholas and his assistant Helen went to visit the manager who 'owned' the timetable, to utilise the database that stored the information. It turned out there wasn't one. If a number needed changing, the next time the timetable went to the printers it would be updated.

The only way to get the contact information into digital format was via OCR – optical character recognition - scanning the data into a computer. The OCR programs at the time were not very good.

It was approaching Christmas, and everyone else had gone home. Nicholas and Helen remained in the office, proof-reading the results of the scan. This took some hours. All the while Helen's father was sitting in his car at the front gate waiting to take her home for Christmas. Eventually it was done, the files were emailed to the site developers, and Nicholas and Helen went home.

It wasn't quite over for Nick however. The next day was Christmas Eve, and he stayed working over a dial-up connection with the web developer he'd selected, making changes to the site. The 'Start' button was eventually pressed five minutes before Christmas 1995 – and so BA's deadline of going live before Christmas was met! In the following year the airline started some of the world's first online selling, and Nicholas was given a management grade.

Over subsequent years Nicholas worked in a number of roles that were about the application of IT to marketing-related areas of the company. He worked for some months in Australia, based in Sydney at the local head office. Although he travelled to most of the main cities and briefly to New Zealand, he saw little of the countries, as he only took a couple of days off in his time there. It was summer in the UK when he left for Australia, and so it was coming into summer there. When he came back to the UK for Christmas, he described it as 'living in a cave', an experience maybe accentuated by years spent in the Med.

Nicholas has continued to work on the ba.com website. One of his specialities - managing a team of designers and usability experts - is testing new developments on customers to see if new pages on the site are easy to use – a perfect fit with his psychology degree. In 1999 he married his long-time girlfriend, Helen, and they are still happily together.

Jeremy, in the midst of his Uni applications had to face a big career problem. His fame as an engineer was, as the book demonstrates, known around the rather incestuous world (then at least) of Med marinas. At the age of seventeen, he was offered the job of chief engineer on a one hundred foot yacht, based in Cannes, owned by a millionaire. Terms were five thousand pounds a year (in the 1980's), and all found. Jeremy's love was boats, engines, electrics, electronics and doing things with his hands. Somehow he turned it down as a long-term option; maybe his parents had something to do with it, thinking he should go on to University, and they have felt a bit guilty ever since.

He writes however: *'I did the job on 'Sophisticated Lady' out of Cannes for the summer. The skipper Dudley Stafford was the oldest (mid 30's) and I was the second most senior crew on board out of the crew of six. We had a great time. The boat had two generators, the smaller one incapable of running the air con. The skipper explained that it was too small and had never been able to run it. This didn't make sense to me, so I investigated and found the air filter incorrectly fitted, so blocking the intake. I fixed it and the genny then happily ran the whole ship's air con. From then on I couldn't do wrong in the eyes of the skipper.'*

He was then employed for the summer on the yacht of a member of the well-known Swarovski family. This led him to another extraordinary adventure for a seventeen-year old. He was asked by the family to go to supervise the engine-room work for a yacht being built for them in a Turkish yard. There, the young boy had to control the work of men who believed they knew it all. There were rows. But Jeremy never lost control. He insisted on meticulous attention to detail of the building of the diesel fuel tank.

When a Lloyd's surveyor subsequently surveyed the finished craft he said he had never seen such a perfectly built tank. He could have stayed as engineer with the Swarovski family's yacht but decided instead to return to the UK and Uni.

Jeremy has unquestionably oft regretted his missed boat-working opportunities to this day. After Manchester University his love of cars and hifi led him to design a new type of car-audio system that produced high-quality sound from a very small, cold unit. He raised funding to develop, manufacture and market it, fitting it as standard equipment to Aston Martin cars as well as selling to other manufacturers such as Rolls-Royce. But the major audio manufacturers simply priced him out of the market.

Jeremy and I worked together for a time on the first uses of the internet. After an economics degree at University College in London I had first worked as a journalist for national newspapers and magazines and then started some of the earliest computer companies. So I was able to pick up on the internet. But once again, I did not understand how Jeremy learned all the programming detail that was needed to create some of the first web sites.

In 1994 the Sunday Times held an industrial exhibition in London. There was a special innovation section. Our company was there alone providing, for the first time ever in public, a demonstration of the use of the Internet for business.

But I learned in my early computer days that it is possible to be too far ahead of the market. And so it was this time too. Only a single journalist, from the *Times*, visited our stand, and he was sceptical. Marketing managers in business understood conventional print, and could not conceive of multi-media for marketing and selling.

Many clearly felt threatened by new technology they did not understand in their area of expertise. They could never imagine that one day there would be a desktop computer in millions of homes, linked by the Internet. We were often told the Internet was impractical because there were, and would be always, too few computers connected - in business, let alone by home users.

We did find one large company prepared to look forward. For Knight-Ridder Financial services a major U.S. company, we created one of the world's first interactive financial services web sites.

It was a difficult period with long hours of graphic development work, large numbers of visits over large distances making presentations to prospective clients, most with little comprehension, and even less belief, in the new business environment we were demonstrating.

We were making no commercial progress. Jeremy, now with some quite exceptional experience in digital compression and interactive multimedia, was offered a managerial job with a start-up high-tech company, and took it.

As for me approaching the age of seventy, my days of pioneering had come to an end.

Jeremy went on to work as an IT contractor. He was much in demand but he found it a dispiriting world. He couldn't get his hands dirty. He couldn't end any day looking at the results of his hard work. Contract work means working for teams often commissioned by bureaucrats or businessmen who may know what they want but do not understand they should stay out of the implementation of their project by specialist teams. It is common for them to change specs at any time without understanding it could foil the whole project. Hence billions wasted on projects that never work. More and more dispirited Jeremy finally quit.

Just as in his Med days he had no professional engineering or electrical qualifications. So in these correct days nobody could employ him in that field – nobody could again make him the offer he first received when aged seventeen.

Jeremy's other love was photography. I gave him his first SLR camera aged ten – he still has it. He took the gamble and, with a wife, children and mortgage, gave up highly paid contract work to become a professional photographer. As in engineering, Jeremy understands every dot and comma of the smallest details about how to get perfect photographic images. It took him two years to build a successful business.

He specialises in events. This often involves photographing people in the poor light, say, of a school theatre, and yet producing instant images of studio portrait quality. At Xmas for example the events can come thick and fast. After the event – for which he may drive countless miles – he arrives home in the early hours, to update images, CDs, and his website (*Photoviva.co.uk*). Next day it could all be repeated.

It is high-pressure work and he is often exhausted. But, he says, he always has the satisfaction of daily seeing the results of his work and has never for one moment regretted leaving computer consulting. And he is now beginning to make a reputation here too – his work attracting the attention of the theatrical world. And also attracting the attention of the photographic profession for the high quality, artistic images he can produce regularly working at 12,800 ISO (i.e. in extremely low light).

So no more boat engineering work? Not quite. While still working in Monaco he met the lady who is now his wife. His daughter Eleanor, at the age of fifteen wrote a best-selling Amazon book about how to bring up children – 'How Teenagers Think'. She became a highly employed social media consultant on young people, appearing on TV and dubbed by The Guardian as 'The voice of the MSN generation'. With the money generated by her success and inspired, she says by 'Family Aweigh' published on Kindle she bought a 37ft yacht and has since the age of eighteen lived on it in the south of England. Many trips by her dad have kept it repaired and updated.

Nor is that the end of it. She bought 'Elizmor', a 53ft 1948 wooden Scottish ex-ringnetter fishing boat which had been sitting on the hard in Preston for more than ten years. With a friend she started the work required to recommission the boat into her natural habitat intending to sail her gloriously back south.

But her dad it was, driving regularly seven hours up the motorway from the south who was checking and refitting all the wiring, electronics, bilge pumps, engine controls etc to make her worthy for her new sea challenge. Hard work and a long tiring drive but he was happy. He also fitted a smoke alarm in the engine room, even though not specified by the insurer's surveyor – and laughed at by some other mariners when it had a few false alarms.

He was then aboard as, finally, the neglected old girl, with all her new finery was launched back into the sea. They sailed her for some days down the Irish sea to her new berth and home in Brighton .

But after rounding The Lizard Jeremy's much derided smoke alarm it was that told them of a fire in the engine room. They stopped the engine. He found the fire was started from a wood coating to the exhaust, installed above head-height by previous owners on the hard. It was extinguished by Jeremy speedily coupling a spare pump lying about to a battery (getting a shock in the process) so he could squirt water from buckets upwards.

The fire out, he was mortified he couldn't put her into Falmouth under her own power, by restarting the engine. Ellie had quite properly called 'Pan Pan' to coastguards immediately after stopping the engine. A lifeboat had by now arrived to tow them in, which they had to proceed with.

Jeremy's love of cars has been transferred to his son Alexander who after winning loads of cups at karting became a champion of the MR2 racing series, doing 120 mph at the front around the race tracks of England before he had a licence to drive on the roads. More recently he was awarded best apprentice at BAe and is going on to an engineering degree.

Carolyn's love of the sea did not end. She forsook University and went off to crew sailing boats for a Med touring company, and eventually has settled with a

French husband in a Med coastal town in France where she has brought up two lovely daughters, now grown up. In the process she became the local ladies' wind-surfing champion and master – like Jeremy - of the wind-sailing art; and among other initiatives, taught English in schools and to French pilots.

But we must return to 'Jernica'. With all the children gone, there came the first time Rosemarie and I faced up, with just a little trepidation, if we were honest, to crewing the boat alone. We set off to scrape off the barnacles and anti-foul the hull in Monaco. It was the first time, crewless, we couldn't tackle it ourselves.

The work completed, we came off the slip to stop at the adjacent diesel pump. As we arrived there I heard the bilge alarm go off. I flew down the iron ladder to the engine room. I soon saw water seeping a-plenty through a hole in the hull. I gave Rosemarie a large cloth and told her, without much gallantry but some practicality, to hold it in the hole – and started to steer back to the slip. With Rosemarie spread-eagled all the time in the bilges, I got on the VHF to advise the slip we had a hole in the hull and had to return. They refused to allow us back in as they had another boat due in. "But we're filling with water," I shouted. I could virtually see the shrug at the other end of the VHF as the slip replied, 'Pas possible, M'sieur'.

But I hadn't spent years in the Med for nothing. I did the thing one does – or at least did then, in the Med. I ignored their words and took the practical step of heading directly to the slip, and blocking it for any other boat hoping to access it. As usual the pragmatic Med principle of doing the obvious pertained, and we were pulled in, albeit reluctantly, and Rosemarie could abandon her heroics spredeagled in our dyke. The hole in the hull was eventually repaired. I think Jeremy/Nick were sure when told that it was electrolysis but as the hard was also available to pedestrians and the hole was perfectly rounded I also wondered if some joker with a drill had had fun and games with it in the night.

Rosemarie and I now had to decide. What was to be our future? The thought of leaving our beloved 'Jernica' was so difficult to face. One possibility was to follow the lead of others and become a charter boat. But somehow the idea of hiring strange crew rather than having the family around and having strangers bossing it on the deck was hard for me to grasp.

The only alternative was to part with 'Jernica', and start a new life ashore. We moored in Antibes – (and it's a strange fact that we had walked around the marina countless times in the past, but it seemed a totally different place when we had a berth there.) The day came when we had a good offer for the sale of our boat. I recall having words with the 'expert'/new-to-be skipper who came to assess her for the new owner. He was convinced there must be something wrong with the engines because I'd gone down to the engine room a couple of times during her sea trials with him.

I asked him if he didn't do that at intervals when he was skippering a boat at sea, to check for possible problems. He looked at me as though I was having him on. I looked at him as though he was a simpleton, which he was engine-wise. I so remembered Jeremy threatening me with all sorts of fates if I didn't go down and look around, when he was having a rest on one of our longer journeys.

When I agreed the 'Jernica' sale and returned to tell Rosemarie, she said she'd never talk to me again. I learned to know the truth of what it meant to be 'so choked he couldn't speak'. As I walked off our gangplank for the last time I tried to say the word 'goodbye' but the words literally stuck in my throat. For Jeremy, there could be little compensation for the loss of a loved one which had looked after him at difficult moments at sea, and to which he had extended such daily care. But a little came his way some time later when for his birthday Rosemarie and I presented him with a large picture frame which contained the steel plate from Jernica containing the maker's name, date of build and shipyard number, together with photographs of his long-time charge, and of the family crew.. The tears as he saw it were not unexpected.

As will now be clear, much water has passed under many keels since our joy at first heading for the open sea out of St. Raphael. And so that it would not interfere with any pleasure readers would have experienced joining us on the voyage, I have saved the bad news until last. Rosemarie, a great heroine of our journeys, unfailingly unflappable, calm in dealing with any seagoing situation, a stalwart of daily maintenance of boat and home, all the while caring for her family, and loved by everybody, passed away in my arms three years ago after a long illness. We had been married fifty-seven years and needless to say a large hole has been left in my own life and that of the family.

This epilogue is created in loving memory.

As for myself, the crew are still around when the gales of life blow and they have to step forward. I am getting on a bit, have a serious illness and was admitted to hospital. After a couple of days, it was suddenly realised on examination of a scan that unless I had an operation in very short order, my time was up.

There was only one problem. A doctor had earlier prescribed me a blood-thinning drug as a solution to a major blood clot. Hurriedly this was now changed to intravenously feeding me a blood-clotting drug. No operation was possible until that had taken effect. Nicholas was at my bedside sharing a few jokes during some long hours of this little drama with surgeons and a (wonderful) young lady-registrar explaining calmly I was in a very serious way.

It was finally 4.30 in the morning when they rushed me down to the operating theatre with a less than 50/50 chance. But when I was received at the entrance to the theatre by the registrar, and she gave me a lovely smile and grasped my hand as I entered I had no doubt I would be OK. If survival depends on strength of mind, this lady gave it to me.

I came round two days later. It was again in the early hours of the morning. The first person I saw in the intensive care unit was Nick, with a smile and some joke or other I can't quite remember. He had also accompanied me down to the theatre in the early hours two days earlier.

The crew was, as ever, solidly reliable when the skipper might have been heading for the rocks.

So here I am still able to steer until the end of this epilogue.

As for 'Jernica', she's an old soldier who won't fade away. She sails on. We last heard of her as a charter boat out of Turkey. We thought once or twice of maybe chartering her – but really always knew the emotional effect would be too much.

With the wonders of modern technology, I'm happy that readers are now able to view at the Photobucket website http://tinyurl.com/Ifrsabm photos of Jernica, incidents described in the book, and the family crew at work and play. I hope you won't mind that I've deliberately left this tidbit to the end, as I think a book is written in partnership with the free-flowing imagination of the reader. I sincerely hope however that the photos at this stage may prolong your enjoyment, as you relate them to the story you are now ending, of our family aweigh.

With apologies the photos are grained as there were no digital cameras at the time of our travels and it was difficult to find places to develop negatives around the Med. My digital editing could have been a lot better too, but you can now see us well enough to say hello.

But now, I'll say good-bye and thank you so much for choosing to accompany us on the eventful journey we made to live a dream.

This is 'Jernica', 'Jernica', out.

Mike

39547125R00209

Made in the USA
Charleston, SC
14 March 2015